The Real Estate Litigation Handbook

David A. Soley

FIRST CHAIR
PRESS

AMERICAN BAR ASSOCIATION
Section of Litigation

Cover design by ABA Publishing.

Printed in the United States of America.

14 13 12 11 10 5 4 3 2

Cataloging-in-Publication Data is on file with the Library of Congress.

The Real Estate Litigation Handbook
David A. Soley
ISBN. 978-1-60442-644-1

Discounts are available for books ordered in bulk. Special consideration is given to state bars, CLE programs, and other bar-related organizations. Inquire at Book Publishing, ABA Publishing, American Bar Association, 321 North Clark Street, Chicago, Illinois 60654-7598.

www.ababooks.org

CONTENTS

PREFACE

To the island of Huahine, French Polynesia—which inspired these reflections and writings.

Real estate is the American dream. The litigation over its bounties is one of the most complex and aggressive pursuits in the law. Wars have been fought over its nuances. For the trial attorney, real estate litigation poses the immense challenge of hardened combatants, unique legal principles, and a distinct body of practices, strategies, and experts. The book serves as a guide for successfully getting you through all of its exciting twists and turns.

There is a story about the great Jewish Hasidic scholar named Baal Shem Tov, who found himself lost in a dense forest. The more he walked, the more lost he became. After walking for a long time, he saw a light. He followed the light until he found a man. "Do you know where we are?" asked the great Baal Shem Tov. "No," responded the man with the light, "I am also lost, but working together we will succeed in finding where to go."

This book contains many answers to litigating complex cases involving boundaries, easements, access, title, and other real estate disputes. Contemplate and learn from these pages, add your own style and experience, and, together, we will conquer the mysteries and intricacies of complex real estate litigation.

ABOUT THE AUTHOR

David A. Soley heads the Real Estate Litigation Group at the law firm of Bernstein Shur in Portland, Maine. In his more than twenty-five years of experience as a trial lawyer in both Maine and Washington, D.C., Mr. Soley has handled many hundreds of trials, contested hearings, and depositions. He regularly represents entrepreneurs, property owners, developers, title insurance companies, real estate brokers, and financial institutions in disputes over boundaries, titles, easements, access to properties, warranties, purchase and sale agreements, leases, and other real estate issues.

Mr. Soley is AV-rated by Martindale Hubbell. In 2006, he received the Award of Excellence from the ABA's Litigation Section. He is currently a leader in the ABA Section on Litigation and has served as the Chair of its Advanced Planning Committee, Trial Practice Committee, and Business Torts Committee. He is also the editor of the ABA's *Business Torts Handbook*, and regularly gives seminars on real estate litigation and other trial issues throughout the United States.

Mr. Soley graduated with honors from Bates College in 1980. He also graduated from the Emory School of Law in 1984, and served as the Notes and Comments Editor of the *Emory Law Journal*. He is admitted to practice in the States of Maine, Georgia, Maryland, and the District of Columbia, as well as the U.S. Supreme Court, and the U.S. Courts of Appeal for the First, District of Columbia, and Federal Circuits.

When he is not practicing law, Mr. Soley exhibits his passion for real estate by developing commercial properties in the Greater Portland, Maine area. With his brothers, he is currently the owner of more than a dozen office and retail projects. He is the son, grandson, and great-grandson of real estate entrepreneurs.

Mr. Soley lives with his family on the coast of Freeport, Maine, where he has served two terms as the Chair of the Freeport Town Council.

INTRODUCTION

Know Real Estate

Property is the fruit of labor; property is desirable; it is a positive good in the world.
—Abraham Lincoln

Justice Louis Brandeis wrote an important note to himself: "I know not only whole cases, but whole subjects . . . know not only those facts which bear on direct controversy, but know all the facts and law that surround."

Real estate litigation is a unique and complicated area of the law. To be successful, you need to love property law and you need to have a solid understanding of real estate. Sit down with texts and statutes in your jurisdiction. Learn everything you can about boundaries, easements, deeds, warranties, surveys, roads, mortgages, and liens.

Go to the Registry of Deeds and learn how to do a title search. Study the indices and the plan depositories at the Registry. Go into the field with a surveyor. Learn the instruments, the concepts, and the mathematics involved in surveying a piece of land. Watch how the surveyors find old boundaries and monument markers.

Go to the closing of a real estate transaction. Pay close attention to the transaction, and all of the documents associated with it. Learn how the Purchase and Sale Agreement is negotiated and how the deeds and loan documents are drafted.

Meet with a landlord. Learn everything you can about the acquisition, financing, management, and sale of real estate. It is an extremely complicated and sophisticated business, if done correctly. The best-run commercial building will fail if not structured and financed properly. The best-financed buildings will fail if not managed properly.

Real estate development and acquisition also involves a tremendous amount of entrepreneurship and independent spirit. You cannot fully comprehend real estate law—or your own clients—without a keen understanding of what motivates people who play in this field. You need to walk in their shoes and breathe their air in order to be successful and to enjoy what you do.

If you know and enjoy the business, you will be stimulated by real estate litigation—and it will show. While most judges may not have expertise on real estate issues, they know who does, and that should be you. Jurors and judges alike pick up on confidence, and confidence is acquired through experience, expertise, and love of the topic.

CHAPTER 1

The Client Interview

In the middle of every difficulty lies opportunity.
—Albert Einstein

Real estate litigation generally involves clients at their worst. Americans tend to be deeply attached to their land. Disputes over real estate, especially between neighbors, can involve tremendous tension. By some accounts, more real estate litigators are attacked than divorce lawyers. Americans, it seems, are far more attached to their land than their spouses.

The real estate trial lawyer must vigorously represent the interest of his client, while simultaneously exuding professionalism and defusing unnecessary tension. The first substantive meeting with the client is key.

Set up a person-to-person meeting with the client as soon as possible. Before the meeting is held, review all documents, plans, tax maps, and pleadings that are readily available. You want to attend the first meeting with a preliminary understanding of the issues. After reviewing the available materials, make a list of educated questions that you need to ask the client.

The first meeting with the client—if at all possible—should be at the site. Promptly viewing the actual "lay of the land" is absolutely critical for the effective trial lawyer. Plans, deeds, and other documents can never convey the full story on the proximity of the parties, the location of an easement, or the terrain involved in a boundary dispute. Meeting the client at the site is the only way to fully understand the issues at hand in a real estate dispute.

Do not place any artificial time limits on the first meeting. The best way to begin evaluating a contentious real estate case is to give your client a complete opportunity to express the entire story. Try not to ever interrupt—unless you simply cannot understand what is being explained. Afford your client the time to get everything off his chest, and to fully describe all of the facts and contentions. As most mediators will tell you, tensions decrease when a client truly feels that he has explained the entire story to an avid listener. Listening also creates the bond of trust that is essential in the effective representation of a client. Hearing the complete story gives you a better opportunity to create effective litigation strategies.

Walk the property, especially all disputed boundaries or easements. Personally examine all characteristics of the property involved in the dispute. Look for all signs of evidence that benefit or harm your case. As you walk the property, try to wear the shoes of the opposing party. What will he claim? What would you do if you were representing the other side? Note, as soon as possible, all strengths, weaknesses, and problems with your case.

At the initial conference, press the client to provide you with all relevant documents. Depending on the facts and issues, relevant documents may include the following:

1. Deeds, easements, and other recorded documents
2. Plans and surveys
3. Contracts and Purchase and Sale Agreements
4. Closing binders
5. Correspondence and e-mails
6. Appraisals
7. Title insurance policies and comprehensive general liability insurance policies
8. Photographs
9. Files from prior litigation regarding the same property
10. Prior deposition or trial transcripts concerning the parties

Ask your client to identify all people who have information that will be helpful. Try to determine the potential witnesses—and ask about professionals whom one side or the other may be looking to for expert testimony: surveyors, title searchers, appraisers, accountants, contractors, architects, or historians.

Note: Clients tend to bring surveyors or other nonattorney professionals with them to lawyer meetings. It is very helpful to meet these professionals and to have them walk the boundaries and detail the critical aspects of the dispute. However, communications with nonattorney professionals generally are not privileged—especially if the professional is going to be your expert at trial. Make sure that you politely excuse the consultant or expert when you communicate with your client concerning facts, opinions, goals, and strategies.

While in the initial privileged conversation with the client, thoroughly explore whether insurance might cover some of the cost of litigating the dispute. Title insurance provides defense costs and coverage for certain unanticipated easements and other encumbrances on the property or the title. General comprehensive homeowners or business liability insurance often provides a defense and/or coverage for claims of trespass. **Note**: These coverages may be *voided* by the failure to give proper notice to the insurance company. Be careful not to waste the client's resources by proceeding down a path only to find out later that an insurance company would have reimbursed your client for your work if it had been given timely notice of the claim.

And, possibly most importantly of all, discuss the parties' past settlement efforts and all of your client's thoughts on settlement. Are the parties far off? Are there easements that can be traded for land? What does each party have that will benefit the other side?

Exploring settlement at the beginning of a case is a sign of experience, not weakness. Given the very high costs of real estate litigation, the experienced real estate trial lawyer will spend the beginning of every case looking for a "win-win" between the parties. This is cost effective to do at the beginning of the case, but not after both sides have spent substantial money and are ready for trial.

A thorough understanding of settlement options is also key because real estate disputes—unlike contract actions or most other litigated disputes—afford the potential for unique solutions. While a court is limited to a declaratory judgment, injunction, or financial award, a win-win settlement can carefully redraw boundaries, create or modify easements, and establish a myriad of other property rights benefiting the other parties. For more on this topic, see Chapter 14, "Settlements and Consent Final Judgments."

Note: Always have an accountant review the tax consequences of a potential settlement before signing off on it. If there are known tax issues involved from the start, consult the accountant before entering into settlement negotiations.

A helpful **checklist** for the initial client interview is as follows:

The Dispute

- Describe the problem
- What is the history of the dispute?
- Tour the property

The Client

- Education
- Occupation
- Experience with real estate
- Length of time property has been owned
- What does the client want?

The Opponent

- Education
- Occupation
- Background
- How long have you known the opponent?
- Intelligence level
- Temperament
- What "buttons" have an effect?
- What does the opponent want?

The Documents

- Purchase and Sale Agreement
- Closing binder
- Deeds
- Plans and surveys
- Communications (letters and e-mails)
- Photographs

Witnesses and Professionals

- Witnesses
- Prior owners
- Abutters
- People who grew up on the property

- Renters
- Employees
- Surveyor
- Closing attorney
- Title searcher
- Accountant
- Architect
- Appraiser

Insurance

- Title insurance
- General comprehensive insurance

Settlement

- History of settlement discussions
- Possible middle grounds
- What can we give the other side?
- What are we OK with giving to the other side?
- Tax implications

Credibility

- Prior litigations
- Prior testimony at depositions and trials
- Criminal convictions
- Other skeletons

CHAPTER 2

The Story

Music is a moral law. It gives soul to the universe, wings to the mind, flight to the imagination, and charm and gaiety to life and to everything.
—Plato

Whereas the law is passionless, passion must ever sway the heart of man.
—Aristotle

A simple and convincing story is absolutely essential to winning a real estate case. It is the theme that holds the case together. It provides the momentum to take the case from the initial client interview through to the verdict.

Many trial lawyers do not work on their story until preparing for the opening statement of the trial. This is a mistake. By the time of trial, your story will be subsumed by the other side. Do not wait for the other side to develop *their* story or to seize the power of the momentum and the facts.

After the initial client meeting, the site visit, and the review of deeds, plans, and other documents, go for a walk, relax, close your eyes, clear your head, and then become vigorous. Allow your mind to be taken over by "A" waves, and then permit the facts to come together into a story that will carry the momentum of the case.

Your story must be interesting. It must hold the imagination and sympathy of the finder of fact. It must also be true and faithful to the actual evidence.

Look at the case from your client's perspective; walk in his shoes. Use all of your senses to better hear, see, smell, taste, and feel the true advantages and predicaments surrounding you. Open up all of your perceptions and instincts to fully appreciate the evidence, and then begin writing the imagery and sensory perceptions so important to an appealing story.

For example, assume that your clients' access to their summer residence has been blocked by a neighbor. The neighbor claims that the access trespasses over his property and that your clients have no deeded easement.

You, of course, meet the clients, walk the property, traverse the disputed access, and view the key plans and documents. You then develop your story:

> In my hands is a piece of the heavy chain that Evil Neighbor has unilaterally placed across the driveway leading to the home of Joe, his loving wife Betty, and their two young children. Joe and Betty have a beautiful and happy home at the end of the driveway. The driveway is their only means of accessing their home, which they have continuously lived in—unmolested—for over twenty years. Now, all of a sudden, Evil Neighbor has placed a huge iron chain across the road—preventing Joe, Betty, and their children from getting to their beautiful home. What the Evil Neighbor has done is very wrong, and we ask the Court to hold that Joe, Betty, and their children have a legal right to get to their home.

This story must be established as the theme of the case from the outset. It should be researched by the title searcher, surveyor, and other experts:

1. Does the property abut a public road?
2. Do the deeds, in the chain of title of either party, reference an easement?
3. Do any plans or surveys show an access way?
4. Does the building permit, or municipal records, reflect a way to the home?
5. Do any historical records show a way?
6. Is there any prior use of the easement?
7. Is there evidence of a traveled way on the ground?
8. Is a right-of-way depicted on any historical aerial photographs?

The story should be expressly set forth in the first paragraph of the Complaint. It should also be reflected throughout its factual allegations and causes of action. The story is the one strong theme that is described in the Complaint—and then consistently echoed in all actions and pleadings—through to the closing statement and jury instructions. It is the theme that binds the case together.

Discovery is the tool that real estate trial lawyers use to gather evidence for the story. The picture painted in the Complaint must be substantiated with materials and information that are often held by the other side. Accordingly, in addition to determining what the other side will be using against you, discovery is an opportunity to require the opponent and third parties to produce documents, to get written answers to questions, to gather admissions, and to conduct oral examinations of opponents and hostile witnesses under oath.

The story, or theme of the case, must be kept carefully in mind throughout the discovery process. With respect to document requests, demand (1) communications between the parties, (2) surveys, (3) deeds, and (4) photographs. Serve interrogatories that solicit information on the history of the access, the factual predicates of a prescriptive easement, and the opposing party's contentions. Use the requests for admissions to obtain admissions on the components of the story and to authenticate documents evidencing the story:

1. Admit that Joe lives in the home.
2. Admit that Betty and her two children live in the home.
3. Admit that Joe and Betty have owned the home for 25 years.
4. Admit that Joe and Betty have accessed their home by traveling from Cold Spring Lane, over a driveway, to their home.
5. Admit that Cold Spring Lane is a public road.
6. Admit that Joe and Betty have used the driveway, from Cold Spring Lane to their home (the "Driveway"), for 25 years.
7. Admit that the Driveway is at least 25 years old.
8. Admit that the Driveway is the only access to the home of Joe and Betty.
9. Admit that, for the last 25 years, the Driveway has been the only motor vehicle access to the home of Joe and Betty.
10. Admit that you have continuously seen Joe and Betty use the Driveway, for the last 25 years, to access their home.
11. Admit that Joe and Betty have openly used the Driveway.
12. Admit that you have never given permission to Joe or Betty to use the Driveway.
13. Admit that you have put a chain across the Driveway.
14. Admit that your chain prevents motor vehicle access to the home of Joe and Betty.

The depositions of the parties, neighbors, predecessors-in-title, and witnesses must follow this same theme—and be aimed at garnering evidence where you have been unable to obtain admissions or stipulations.

If sufficient material facts have been proven, file a motion for summary judgment on all or part of the story. A motion for summary judgment allows for the case to be resolved, without going to trial, where the important (or material) facts are not in dispute. If there are still material facts in contention—or if the motion is not successful—go to trial and tell the story of your clients:

> This is a case about the wrongful and overreaching efforts of the Evil Neighbors to deprive Joe and Betty—and their children—of access to their home of 25 years. We ask you to find that the Evil Neighbors have violated the law and to find that Joe and Betty have lawful access to their home.
>
> Joe and Betty bought their home, off of Cold Spring Lane, 25 years ago. They moved in and have continuously used it as their home for 25 wonderful summers. Their two children were born at the home—and have spent every summer of their lives living there. It was in this home that little Johnny learned to fish and to sail. Little Sally learned to play piano in the parlor and has spent countless hours sitting on the beach, reading, and writing poetry. At the beginning of each summer, the kids eagerly look forward to living at their home.
>
> This all came to a rude halt when the Evil Neighbors barred access to Joe and Betty's home with a 500-pound iron chain. The kids stared at the iron chain and cried. Their family has no way to access their beautiful home other than over the driveway.
>
> The Evil Neighbors' actions are wrong. The law provides that there is an unwritten, but legal, easement—a right-of-way—that allows people access to property where there is a 20-year continuous history of open and notorious use of a way, under a claim of right. This is called a prescriptive easement, and the law exists for precisely this kind of case—to allow Joe, Betty, Johnny, and Sally to continue to use their driveway, unmolested, to get to their home. Please apply the law, and find that this wonderful family has a prescriptive easement to get to their home.

This is how you carry your theme from the initial meeting to the trial. It requires doing much more work up front, but that early preparation ultimately saves substantial time and money—and gives your case a significant edge in real estate litigation.

Note: Do not put your head in the sand if facts are developed that place the story in serious question. Be prepared to ask the right questions of the client and adjust to reality. Never underestimate the other side.

Fortunately, most well-prepared cases and well-thought-out themes will not have major setbacks. By grasping the essential facts of the case, the needs of the client, and the lay of the land—early in the proceedings—you will have smooth sailing and confidence in all stages of the litigation.

CHAPTER 3

Exploring the Title

What we call real estate—the solid ground to build a house on—is the broad foundation on which nearly all the guilt of this world rests.
—Nathaniel Hawthorne

Title to real estate and the rule of law is at the foundation of a free enterprise society. A person who buys a home gets a deed. The deed is recorded at the Registry of Deeds and is indexed under the names of both the seller and the buyer. The recording of the deed at the Registry safeguards the purchase and secures the property rights of the new owner.

The rules of conveyances have not changed dramatically since the common law came into being in 1066. In addition to conveyances by deeds, the title to property can also generally be transferred by a will, by intestate descent (inheritance where no will exists), by foreclosure of a mortgage or lien, by court order, or by operation of law. With the exception of adverse possession and some other forms of unrecorded transferring (discussed later in this chapter), all of these methods of conveyancing should be recorded in the local Registry of Deeds so that they can be examined by a title searcher.

Similarly, easements can be created or transferred by an express grant, reservation, or exception in a deed. They can also be created by prescription (adverse possession of an easement), implication, and estoppel, and by statutory proceedings.

Searching the title is, essentially, an audit of all records relating to the title. The title search traces the ownership of the property, examines the property description, and reveals all recorded encumbrances on it. It cannot uncover prescriptive transfers or unwritten easements. Most conveyances are by deed.

The deed, of course, describes the property purchased in a manner so that it can be located on the face of the earth. By reading the unique property description, a title examiner can differentiate it from other properties and research it. An example of a property description is the following:

> A certain lot or parcel of land, with the buildings thereon, situated at Spar Cove Point, so-called (formerly known as Staples Point) in the Town of Freeport, County of Cumberland, State of Mind, and bounded and described as follows:
>
> Beginning at the mean high water line of the Harraseeket River at the southerly corner of Lot No. 30 as delineated and set forth on Plan of Spar Cove Point recorded in Cumberland County Registry of Deeds Plan Book 54, Page 6; thence N 58° 09' W along the division line between Lots No. 30 and No. 29 one hundred fifty-two (152) feet, more or less, to the easterly corner of a ten (10) foot square well lot conveyed herewith; thence southwesterly nine and fourteen hundredths (9.14) feet, northwesterly ten (10) feet, and northeasterly nine and fourteen hundredths (9.14) feet to the northerly corner of said well lot; thence continuing along the southwesterly line of Lot No. 30 N 58° 09' W four hundred forty-five and ninety-five hundredths (445.95) feet to an iron pipe set on the easterly line of a 15 foot right-of-way; thence N 14° 58' E along said right-of-way one hundred eighty (180) feet, more or less, to the mean high water line of Spar Cove; thence easterly along the mean high water line six hundred fifty (650) feet, more or less, to Spar Cove Point, so-called, also known as Staples Point; thence southerly and southwesterly three hundred sixty (360) feet, more or less, to the point of beginning, containing three and fifty-five hundredths (3.55) acres, more or less, and being Lot No. 30, a small part of Lot 29 containing a well, and all of an unnumbered lot shown on said plan recorded in Book 54, Page 6.
>
> Also, another lot or parcel of land designated as Lot 1-A on said Plan and containing forty-one hundredths (0.41) acres, more or less, and being the lot conveyed by John E. Lavers and N. Mae Lavers to Roderique F. Soule and Audrey J. Soule dated May 23, 1966, recorded in said Registry of Deeds in Book 3073, Page 335.
>
> Also granting and conveying to the Grantees as aforesaid an easement or right-of-way for the purpose of travel by vehicles and/

> or pedestrians in common with others over and along the roadways as shown on the aforementioned plan as well as over and along any easements, rights-of-way or common areas as shown on the plan.
>
> Also conveying to the Grantees with Quitclaim Covenant, all shore rights and any claim to the area between the high water mark and low water mark, in common with others, adjacent to the land in the Town of Freeport, County of Cumberland and State of Mind, that was conveyed to John R. Greenhalgh, Jr. and Carole Greenhalgh by William J. Soule, et al., by Warranty Deed dated November 26, 1975, recorded in said Registry of Deeds in Book 3776, Page 314, and by said John R. Greenhalgh, Jr. and Carole Greenhalgh to John B. Lincoln and Sally B. Lincoln by deed dated October 24, 1983, and recorded in said Registry of Deeds in Book 6317, Page 237.

The foregoing deed has a metes and bounds description indicating the location of the property on the face of the earth. Always check to determine if a boundary description "closes" by having it sketched on paper with a scale and compass. To be effective, the description in the deed must locate the land with such reasonable certainty as to identify it without the aid of extrinsic facts. If the description does not locate the land with reasonable certainty or does not "close," it is invalid. Sometimes deed research into earlier deeds can fix the problem by showing that the description is missing a course, contains a typographical error, or contains incorrect courses or distances.

The above description also references a plan. Reference to a plan in a deed incorporates the plan as part of the deed. It is very important to examine any plans referenced in the deed. Often, plans can be obtained from the Registry of Deeds, the surveyor's office, or the landowner. Look carefully at the plan to determine all easements, conditions, and restrictions that benefit or burden the property.

The above deed also gives the book and page number for its predecessor deed. This is very helpful in tracking the title. If there is no reference to a prior deed, this information can usually be obtained by calling or visiting the local tax assessor. Using the name of the known owners and prior owners, a title searcher must then examine all transactions affecting the land in the grantor and grantee indices at the appropriate Registry of Deeds.

By reviewing these indices, the title examiner can trace the ownership of the property and determine all recorded events that have happened to the property while the current owner owned it—and when all other prior owners owned it. In addition to all conveyances, the title searcher views all encumbrances and benefits such as mortgages, easements, tax liens, judgment liens, mechanic's liens, leases, agreements, seizures, attachments, and court decrees. This constitutes the chain of title for the property.

The importance of all of this deed research can be best illustrated by an example. William McCoy comes to see you. He has hired a prominent surveyor to determine his boundary with Ephraim Hatfield. The survey shows the following:

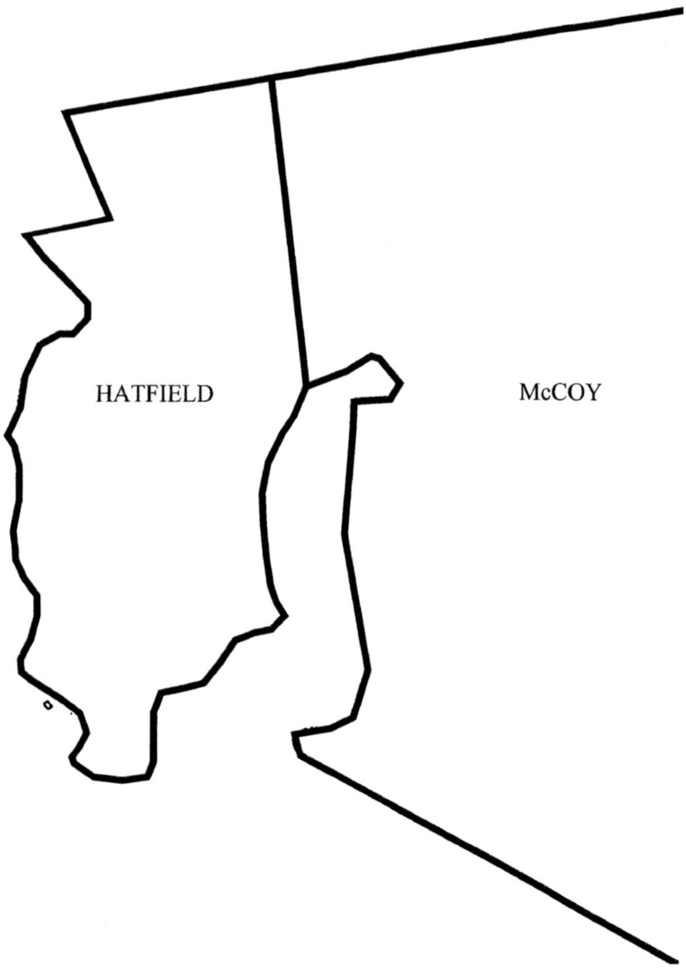

As often happens in boundary disputes, Mr. Hatfield refuses to rely on the McCoy survey. He retains a different surveyor—and comes up with substantially different results:

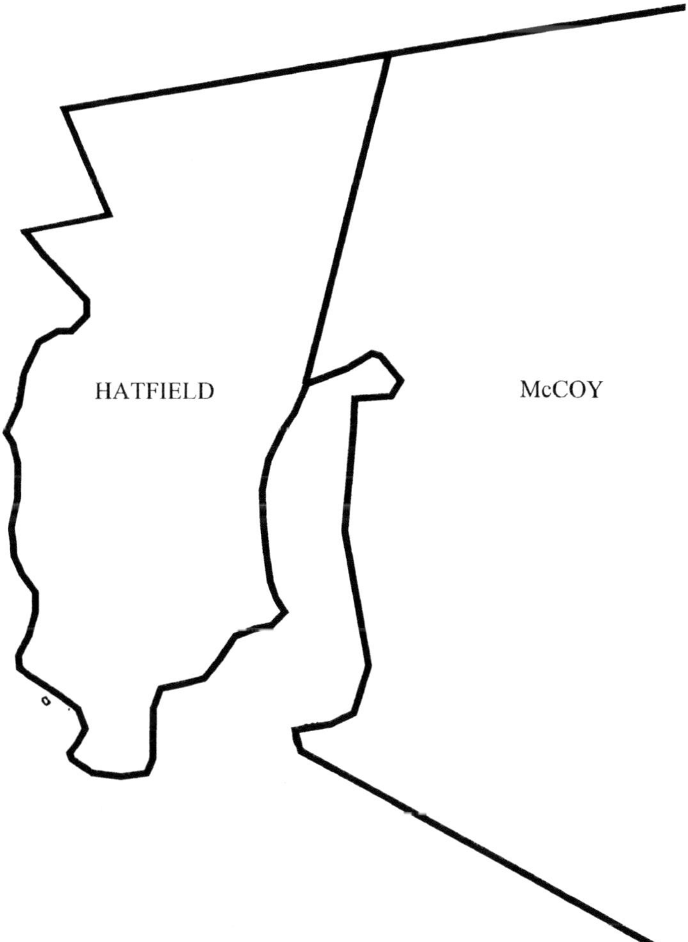

The first thing that you do is a thorough examination of the parties' respective titles. Find the deed into Hatfield and the deed into McCoy. Trace the deeds back in history until both parties' land is owned by a single person. As you go back in history, you must draw a chain of title. In the example of Hatfield and McCoy, the chain of title going back to a common grantor looks like the following:

CHAIN OF TITLE FOR TRIANGLE PORTION OF GOODEN PARCEL - TAX MAP 27 LOT 5
(All deeds in chain of title include the right of way along the former Roaches lot (nka Tax Map 13 Lot 7 -Abstract Appraisal Company))

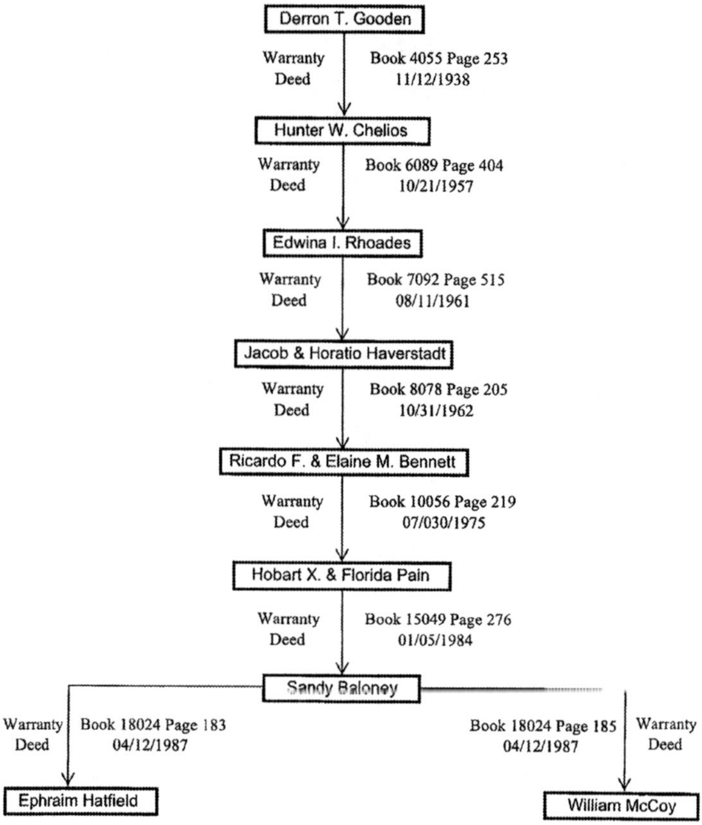

Another more complicated chain of title is the following:

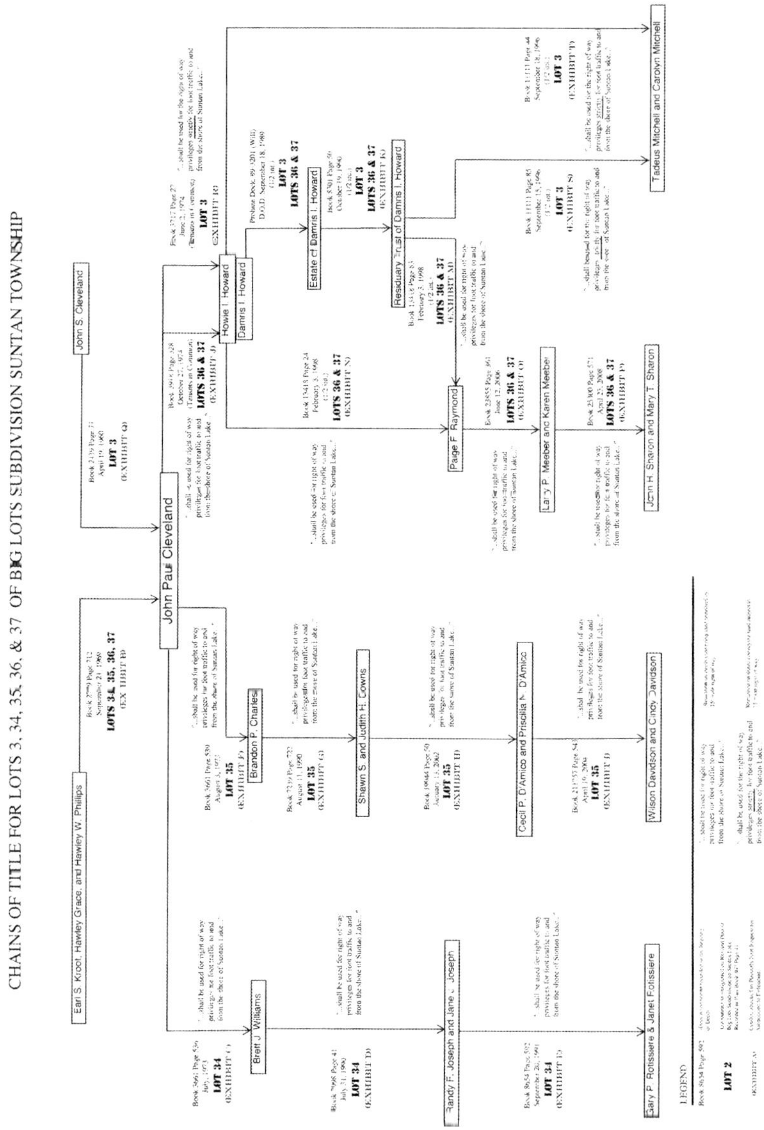

The title examiner should then examine all other relevant recorded events within the chain of title. "Relevant" events include all deeds that describe or change the description of either of the parcels of property. Many states require or recommend that the title examination also look outside the chain of title to look for deeds or liens that have not been timely recorded. Depending on the nature of the property dispute, the title examination may also need to delve into the chain of title for other abutting or neighboring properties.

It is imperative to reiterate that this title examination must be done at the *outset* of handling the dispute. Proper advice and analysis can never be provided in boundary or easement issues without a thorough understanding of the chain of title.

As alluded to above, there are also conveyances of land and creation of easements that *cannot* be identified by a thorough title search. This is why it is important to walk the land and to study surveys.

Specifically, title can be established by adverse possession. This concept, popular when the United States was being colonized or settled, is still the common law or statutory law in many jurisdictions. It provides that a person who openly takes actual control over land—for a continuous period of years—becomes the title owner of the property *even though* the record title is in the name of someone else. A common formulation for adverse possession is that right in title must be established, by a preponderance of the evidence, that a party's use and possession of property is (1) actual, (2) open, (3) visible, (4) notorious, (5) hostile, (6) under claim of right, (7) continuous, (8) exclusive, and (9) of a duration exceeding twenty years. Adverse possession is generally not available against states or political subdivisions. A "permissive" use such as a lease negates adverse possession.

Therefore, the lawyer walking the property must be alert to houses, structures, fences, and enclosures that do not belong to the record owner or that are not permissive uses allowed by the record owner. Check fences and stone walls to ensure that they are not "creeping" over the boundaries.

Title can also be transferred by the common law concepts of "acquiescence" or "estoppel." Acquiescence is where two adjoining landowners have recognized a common boundary for a long period of time. This generally occurs where the neighbors have long recognized a fence, wall, hedge, or marks on trees as their boundary and have "acquiesced" and taken actions in reliance of this boundary. A boundary can be established by acquiescence even when the deed description clearly and unambiguously describes a different boundary.

Title can also be conveyed under the doctrine of estoppel when the record property owner, by his conduct, induces another to act to his detriment in reliance on something not true. This may occur, for example, where a record title owner inaccurately tells a neighbor the location of the property line and then the neighbor, under watchful eye of the record owner, builds a structure or driveway on the record owner's land. The doctrine of estoppel transfers the land under the structure or driveway to the neighbor. Generally, intent to mislead is not required for estoppel to apply, and the neighbor must prove the claim by clear and convincing evidence.

As with adverse possession, real estate litigators must take care to study the property at issue for evidence of such nonrecorded transfers. Surveyors are critical in this effort.

Easements can also be created by nonrecorded circumstances. Just as title to land can be conveyed by adverse possession, a continuous user of a way—who meets all of the elements of adverse possession other than exclusivity—can own a prescriptive easement. Thus, a person who continuously and openly travels over another's property for a long period of time, without permission, may have a permanent legal easement to continue doing so.

In addition, there are easements by estoppel (1) where a lot is sold by reference to a plan conveying rights to streets and ways and (2) where the grantee conveys land bounded by a way—which way is owned by the grantor. In both cases, the purchaser of land has a permanent easement to use the aforementioned way for access to his property.

Furthermore, there are two types of implied easements that generally result in legal rights-of-way without the benefit of any recorded conveyance. An easement by "necessity" generally occurs where a grantor owns land on a public way and sells a landlocked portion of the property. In such cases—for as long as the grantee or his heirs have no other means of access to the "back" lot—he owns an easement by necessity, over the grantor's remaining land, to the public way.

An implied quasi easement is also triggered where a landowner divides property and, at the time of the division, there is a way on the face of the earth from the sold parcel, over the remaining land, to a public road. This type of easement often cannot be determined by an inspection or survey of the premises because it is triggered *at the time* of the division, not the present time. Therefore, these types of easements must be caught in old surveys or aerial photographs. Obviously, it is not cost effective for an attorney or title searcher to thoroughly investigate all of the issues associated with nonrecorded transfers of title and easements. However, the competent real estate litigator must be aware of these issues.

The professional should also be aware that recorded and unrecorded easements can be extinguished by abandonment. To prove abandonment, it must be shown that there is a history of nonuse of the easement coupled with acts or omissions evidencing a clear interest to abandon *or* adverse possession.

The bottom line is that the real estate litigator must be familiar with the twists and turns of all titles involved with the properties in dispute. This is an essential part of preparing the story, the complaint, the discovery, and the trial.

CHAPTER 4

Surveys and Plans

He who builds by the roadside has many surveyors.
—Italian Proverb

As the saying goes, the world is not getting any bigger. Most of the land in the United States has been the subject of a survey at some point in the past. It is of great importance to gather and review those surveys prior to launching a lawsuit.

Some surveys are recorded in the Registry of Deeds. Many surveys, however, are unrecorded. Look through the deeds to find references to unrecorded plans. Clients, predecessors-in-title, and prominent surveying companies are excellent sources of unrecorded surveys.

City and town halls are also good places to look for surveys. Code enforcement officers keep them in their "road" files. Assessors often attach surveys to their tax cards and other records. Municipal planners generally maintain copies of recorded and unrecorded subdivision plans.

The local historical society is also a good place to search for old maps and other geographic plans. Many historical societies have "merchant" maps wherein advertisers disseminated accurate layouts of the municipality—and pinpointed the location of homes and businesses.

Beginning in the 1930s and 1940s, aviators and government officials began taking photographs of land throughout the country. If your case involves old ways or preexisting natural or man-made physical features, it is essential that you seek and gather these old aerial photographs. These old photographs are held by a myriad of private businesses and government officials, depending on the state, and are available for a fee. The archivists of photographs often have people on staff with expertise in interpreting these photographs. Some states have indices listing what land has been photographed, who has the photographs, and other information concerning the altitude of the airplane and the precision of the camera at the time the photograph was taken. Check these indices to see if you can find anything helpful for your case. Generally, planes flying 200 feet or less over property—with a reasonably good camera—have produced excellent photographs of buildings and physical features.

Once the old plans and photographs are accumulated, the fun does not end. It begins. Many old plans were drawn by people with no training or experience in surveying. Some surveys were drawn by trained professionals who—for reasons of cost effectiveness—sacrificed accuracy. As rural farmlands gave way to sprawling downtowns and suburbs, the older "rushed" surveys have led to multi-million-dollar disputes.

The instruments of older surveyors also lacked the precision of today's survey tools. It was not uncommon for a one-mile distance in a deed to be off by as much as 400 feet. A 19th-century treatise observed the following:

> The original surveys of land in the older States of the American Union were exceedingly deficient in precision. This arose from two principal causes; the small value of land at the period of these surveys, and the want of skill in the surveyors. The effect at the present day is frequent dissatisfaction and litigation. Lots sometimes contain more acres than they were sold for, and sometimes less. Lines which are straight in the deed, and on the map, are found to be crooked on the ground. The recorded surveys of two adjoining farms often make one overlap the other, or leave a gore between them. The most difficult and delicate duty of the land-surveyor, is to run out the old boundary lines . . .

Knud E. Hermansen & Donald R. Richards, *Principles and Procedures for the Location of Boundaries* (2006), at 15–16, citing W.G. Gillespie, *Treatise on Land-Surveying* (1881), at 154.

Surveyors sometimes used sixteen-foot (one-rod) flat poles to measure hilly terrain. Chains, from time to time, had missing links. Occasionally, inexperienced surveyors forgot to account for changes in magnetic north. Even when properly accounted for, courses were often distorted by the relatively imprecise compasses used through much of the 20th century. Lawyers would then compound the mistakes.

In short, survey inaccuracies are a fertile source of real estate litigation. It is imperative that surveys—especially older ones—not be taken for granted.

As a result of inaccuracies in deed descriptions and surveys, there is a wealth of case law dealing with inconsistent terms. In general, monuments control over courses (directions), courses control over distances, and distances control over acreage. Thus, if the monuments on a plan do not match the courses, the monuments control and the courses are ignored.

A "monument" is anything referenced as a monument or marker in the deed. Usually, it marks the location of a corner. If a deed describes a boundary as beginning at a hemlock tree and then proceeding 100 feet due north to a stone wall, both the hemlock tree and the stone wall are monuments. Iron pins, stone walls, and granite markers *not* mentioned in the deed *cannot* be monuments.

As set forth above, undisturbed monuments take precedence over courses. Natural monuments also control over artificial markers.

Courses—which describe the direction from one monument to another—control over distances. Assume, all things being equal, that a course which says "N 35° E for a distance of 100 feet" ends in the ocean. This would mean that either the course or the distance is wrong. As the course has priority over the distance, you hold the course until you hit the ocean, and ignore the distance.

Distances control over acreage. The general rule is that—all things being equal—you follow the monuments, courses, and distances. If this creates a 20-acre parcel, and the deed says 10 acres, you ignore the deed reference to 10 acres.

Finally, area controls where there is no better information as to what controls. Area—or acreage—rarely comes up as controlling in real estate litigation. References to area in deeds are usually imprecise and not reliable. Area is only used to determine a boundary in a deed that contains no monuments, courses, or distances. Such a deed would presumably contain language describing it as being west of a certain property, with parallel northerly and southerly boundaries, and containing 10 acres.

All of these legal principles are involved in determining a boundary. Thus, defining a boundary is a question of law. However, locating a boundary (applying these legal principles) is a question of fact. Surveys and surveyors, including the plans and deeds of abutters, are key ingredients in resolving these issues of fact.

CHAPTER 5

The Expert Witnesses

There are as many opinions as there are experts.
—Franklin D. Roosevelt

Real estate cases cannot be won without high-quality experts. Choose experts *very* carefully. They must be accomplished, articulate, experienced, and professional in appearance.

The typical judge or juror does not have a lot of experience when it comes to the facts or law of real estate. They go into these cases relatively open minded—but can be counted on to spot an inexperienced "expert witness." Therefore, care should be taken to choose experts who are accomplished: who have a good grasp of their field, who are confident in their level of expertise, and who can be counted on to stand up for their convictions.

The expert must also be articulate. Most judges know little of the complexities of property law. Most jurors know nothing. This means that the finder of fact needs to be able to digest complex information quickly and simply. The expert must be able to speak and convey information on the same fifth-grade reading level as most local newspapers. He must be able to speak in simple sentences—without long clauses or pontifications. This comes naturally to some experts, but not to all.

Note: If your potential expert cannot, after reflection, explain his summary position in a two-minute spiel, get another expert. There is no substitute for the ability to quickly and convincingly get to the bottom line. Spend time with the prospective expert before finalizing your choice. Be sure that he will have a good rapport with you and the finder of fact.

The expert must also be intelligent and experienced. In real estate litigation, knowledge is valuable—and a judge is quick to pick up on the fact as to whether an expert is duly qualified. In general, experts should have at least ten years of continuous experience in their field.

In addition, the expert needs to be professionally attractive. For better or worse, judgments are often based on first impression. Know your local audience. Ensure that the expert is dressed appropriately, in light of his profession, and looks neat, honest, and well groomed. Regardless of an expert's knowledge and experience, reject him immediately if he cannot look you in the eye, speak in plain English in short and pointed sentences, and generally appear professional.

The first expert that real estate trial lawyers typically seek out is the title expert. The role of the title expert is to identify and describe the relevant deeds, as well as to testify about the respective parties' chains of titles. While this expert can possibly be eliminated if the parties mutually authenticate deeds and chains of title, it is hard to convey the theme of the case to a finder of fact by simply introducing stipulations concerning multiple deeds and title chains. The flow of the case is far improved if you have an expert who can explain how the property moved from one person to another, and who can easily express the critical nuances in various deeds.

The first place to look for the title expert is at the office of the title attorney or closing agent who researched the title as part of the purchase and sale of the property at issue. In order to close the property transaction, the closing attorney performed a title search or wrote a title opinion. If this attorney did a thorough title job—and fits the other criteria for a high quality expert—your search for a title expert may have ended, provided that the title attorney is not too strongly linked to the client.

Note: Do not use an attorney, paralegal, title searcher, or abstractor from your own firm. This unnecessarily exposes your expert to claims of bias.

The next most common expert in a real estate dispute is the surveyor. The finder of fact often is loath to do a site visit to the property and, even if the judge or jury visits the site, they do not know where to place their focus. The expert surveyor needs to be the eyes of the judge: introduce plans that both describe the land and point out the monuments, boundary markers, distances, courses, and physical characteristics of the property at issue. The surveyor often is used to submit multiple plans, over various time frames, that show how boundaries, easements, ways, or other features have changed over time.

Many surveyors have taken courses in aerial photography. If your case involves the need to review and interpret aerial photographs, look for an expert surveyor who has experience and training to interpret aerial photographs.

To locate a surveyor, look initially at all the plans that already have been done for the property and for abutting properties. If there is a particularly good plan that you will be introducing at trial, consider the author of that survey as a potential expert.

Many real estate disputes have a money damages component. If the damage at issue is the value of a parcel of property—or the difference in value before or after some occurrence—you will need a certified real estate appraiser. As with the other experts, this person should be chosen up front. Get someone who is very familiar with the type of property at issue and, as set forth above, is straightforward and well-spoken. Most real estate appraisers devote their life to the formulaic work surrounding commercial and residential closings and refinancings. You will generally need an appraisal expert who is more creative than most of his peers, and more willing to think "outside the box."

Appraisers are also limited to determining land value based on comparable sales and discounted cash flow analyses. For complicated mathematical calculations involving income-producing properties or investments, you should hire an expert accountant.

In cases involving old roads or ways, consider a historian. Historians are often used to testify as to the location of old streets and the history of the municipality in maintaining and using them. They can also be used to research and testify concerning code enforcement files, road commissioner reports, town line movements, and other historical events. These historical experts can often be found at local universities or historical societies.

In some cases, real estate trial lawyers have needed to retain expert archaeologists to excavate an area in contention to look for remains of ancient boundaries, roads, or landmarks. Tree experts may also come into play where trees or timber have been damaged or destroyed.

The key is to get knowledgeable and competent-looking people who tell a nice story in a sincere, credible manner. While the expert is required to be independent, he is an important part of the team striving to achieve your client's objectives.

CHAPTER 6

Filing the Complaint and Determining the Causes of Action

Complaint is the largest tribute Heaven receives.
—Jonathan Swift

The Complaint is the embodiment of your story, the theme of the case. It introduces the court to what you want—and why. It is an important advocacy piece of first impression. Before drafting the complaint, send a demand letter to the other side putting them on notice of your claim and the relief sought. The reason for the demand letter is twofold: (1) to determine whether the case can be resolved without the cost of litigation and (2) to serve as an attachment to the subsequent Complaint—letting the court know that you tried to be reasonable, but that reason has not prevailed (this also is a necessary element for the "controversy" aspect of a declaratory judgment claim). The demand letter, therefore, is written with an eye to inform the judge that you are on the side of goodness and justice. An example of a demand letter is as follows:

> Dear Evil Neighbor:
>
> This firm has been retained by Joe and Betty to request that you immediately remove the heavy iron chain barring access to their home, and to have you recognize their right to travel along the driveway to their home. It is our hope that this can be achieved without litigation.
>
> As you know, Joe and Betty have continuously, notoriously, and openly used the driveway for over 25 years—as their only means of getting to their home. This was done, at all times, with your knowledge and under a claim of right. Under the law, Joe and Betty have a legal

> and prescriptive easement to use the driveway to access their property. Your unilateral blocking of their right is contrary to the law.
>
> Kindly remove the chain immediately. If you have any questions about any of the above, please have your attorney call me within the next ten days.
>
> Very truly yours,

This letter is a very straightforward statement of the claim and a reasonable request for relief. Once it is attached to the Complaint, the judge will appreciate the fact that you made a reasonable effort to resolve this dispute honorably—and that it was the other side, by its unreasonableness, who forced the commencement of litigation.

Note: Sending a demand letter exposes your client to the risk that the other opposing party will seek to seize the momentum by using the demand letter as the basis for a complaint for declaratory judgment against *you*. By filing first, the opposing party may bring the case in an undesirable forum, or present the facts to the court in a way that—upon first impression—makes you look less reasonable. However, in balance, the straightforwardness and reasonableness of the demand letter, and the potential upside of avoiding litigation altogether, generally dictates in favor of sending a demand letter in advance of filing a lawsuit.

The Complaint is an important document that is usually read by the judge and should be carefully and thoughtfully written. Since this is likely to be the first pleading seen and reviewed by the court, it is an excellent opportunity to succinctly present your story.

DRAFTING THE COMPLAINT

The first paragraph of the Complaint should be the Preliminary Statement—a "press release"—which precisely and positively sums up your case and the relief sought. As with any concise written piece of persuasion, use power draftsmanship: focus on short sentences beginning with a noun and quickly followed by a verb. Try to stay away from clauses and complicated or ambiguous thoughts. Limit the use of punctuation. An example of a Preliminary Statement is the following:

> The Evil Neighbors have unilaterally and wrongfully barred Joe's and Betty's access to their home by placing a heavy iron chain across their driveway. Joe and Betty ask this Court to order that the

chain be taken down immediately and to declare that Joe and Betty have a permanent prescriptive right to access their home due to their continuous, notorious, and open use of the driveway for more than 20 years, under a claim of right.

After identifying the parties and the grounds for jurisdiction and venue, the Complaint should tell the story in short and simple paragraphs. By concisely going over all of the facts in the story, the judge will be able to easily understand and appreciate the factual basis for the legal claims. In addition—to the extent that the opposing party admits some of your paragraphs—needless fighting and expense will be avoided. The story should be presented chronologically for ease in comprehension. Important documents should be attached to the Complaint and authenticated.

As recently declared by the U.S. Supreme Court in *Bell Atlantic Corp. v. Twombley,* 550 U.S. 544 (2007) and *Ashcroft v. Igbal,* 129 S. Ct. 1937 (2009), a Complaint must contain more than conclusory statements or a "formulaic recitation" of a cause of action. Instead, the factual allegations must be concrete and specific. There must be enough factual detail to demonstrate a plausible claim for relief. In other words, the Complaint must contain enough factual matter to plausibly show that the claims are true. This command from the U.S. Supreme Court has always been good practice in real estate litigation—and has been adopted in other jurisdictions.

Following the factual allegations (or "story") portion of the complaint, consider a heading entitled "Defendants' Wrongful Conduct." This is where you state, in no uncertain terms, the bad things done by the other side: the refusal to remove the chain, the trespass onto your property, the blocking of the view easement, the failure to recognize the correct boundary, or whatever wrong has been committed. Emphasize that this wrong has continued despite *notice*—and attach the demand letter wherein you sought a reasonable resolution prior to bringing this matter before the judge.

CAUSES OF ACTION

The next heading of the Complaint should be entitled "Defendants' Violations of Law." This is where you assert your counts. Each count must contain a complete cause of action and all of the elements of the claim.

One of the most popular and useful causes of action in real estate litigation is the declaratory judgment. This is where you explain to the court that there is a bona fide dispute between the parties and that the court has standing to resolve the dispute. Declaratory judgment counts are routinely used to establish boundaries, to assert or denounce easement claims, and to grant or deny access to property.

Note: Some jurisdictions require that Complaints asserting declaratory relief state this fact in the caption of the complaint by stating, for example, "Complaint for Declaratory Judgment." It is important to make sure that you know all rules of court pertaining to real estate litigation before filing the Complaint.

Another popular cause of action is a claim for injunctive relief. This is addressed in more detail in a subsequent chapter. For purposes of drafting the Complaint, injunctive relief should be a separate count (or in some jurisdictions a remedy).

Certain courts also require that the caption of the complaint reflect the fact that injunctive relief is sought by stating, for example, "Complaint for Injunctive Relief and Damages."

Intentional or negligent trespass is an additional cause of action routinely associated with real estate litigation. Most jurisdictions have common law and/or statutory causes of action for trespass. Some states have special trespass statutes for specific claims such as tree cutting or waste of property.

Note: A trespass claim can, under certain circumstances, trigger insurance coverage or defense under a comprehensive general liability insurance policy. Depending on the jurisdiction and the wording of the liability policy, a trespass claim may sound in "negligence" for purposes of insurance coverage. If the potential damages arising from a trespass claim are minimal, you may consider avoiding the trespass claim so as to preclude the other side from having access to a "free" attorney.

In many cases, it makes sense to file a claim for breach of warranty. Warranty deeds and, in some cases, quitclaim deeds with covenants, ensure many of the most important qualities of land titles, including an assurance that the prior sellers own the land and that the land is being conveyed without unspecified encumbrances.

Specifically, in cases where your client does not fully own all of the property described in the deed—or where an unanticipated easement runs through or encumbers it—you have a claim for breach of warranty against all prior owners who conveyed the same property by warranty deed. The grantor of a warranty deed covenants with the grantee, and all subsequent owners, that he owns the property, that there are no undisclosed encumbrances, that he has good right to sell the property, and that he will warrant and defend the same to the grantee against all lawful claims and demands of third parties. Where a boundary description is challenged or an easement is claimed against your client, you have a claim against such prior owners "in the alternative": "Joe and Betty vigorously contest the claims set forth in Defendant's Complaint but—in the alternative—they bring this claim against Mr. Prior Warranty Deed Conveyancer in the event that Defendant's claims are proved at trial."

"Partition" actions are a very useful tool where two or more owners of land who do not get along can divide the property or its proceeds. In most states, any person with a fee interest in land can force the land to be sold or divided. The Complaint simply states that he owns an undivided fee interest in the property and demands partition. In an action for a "physical" partition, the property is divided and each owner receives a piece of the property commensurate with his ownership interest. Most jurisdictions allow bona fide physical partition actions to circumvent state and municipal land use rules on subdividing property.

"Equitable" partition actions are more common. Here, the complainant must allege that physical partition is impractical and that the property should be sold, and the sale proceeds divided by the percentage of each owner's interest in the land. Where three persons own an equal, undivided fee interest in a single family home on a small lot, a physical division of the land obviously makes no sense and the only equitable solution is to sell the property and divide the net proceeds of the sale.

Where persons in a dispute have invested or received differing amounts of money from property, the complaint needs to include a cause of action for an accounting. This allows a "true up" of each litigant's investments and receipts, pro rata with the percentage of ownership interest.

Note: Some jurisdictions limit the accounting to time periods within the statute of limitations—although the better policy approach is to consider the falling out of the partners as the starting period for the accrual of the action. Many jurisdictions also hold that a joint tenant or tenant-in-common has a legal right to live on the property "rent free" as long as he is paying all routine expenses and costs of maintenance (as opposed to capital improvements).

Another real estate cause of action is the somewhat antiquated claim for "quiet title." This cause of action is used to clear title where the whereabouts of owners are unknown, or where title to the property is somewhat murky as a result of a tax foreclosure. Each jurisdiction has a distinct statutory process for bringing such claims. Many jurisdictions prefer to reach the same result through a declaratory judgment proceeding.

Other causes of action to consider:

- **Nuisance.** A "private" nuisance is defined by Section 29.02 of the *Restatement (Second) of Torts* as "a nontrespassory invasion of another's interest in the private use and enjoyment of land." Generally, a physical invasion onto land is trespass. According to the *Restatement*, "fumes, smoke, light or other nontrespassory conduct are governed by nuisance principles." A "public" nuisance involves a condition that is generally harmful to health, offensive, or creating a public harm. Jurisdictions vary as to whether an individual can prosecute a cause of action for public nuisance.
- **Fraudulent conveyance.** A fraudulent conveyance is where a debtor transfers his property to hinder, delay, or defraud a creditor. This statutory cause of action allows a claim to be brought against the third person who receives the assets, and usually involves double or triple damages, as well as reimbursement of attorney's fees.
- **Slander of title.** The *Restatement of Torts* describes slander of title as untrue statements disparaging one's title to property under circumstances likely to cause harm. Many jurisdictions treat this cause of action similarly to a claim for fraud.

Each jurisdiction also has unique statutory and common law causes of action. You need to make sure you are familiar with all of these before filing the Complaint.

REMEDIES

Following the counts and/or causes of action in the Complaint, there is generally a "Wherefore" or remedies section. Given that land is unique and that judges in real estate litigation have broad equitable powers, you do not need to limit your remedy to dollar damages. In enforcement of a purchase and sale contract, specific performance—or requiring that the contract be performed—is common. Defenders of such actions frequently claim rescission, which voids the contract and puts the parties where they would be but for the signing of the contract.

There is tremendous latitude to fashion a myriad of other remedies. Courts have the equitable power to move easements, to change property descriptions and boundaries, and to grant or deny access to property.

OTHER CONSIDERATIONS

In cases involving title, make sure that you list all mortgage holders and other lien holders as parties in interest. There is nothing worse than winning a case—and finding out that your victory is not binding on a bank because it has not been named a party. You could, for example, win a case against the defendant, and find that the defendant has been foreclosed upon and replaced as owner by the bank. In order for the bank or other pre-existing lien holder to be bound by the judgment, it must be a party to the Complaint.

Care should also be taken in the Complaint as to the choice of forum. Generally, federal judges (where diversity exists) have less knowledge of real estate law than state judges. As a rule of thumb, it is best to bring a real estate dispute in the court closest and conceivably most familiar with the property. The familiarity of the applicable state court judge with real estate—and the convenience of you and your clients—must also factor into the equation and the choosing of a forum.

Some jurisdictions also require that the Complaint state whether or not a jury trial is being asserted. Many other jurisdictions require that a jury trial "demand" be made very soon after the filing of the Complaint. As a general rule, jury trials add little to real estate litigation other than expense. Jurors also cannot make a determinative decision on any equitable considerations in the case. Of course, a jury trial may be preferred where there is a large dollar damage component to the case and where you are in a jurisdiction where such jury damages tend to be higher than judge verdicts. This is discussed in more detail in chapter 12, "The Trial."

Exemplars of different Complaints in the below-listed types of real estate litigation follow for your guidance and inspiration:

- Access via an Old Easement
- Right-of-Way to a Dock
- Implied Easement/Slander of Title
- Blocking of Access/Nuisance
- Road Access—Public or Private Prescriptive Easement
- Breach of Mortgage/Discharge of Mortgage/Equitable Subordination
- Abandonment of Public Road/Declaratory Judgment Regarding Prescriptive Rights
- Breach of Warranty/Easement by Necessity
- Breach of Warranty/Fraudulent Transfer
- Specific Performance of Contract
- Partition

ACCESS VIA AN OLD EASEMENT

STATE OF MIND SUPERIOR COURT

EPHRAIM M. HATFIELD,)
Plaintiff)
)
v.)
) Civil Action No. ________
WILLIAM B. MCCOY,)
Defendant)
)

COMPLAINT FOR DECLARATORY RELIEF, PERMANENT INJUNCTION, AND DAMAGES

(Title to Real Estate Is Involved)

Plaintiff Ephraim M. Hatfield ("Hatfield") by his undersigned counsel, states the following as his Complaint against Defendant William B. McCoy ("McCoy"):

Preliminary Statement

1. Hatfield brings this action to enjoin McCoy from blocking access to the rear of Hatfield's building, and his parking spaces, in Bar Harbor. Hatfield, and his predecessors in title, have long held an express deeded right-of-way (the "ROW") to the rear of the building. In the 1970s, McCoy blocked the ROW when he constructed a parking lot. After the Hatfield predecessor immediately filed a legal action to enjoin the blocking of the ROW, the parties (McCoy and the Hatfield predecessor) agreed to give the Hatfield predecessor an alternative access to the rear of the building. McCoy has now flagrantly breached both the express easement and the agreement by once again blocking the access to the building's rear—which access is critical for supplying the Hatfield business and is the parking area for the Hatfield building and its tenants.

The Parties

2. Plaintiff Ephraim Hatfield is a citizen who resides in Bar Harbor.

3. Defendant William McCoy is an individual who resides in Palm Beach, Florida.

The Facts

4. Mr. Hatfield owns a certain lot or parcel of land located in the Town of Bar Harbor, more accurately described in a deed dated November 1, 2005, and recorded in the Hancock County Registry of Deeds in Book 4333, Page 64 (the "Hatfield Property").

5. A true and accurate copy of the deed to the Hatfield Property is attached hereto as Exhibit A.

6. The Hatfield Property is depicted on Bar Harbor Tax Map 104, Lot 128.

7. A true and accurate copy of Bar Harbor Tax Map 104 is attached hereto as Exhibit B.

8. The Hatfield Property is located at 100 Main Street in Bar Harbor, in an area of retail establishments, including storefronts, galleries, and restaurants.

9. The Hatfield Property is improved by a two-story building, with retail space on the first floor and a residential living space on the second floor (the "Building").

10. Hatfield operates a pastry business in the retail space located on the first floor of the Building.

11. Customers enter the pastry business through the Building's front entrance, on Main Street.

12. The Hatfield Property includes a lot with parking spaces located immediately behind the building (the "Hatfield Parking Lot").

13. Until 1978, the Hatfield Parking Lot was accessed via a right-of-way set forth in a deed dated December 8, 1893, and recorded in the York County Registry of Deeds in Book 277, Page 136 (the "ROW"), a true and accurate copy of which is attached hereto as Exhibit C.

14. The ROW expressly sets forth an easement to what is now the Hatfield Property:

> Together also with and as appurtenant to the above described lot a right-of-way over all parts of a strip of land adjoining the above and bounded on the North by said land formerly owned by the Eastern Railroad company; on the East by the lot of land above described and conveyed; and on the South and West by land of T. and S.H. Rodick. Said right-of-way however to be [held] and enjoyed by the Grantees

> only in common with the Grantor his heirs and assigns and all persons to whom he may grant similar rights.

15. Hatfield and/or his predecessors-in-title made and received deliveries over the ROW.

16. Hatfield and/or his predecessors-in-title regularly used the ROW for vehicular access to the Hatfield Parking Lot.

17. Hatfield and his predecessors used the ROW to allow maintenance and repair workers to access the Building.

18. McCoy owns a certain lot or parcel of land located in Bar Harbor, which is more accurately described in a deed dated April 4, 1978, and recorded in the Hancock County Registry of Deeds in Book 1321, Page 136, a true and accurate copy of which is attached hereto as Exhibit D (the "McCoy Property").

19. The McCoy Property is depicted on Bar Harbor Tax Map 104, Lot 131.

20. The McCoy Property was and is encumbered by the ROW.

21. In the late 1970s, McCoy, and/or his predecessors in title, began construction of a parking lot on a portion of the McCoy Property (the "McCoy Parking Lot").

22. The plans for the construction of the McCoy Parking Lot included a retaining wall, which blocks the ROW.

23. At the time the construction of the McCoy Parking Lot began, the Hatfield Property was owned by Phillip and Nathan Winslow, as more accurately described in a deed dated February 16, 1972, and recorded in the Hancock County Registry of Deeds in Book 1136, Page 452.

24. The Winslows immediately initiated legal action against McCoy to halt construction of the McCoy Parking Lot, and to preserve their deeded access, over the ROW, to the Hatfield Parking Lot.

25. During the course of the litigation, Phillip and Nathan Winslow negotiated an agreement with Joseph Davis and Michele Davis, predecessors to McCoy's title, in which the Winslows consented to conditionally suspend their access over the ROW, provided an alternative means of access was made available over the McCoy Property.

26. Phillip Winslow, Nathan Winslow, Joseph Davis, and Michele Davis executed an agreement providing alternative access over the McCoy Property in a document dated June 2, 1978, executed on February 27, 1981, and recorded in the Hancock County Registry of Deeds in Book 1399, Page 182 on March 2, 1981 (the "Agreement").

27. A true and accurate copy of the Agreement is attached hereto as Exhibit E.

28. Phillip Winslow and Nathan Winslow did not abandon the ROW when they executed the Agreement, they simply agreed to conditionally use an alternative access.

29. No party in the chain of title to the Hatfield Property has ever abandoned the ROW.

30. The ROW is a permanent easement, and remains in place.

31. McCoy, and/or his predecessors-in-title, completed construction of the McCoy Parking Lot, including the installation of a retaining wall which blocked access to the Hatfield Parking Lot by means of the ROW.

32. A certain plan completed on McCoy's behalf dated December 13, 2001, and recorded in the Hancock County Registry of Deeds in Plan Book 30, Page 146 (the "McCoy Plan"), depicts the McCoy Property, the Hatfield Property (then owned by High Seas, Inc.), and the McCoy Parking Lot.

33. A true and accurate copy of the McCoy Plan is attached hereto as Exhibit F.

34. In an area on the McCoy Plan captioned "Easements, Rights of Way and Encroachments," paragraph (1) states:

> Rights . . . High Seas, Inc. to access [its] property over the backyard lot, so called, reference is made to the language contained in the deeds for these parcels as referenced on this survey plan. The location of these rights are not specifically defined and cannot be precisely located on the face of the earth.

35. High Seas, Inc. is a predecessor to Hatfield's title to the Hatfield Property.

36. In each deed transferring the Hatfield Property subsequent to the execution of the Agreement, the transfer is made subject to the Agreement, beginning with a deed dated November 20, 1984, and recorded in the Hancock County Registry of Deeds in Book 1519, Page 504, a true and accurate copy of which is attached hereto as Exhibit G.

37. McCoy, and/or his predecessors in title, continuously honored the Agreement until the Summer of 2007, permitting owners of the Hatfield Property to access the Hatfield Parking Lot from Main Street over the McCoy Property.

38. In the Summer of 2007, however, McCoy abruptly breached his easement and Agreement by blocking access to the Hatfield Park-

ing Lot by parking, or permitting the parking of, an automobile on the McCoy Property directly in front of the access path to the Hatfield Parking Lot.

39. Hatfield repeatedly asked McCoy to remove the automobile obstructing access to the Hatfield Parking Lot.

40. In violation of the easement and Agreement, McCoy did not remove, or cause the removal of, the automobile obstructing access to the Hatfield Parking Lot.

41. The obstruction has continued, and access to the Hatfield Parking Lot remains obstructed.

42. As a result of the obstruction, Hatfield and his tenants have been unable to utilize the Hatfield Parking Lot for parking, and have been forced to locate parking elsewhere in a congested area where little parking is available.

43. As a result of the obstruction, Hatfield has been unable to take deliveries through the Hatfield Parking Lot.

44. As a result of the obstruction, Hatfield and his tenants have effectively been unable to utilize the rear entrance to the Hatfield Property for any purposes.

45. As a result of the obstruction, public safety vehicles could be prevented from gaining access to the Hatfield Property.

46. As a result of the obstruction, Hatfield has been unable to rent the living space on the second floor of the Building.

47. As a result of the obstruction, Hatfield has been forced to take deliveries to his retail store through the Main Street entrance of the Building, causing disruptions to the Hatfield business operations.

48. Defendant's failure to honor the Agreement has negatively impacted the value of the Hatfield Property, and has interfered with Hatfield's use and enjoyment of his property.

COUNT I

Declaratory Judgment and Permanent Injunction

49. Hatfield repeats and realleges herein each and every allegation set forth above in the preceding Paragraphs.

50. There is a real and substantial controversy between the parties in that McCoy has violated the Agreement, and has obstructed the ROW with the construction of a retaining wall.

51. Hatfield has a permanent easement in place.

52. Hatfield has standing to raise this issue before this Court.

53. This Court has jurisdiction to determine the legal rights of the parties concerning the continued existence of the ROW pursuant to 14 M.R.S.A. §§ 5951 et seq.

WHEREFORE, Plaintiff Ephraim Hatfield respectfully requests that the Court declare that the ROW remains in place over the McCoy Property; issue a permanent injunction requiring McCoy to remove the retaining wall obstructing access via the ROW; award Hatfield interest and costs; and grant such other and further relief as the Court deems just and appropriate.

COUNT II

In the Alternative, the Agreement Is a Valid and Binding Agreement That Runs with the Land, and the Defendant Has Breached His Contract

54. Hatfield repeats and realleges herein each and every allegation set forth above in the preceding Paragraphs.

55. The Agreement contains binding and enforceable promises made by the Defendant to Hatfield's predecessor in title.

56. The Agreement obligates the Defendant to provide Hatfield, his family members, his tenants and delivery personnel with unlimited and free access to the Hatfield Parking Lot via the McCoy Property.

57. Hatfield, as beneficiary of the obligations contained in the Agreement, which permitted McCoy and/or his predecessors in title to construct a parking lot obstructing the ROW, has the ability to enforce those obligations.

58. By the conduct set forth above, the Defendant has breached his obligations under the Agreement.

59. Hatfield has satisfied all conditions precedent to the contractual obligations contained in the Agreement.

60. Hatfield has not breached the terms of the Agreement.

61. As a result of the Defendant's wrongful conduct, Hatfield has suffered, and will continue to suffer, substantial damage.

62. If, *arguendo*, the Court determines that the ROW is no longer valid, the Agreement represents a valid and binding right of access that runs with the land, burdening the McCoy Property and benefiting the Hatfield Property.

WHEREFORE, Plaintiff Ephraim Hatfield respectfully requests that in the event the Court finds the ROW invalid for any reason, the Court declare that the Agreement is binding on all parties; that it burdens the McCoy Property; that it benefits the Hatfield Property; and that it runs with the land in perpetuity. Hatfield further requests that the Court award damages in his favor, and against Defendant William McCoy, in an amount consistent with the evidence in this case, together with interest, costs, attorney's fees, punitive damages, and such other and further relief as the Court deems just and appropriate.

COUNT III

Intentional Trespass and Interference with Easement Rights

63. Hatfield repeats and realleges herein each and every allegation set forth above in the preceding Paragraphs.

64. With his actions to construct a parking lot and retaining wall, McCoy obstructed the ROW and interfered with access to the Hatfield Property.

65. McCoy knew and intended that his actions would enter onto the land burdened by the ROW, and that his actions would obstruct the ROW.

66. McCoy's actions directly interfered with the rights of Hatfield and Hatfield's predecessors in title to possess his deeded rights in the ROW.

67. McCoy's actions are the direct cause of interference with Hatfield's use of the ROW and the Hatfield Parking Lot, and are the proximate cause of interference with Hatfield's ability to conduct business in the Building.

68. McCoy's actions, as described above, amount to intentional trespass and interference with Hatfield's easement rights.

69. As a result of the Defendant's wrongful conduct, Hatfield has suffered, and will continue to suffer, substantial damage.

WHEREFORE, Plaintiff Ephraim Hatfield respectfully requests that the Court award damages in his favor, and against Defendant William McCoy, in an amount consistent with the evidence in this case, together with interest, costs, attorney's fees, punitive damages, and such other and further relief as the Court deems just and appropriate.

RIGHT-OF-WAY TO A DOCK

STATE OF MIND SUPERIOR COURT

EPHRAIM M. HATFIELD,)
Plaintiff)
)
v.)
) Civil Action No. ________
WILLIAM B. MCCOY,)
Defendant)
)

COMPLAINT FOR DECLARATORY JUDGMENT AND DAMAGES

Plaintiff Ephraim M. Hatfield, by his undersigned counsel, hereby states the following as his Complaint:

Preliminary Statement

1. Mr. Hatfield has an express deeded easement over the Boothbay Harbor property of Mr. McCoy to use a dock, runway, and float. In fact, Mr. Hatfield and his predecessors have used the deeded right-of-way continuously for over twenty years and have regularly paid their share of dock improvements and maintenance. In a sudden change to the status quo, Mr. McCoy claims that Mr. Hatfield is no longer allowed to access his express easement and dock. Mr. Hatfield requests that the Court declare that the easement is valid and binding, and award damages in his favor.

The Parties

2. Plaintiff Ephraim Hatfield is a citizen of Boston, Massachusetts.
3. Defendant William McCoy is a citizen of New York, New York.

The Properties

4. Mr. McCoy's property is on the ocean in Boothbay Harbor, and is enumerated as Lot 17 on Boothbay Harbor Tax Map No. 13. A true

and accurate copy of the Boothbay Harbor Tax Map No. 13 is attached hereto as Exhibit A.

5. Mr. Hatfield's property is Lot 12 on the same tax map. Mr. Hatfield accesses the McCoy property over Cove Road.

6. Mr. Hatfield and his predecessor have—for over 20 years—accessed the ocean and their dock, runway, and float by crossing over McCoy's property.

7. Mr. Hatfield's property is Lot 12 on the same tax map. Mr. Hatfield accesses the McCoy property over Cove Road.

8. The property owned by Mr. McCoy was previously owned by Clara Bartlett and Sam Bartlett, husband and wife, as joint tenants.

9. The property owned by Mr. Hatfield was previously owned by Clara Bartlett, the wife of Sam Bartlett.

10. Upon Clara Bartlett's death in 1961, she left her property to the children of herself and Sam Bartlett.

11. In 1976, Sam Bartlett—now sole owner of what would be the Hatfield property—died, leaving a Will that directed his Executors to sell his property and to give the proceeds to his heirs (who were the same people as the heirs of Clara Barlett).

12. When the children of Sam Bartlett and Clara Bartlett sold their father's property, through his Executors, they reserved for themselves an express deeded right-of-way—over what is now the Hatfield property—to access their dock, runway, and float.

13. Today, this easement benefits Hatfield and burdens McCoy.

McCoy's Chain of Title

14. On October 11, 1935, Sam Bartlett and Clara Barlett, husband and wife, and as joint tenants, bought the property—which included McCoy property—in Boothbay Harbor, from Lizzie J. Burgess. The deed conveying the property was recorded in the Lincoln County Registry of Deeds at Book 411, Page 107. A true and accurate copy of the deed is attached hereto as Exhibit B.

15. Sam Bartlett and Clara Bartlett had four children: Philip Bartlett, Margaret R. Harris, William Bartlett, and Carolyn Williams.

16. The property purchased by the Bartletts, as joint tenants, was on the ocean and included a dock, runway, and float "running from the shore of said property into the channel . . ."

17. Clara Bartlett died on April 25, 1961. By operation of the law of joint tenancy, the foregoing property became owned solely by Sam

Bartlett. Upon her death, her heirs were Phillip Bartlett, Margaret R. Harris, William Bartlett, and Carolyn Bartlett.

18. Carolyn Bartlett later married and, on her death on August 7, 1976, was named Carolyn Williams. Her heirs were David G. Williams, Betty H. Williams, Sandra H. Williams, and William Williams.

19. Sam Bartlett died on October 10, 1976. In his Will, he directed his Executors to, among other things, sell his real estate and provide the proceeds to his children and the children of his pre-deceased daughter, Carolyn Bartlett, aka Carolyn Williams.

20. On his death, the heirs of Sam Bartlett were the following: Philip Bartlett, William Bartlett, Margaret R. Harris, David Williams, Betty Williams, Sandra Williams, and William Williams.

21. Prior to the sale, the heirs of Sam Bartlett and Clara Bartlett owned both the Hatfield and McCoy lots. They then sold the "McCoy" portion, but reserved to the nearby "Hatfield" lot an easement and right to use the dock, runway, and float.

22. Philip Bartlett and William Bartlett, sole acting Executors of the Will of Sam Bartlett, sold the property—now belonging to Mr. McCoy—to T. Scott Kennedy and Judith C. Kennedy on December 14, 1977. The deed conveying the property was recorded in the Lincoln County Registry of Deeds at Book 942, Page 43. A true and accurate copy of the deed is attached hereto as Exhibit C.

23. The Executors of the Estate of Sam Bartlett sold the land ***subject to an express deeded right-of-way***:

> The above-described premises are conveyed subject to a certain right-of-way which is described as follows:
>
> A right-of-way running from the terminus of Cove Road, southwesterly to the wharf extending into Cove; the southerly boundary of said way being a 12 foot parcel of land owned by Pomerantz and Ramsey and which extends S. 72° 38' W. two hundred eighty six and one-tenth (286.1) feet from a pipe in cement at said terminus, to a bolt in an off-shore ledge. The north boundary of said way begins at a pipe in rocks located N. 26° 28' E. and eleven and two-tenths (11.2) feet from aforementioned pipe in cement and runs thence S. 72° 38' W. one hundred forty-four and two-tenths (144.2) feet to a pipe in large rocks; thence S. 78° 01' W. eighty and eight-tenths (80.8) feet to a pipe in rocks at high water mark, which pipe is also four and five-tenths (4.5) feet northerly from the wharf.

> The right to maintain or replace the dock, runway and float, within the westerly extension of the S. 78° 04' W. line, on the north, and the westerly extension of the S. 72° 38' W. property line of the land herein conveyed, shall be a part of the right-of-way herein granted.
>
> The use of the above described right-of-way and the dock, runway and float shall be restricted to the owner or owners of the premises described in the Deed of Chester A. Swett to Clara Bartlett dated October 24, 1939 and recorded in Lincoln County Registry of Deeds, Book 427, Page 458 (the "Swett Deed"), which owners currently are Philip Bartlett, William Bartlett, Margaret R. Harris, David Williams, Betty Williams, Sandra Williams, and William Williams, and their guests.

This express deeded right-of-way is hereinafter referred to as the "Dock Easement."

24. The Dock Easement recorded above was expressly restricted to the owners or owners of the premises described in the Deed from Chester A. Swett to Clara Bartlett, dated October 24, 1939, and is the property owned today by McCoy. The deed conveying the property was recorded in the Lincoln County Registry of Deeds at Book 427, Page 458. At the time of the creation of the Dock Easement in the deed to T. Scott and Judith C. Kennedy (see Exhibit C attached and previously noted above), the McCoy property was owned by the heirs of both William Bartlett and Clara Bartlett, who are listed above. Similarly, the reference in the Dock Easement to "Lot 12" refers to the property now owned by Mr. Hatfield and is described in the Swett deed. A true and accurate copy of the Swett deed is attached hereto as Exhibit D.

25. The purpose of the express deeded right-of-way was to benefit the remaining property owned by all of the Bartlett heirs—now Hatfield property—to cross over what is now Mr. McCoy's property to access the dock, runway, and float.

26. Indeed, the Contract for Sale of Real Estate, by and between the Estate of William Bartlett and the Kennedys, expressly provided that a "Right-of-Way shall be granted to the owners of Lots 12 and 19 on the Boothbay Harbor Tax Map #13 and to the owners of Lots 12, 13, and 15 on Map #25 over a parcel of land 20' x 260' on lot #17 bounded on the southeast by Parcel 18 and on the northwest by Lot 17 extending 100' from the waters of Hodgdon's Cove to the Town Road, including

the use of the dock, float, and runway." A true and accurate copy of this contract, dated October 11, 1977, is attached hereto as Exhibit E.

27. The Right-of-Way set forth in the contract, dated October 11, 1977, benefits the property owned today by Mr. Hatfield. The reference to Map 13, Lot 12 refers to the Hatfield property (see Exhibit A attached hereto and previously noted above).

28. On July 16, 1979, T. Scott Kennedy and Judith C. Kennedy sold the aforementioned property to Phippen Sanborn and Catharine C. Sanborn. The deed conveying the property was recorded in the Lincoln County Registry of Deeds at Book 1001, Page 279. A true and accurate copy of the deed is attached hereto as Exhibit F.

29. The Kennedy to Sanborn deed is expressly subject to the Dock Easement.

30. On May 15, 1981, Phippen Sanborn and Catharine C. Sanborn sold the aforementioned property to Defendant William McCoy. The deed conveying the property was recorded in the Lincoln County Registry of Deeds at Book 1064, Page 273. A true and accurate copy of this deed is attached hereto as Exhibit G.

31. The Sanborn to McCoy deed is expressly subject to the Dock Easement.

32. Thus, Mr. McCoy has written notice of the McCoy's easement in their own deed, as well as in their chain of title.

The Hatfield Chain of Title

33. Clara Bartlett bought the property—now belonging to Mr. Hatfield—from Chester A. Swett on October 24, 1939. The deed conveying the property was recorded in the Lincoln County Registry of Deeds at Book 427, Page 458 (see Exhibit D attached hereto and previously noted above).

34. Clara Bartlett died on April 25, 1961, leaving the property to the four children of William Bartlett and Clara Bartlett: Philip Bartlett, Margaret R. Harris, William Bartlett, Jr. and Carolyn Bartlett (later to be known as Carolyn Williams upon her marriage).

35. The heirs of Clara Bartlett regularly crossed over the property—now owned by Mr. McCoy—and used the dock, runway, and float at issue.

36. On September 8, 1978, William Bartlett, as one of the four heirs of Clara Bartlett, conveyed his one-fourth interest in the "Swett Property" (see Exhibit D as previously noted above), along with the Dock

Easement, to Charlotte R. Blaney and Margaret Harris. The deed conveying the property was recorded in the Lincoln County Registry of Deeds at Book 970, Page 276. A true and accurate copy of the deed is attached hereto as Exhibit H. The aforementioned conveyance gave the Purchasers an express right to use the Dock Easement:

> Meaning and intending to describe the same premises as Chester A. Swett conveyed to Clara Bartlett by warranty deed dated October 24, 1939, and recorded in Lincoln County Registry of Deeds in Book 427, Page 458.

Together with a certain right-of-way which is described as follows:

> A right-of-way running from the terminus of Hodgdon Cove Road, southwesterly to the wharf extending into Hodgdon's Cove, the southerly boundary of said way being a 12 foot parcel of land owned by Pomerantz and Ramsey and which extends S. 72° 38' W. two hundred eighty-six and one tenth (286.1) feet from a pipe in cement at said terminus, to a bolt in an off-shore ledge. The north boundary of said way begins at a pipe in rocks located N. 26° 28' E. and eleven and two tenths (11.2) feet from aforementioned pipe in cement and runs thence S. 72° 38' W. one hundred forty-four and two tenths (144.2) feet to a pipe in large rocks; thence S. 78° 04' W. eighty and eight tenths (80.8) feet to a pipe in rocks at high water mark, which pipe is also four and five tenths (4.5) feet northerly from the wharf.
>
> The right to maintain or replace the dock, runway and float, within the westerly extension of the S. 78° 04' W. line, on the north, and the westerly extension of the S. 72° W. property line of the land herein conveyed, shall be a part of the right-of-way herein granted.
>
> The use of the above described right-of-way and the dock, runway and float shall be restricted to the owner or owners of the premises described in the Deed of Chester A. Swett to Clara Bartlett dated October 24, 1939, and recorded in Lincoln County Registry of Deeds, Book 427, Page 458, which owners currently are Philip Bartlett, William Bartlett, Margaret R. Harris, David Williams, Betty Williams, Sandra Williams, and William Williams and their guests. On or about September 8, 1978, Charlotte R. Blaney; Margaret R. Harris; Phillip Bartlett (Margaret and Phillip being sister and brother of William Williams); David G. Williams; Sandra Williams; William Williams (the last three being three of the four children of Carolyn R. Bartlett (Williams)—sister of William Bartlett), conveyed their interest to the Swett Property and the Dock Easement to Charles

S. Yentsch and Clarice M. Yentsch. The deed conveying this interest in the property was recorded in the Lincoln County Registry of Deeds at Book 970, Page 282. A true and accurate copy of the deed is attached hereto as Exhibit I.

37. On or about September 8, 1978, Charlotte R. Blaney; Margaret R. Harris; Phillip Bartlett (Margaret and Phillip being sister and brother of William Williams); David G. Williams; Sandra Williams; William Williams (the last three being three of the four children of Carolyn R. Bartlett (Williams)—sister of William Bartlett), conveyed their interest to the Swett Property and the Dock Easement to Charles S. Yentsch and Clarice M. Yentsch. The deed conveying this interest in the property was recorded in the Lincoln County Registry of Deeds at Book 970, Page 282. A true and accurate copy of the deed is attached hereto as Exhibit I.

38. On or about September 8, 1978, Betty Bartlett as the last of the four children of Carolyn Bartlett Williams conveyed all of her interest in the Swett Property and the Dock Easement to Charles S. Yentsch and Clarice M. Yentsch. The deed conveying this interest in the property was recorded in the Lincoln County Registry of Deeds at Book 970, Page 279. A true and accurate copy of the deed is attached hereto as Exhibit J.

39. The aforementioned deeds to Charles S. Yentsch and Clarice M. Yentsch are all expressly benefited by the Dock Easement.

40. Charles S. Yentsch and Clarice M. Yentsch regularly crossed over the Hatfield property and used the dock, runway, and float at issue.

41. Charles S. Yentsch and Clarice M. Yentsch, by deed dated October 11, 1979, sold what is now the McCoy property to Suzanne R. Buchanan. The deed conveying the property was recorded in the Lincoln County Registry of Deeds at Book 1012, Page 36. A true and accurate copy of the deed is attached hereto as Exhibit K.

42. The Yentsch to Buchanan deed is expressly benefited by the Dock Easement.

43. Suzanne R. Buchanan regularly crossed over the Hatfield property and used the dock, runway, and float.

44. On December 29, 1986, Suzanne R. Buchanan sold the property to Ephraim Hatfield. The deed conveying the property was recorded in the Lincoln County Registry of Deeds at Book 1361, Page 163. A true and accurate copy of the deed is attached hereto as Exhibit L.

45. The deed from Buchanan to Hatfield is expressly benefited by the Dock Easement.

46. Mr. Hatfield has regularly crossed over the McCoy property and used the dock, runway, and float.

Mr. Hatfield and His Predecessors Have Regularly Used, Improved, and Maintained the Dock Easement and Dock

47. Historically, all improvements and maintenance of the dock, runway, and float at issue have been paid equally by Hatfield, McCoy, other abutters, and their predecessors in interest.

48. Specifically, Mr. Hatfield and his predecessors, the Buchanans, have historically used the dock, runway, and float—and have paid their pro rata share of the cost of all improvements and maintenance.

49. On September 17, 1986, for example, Ben's Boatyard sent Mr. McCoy a $21,300 proposal to replace the old dock, to build a new runway, to build a new float, and for other work. A true and accurate copy of the deed is attached hereto as Exhibit N.

50. William McCoy, on September 29, 1986, wrote a letter to Dr. Raymond Buchanan enclosing the Ben's Boatyard proposal for the purpose of having Dr. Buchanan sign the contract and pay his portion of these major dock improvements. A true and accurate copy of the letter is attached hereto as Exhibit O.

51. Dr. Raymond Buchanan's wife is the predecessor in interest to Mr. Hatfield.

52. William McCoy and Raymond Buchanan accepted this proposal and each signed the contract with Ben's Boatyard. A true and accurate copy of the contract executed by and between Ben's Boatyard, Raymond E. Buchanan, and William McCoy is attached hereto as Exhibit P.

53. Mr. McCoy and Buchanan (the predecessor of Mr. Hatfield) subsequently each paid one-half of the total cost of these dock improvements.

54. Ben's Boatyard subsequently sent other bills to the owners of these three properties for dock improvements and all invoices received for maintenance.

55. Mr. Hatfield and his predecessors in interest always paid their pro rata share of all invoices received for the cost of the dock improvements and maintenance.

56. As recently as June 24, 2004, Mr. McCoy has forwarded bills for dock maintenance to his neighbors and asked that his neighbors pay their pro rata share of such maintenance. A true and accurate copy of a letter which William McCoy wrote to Ephraim Hatfield dated June 24, 2004, is attached hereto as Exhibit Q.

Mr. McCoy's Wrongful Conduct

57. On September 30, 2004, Mr. McCoy sent a letter to Mr. Hatfield claiming that Mr. Hatfield does not have a recorded enforceable right-of-way or easement over the McCoy property. A true and accurate copy of the letter dated September 30, 2004, is attached hereto as Exhibit R.

58. On May 3, 2005, Mr. McCoy's attorney wrote a letter to Mr. Hatfield's attorney stating, among other things, that Mr. Hatfield does not have an easement over McCoy's land, dock, and float. A true and accurate copy of the letter dated May 3, 2005, is attached hereto as Exhibit S.

59. Mr. McCoy has also acted wrongfully in refusing to allow Mr. Hatfield to cross his property and to use the dock, runway, and float at issue in this case, and in recording, on November 2, 2004, a Notice denying Hatfield access to his dock easement in the Lincoln County Registry of Deeds at Book. A true and accurate copy of the Notice is attached hereto as Exhibit T.

COUNT I

Declaratory Judgment—Express Easement

60. The foregoing allegations set forth above in Paragraphs 1 through 59 of this Complaint are hereby repeated and realleged herein as if set forth in full.

61. There is a real and substantial controversy between the parties in that Mr. McCoy has refused to recognize Mr. Hatfield's express deeded right to cross McCoy's property and to use the dock, runway, and float at issue in this case.

62. Mr. Hatfield has standing to raise this issue before this Court.

63. This Court has jurisdiction to determine the legal rights of the parties concerning the easement pursuant to 14 M.R.S.A. §§ 5951 et seq.

WHEREFORE, Plaintiff Ephraim Hatfield respectfully requests that the Court declare that he has an easement over the Defendant's land and a right to use the dock, runway, and float at issue in this case;

order the Defendant to cease interfering with Mr. Hatfield's express deeded easement; award Mr. Hatfield interest and costs; and grant such other and further relief as the Court deems just and appropriate.

COUNT II

Declaratory Judgment—Prescriptive Easement

64. The foregoing allegations set forth above in Paragraph 1 through 63 of this Complaint are hereby repeated and realleged as if set forth in full.

65. There is a real and substantial controversy between the parties in that Mr. McCoy is seeking to block Mr. Hatfield's longstanding prescriptive easement to cross his property and to use the dock, runway, and float at issue in this case.

66. Mr. Hatfield and his predecessors in interest have continuously used the easement and the dock, runway, and float for more than twenty years, under a claim of right adverse to the owner, with the owner's knowledge and acquiescence, or has used the dock in a manner which is so open and notorious, visible, and uninterrupted that knowledge and acquiescence is presumed.

67. Mr. Hatfield has standing to raise this issue before this Court.

68. This Court has jurisdiction to determine the legal rights of the parties concerning their prescriptive easement pursuant to 14 M.R.S.A. §§ 5951 et seq.

WHEREFORE, Plaintiff Ephraim Hatfield respectfully requests that the Court declare that he has a prescriptive easement over the McCoy property and a prescriptive right to use the dock, runway, and float at issue in this case; order the Defendant to cease interfering with this prescriptive easement; award Mr. Hatfield interest and costs; and grant such other and further relief as the Court deems just and appropriate.

COUNT III

Declaratory Judgment—Quasi-Easement

69. The foregoing allegations set forth above in Paragraphs 1 through 68 of this Complaint are hereby repeated and realleged herein as if set forth in full.

70. The McCoy property and the Hatfield property was in a single ownership in that they were both owned by the heirs of Sam Bartlett and Clara Bartlett.

71. At the time that the properties were in single ownership, they were owned in a manner constituting a quasi-easement. Specifically, the heirs crossed over the McCoy property to access the ocean and the dock, runway, and float.

72. At the time that the unity of title was severed, it was done in a manner which manifested an intent that the quasi-easement should continue as a true easement.

73. The buyers of the dominant estate (the Hatfield property) have continued their use of this easement.

WHEREFORE, Plaintiff Ephraim Hatfield respectfully requests that the Court declare that he has a quasi-easement over Defendant's land and a right to use the dock, runway, and float at issue in this case; order the Defendant to cease interfering with the Mr. Hatfield's quasi-easement; award Mr. Hatfield interest and costs and grant such other and further relief as the Court deems just and appropriate.

COUNT IV

Promissory Estoppel

74. The foregoing allegations set forth above in Paragraphs 1 through 73 of this Complaint are hereby repeated and realleged herein as if set forth in full.

75. McCoy and his contractors sent Mr. Hatfield and his predecessor bills for the improvement and maintenance of the dock, runway, and float. Mr. Hatfield and his predecessors paid all of their pro rata share of these invoices.

76. Mr. Hatfield and his predecessors paid these invoices pursuant to a reasonable expectation that they had a right to cross over the McCoy property to use the dock, runway, and float.

77. Mr. Hatfield and his predecessors relied on the fact that they paid for dock improvements and dock maintenance because they had an easement over the McCoy property to use the dock facilities.

78. Injustice can be avoided only by the enforcing the longstanding practice of allowing Mr. Hatfield and his predecessors use of the dock facilities.

WHEREFORE, Plaintiff Ephraim Hatfield respectfully requests that the Court declare that he has a right to travel across Defendant's land and a right to use the dock, runway, and float at issue in this case; order the Defendant to cease interfering with Mr. Hatfield's express deeded easement; and award Mr. Hatfield interest, costs of suit, and such other and further relief as the Court deems just and appropriate.

COUNT V

Unjust Enrichment

79. The foregoing allegations set forth above in Paragraphs 1 through 78 of this Complaint are hereby repeated and realleged herein as if set forth in full.

80. The Defendant has been unjustly enriched by the benefits conferred upon him by the fact that Mr. Hatfield has paid charges and expenses in connection with the dock, runway, and float.

81. The Defendant has failed and/or refused to reimburse Mr. Hatfield for these benefits.

82. It would be inequitable for Defendant to retain the benefits conferred upon him by Mr. Hatfield without compensating Mr. Hatfield for the value of those benefits.

83. Defendant has received and accepted the benefit of Mr. Hatfield's payments for repairs and maintenance to the dock, runway, and float, with the knowledge and understanding that he was obligated to pay for such benefits.

WHEREFORE, Plaintiff Ephraim Hatfield respectfully requests judgment against Defendant in an amount that is reasonable under the circumstances, plus interest, costs of suit, and such other and further relief as the Court deems just and appropriate.

COUNT VI

Quantum Meruit

84. The foregoing allegations set forth above in Paragraphs 1 through 83 of this Complaint are hereby repeated and realleged herein as if set forth in full.

85. The payments made by Mr. Hatfield were provided under circumstances that clearly establish Mr. Hatfield's reasonable expectation that he would be compensated by the Defendant for such payments.

86. Defendant benefited from these payments, but has not reimbursed Mr. Hatfield for his share of the aforementioned payments.

87. Defendant is liable to Mr. Hatfield in quantum meruit for the reasonable value of the payments made on his behalf.

WHEREFORE, Plaintiff Ephraim Hatfield respectfully requests judgment against the Defendant in an amount that is reasonable under the circumstances, plus interest, costs of suit, and such other and further relief as the Court deems just and appropriate.

IMPLIED EASEMENT / SLANDER OF TITLE

STATE OF MIND SUPERIOR COURT

EPHRAIM M. HATFIELD,	)	
Plaintiff	)	
	)	
v.	)	
	)	Civil Action No. ________
WILLIAM B. MCCOY,	)	
Defendant	)	
	)	

COMPLAINT FOR DECLARATORY JUDGMENT AND DAMAGES

(Title to Real Estate Is Involved)

I. Preliminary Statement

1. Ephraim M. Hatfield owns a commercial parcel of land in Naples which is under contract to be sold to the ACME Company. It is imperative that the sale go through as soon as possible because Mr. Hatfield needs to pay a lump sum payment to his mortgagee. The ACME Company is anxious to close on this transaction—and Plaintiff is anxious to pay his mortgagee—but Defendant is wrongfully holding up the closing and ACME's proposed project by making a meritless claim that he has an easement by necessity that runs through the middle of Plaintiff's property. In fact, Defendant's property is readily accessible by a public road and there is no evidence on the face of the earth that he has any kind of easement on the property of Mr. Hatfield. Indeed, the evidence indicates that Defendant is trying to hold up the transaction inappropriately so that he can obtain an outrageous sum of money. Mr. Hatfield asks that the Court declare that Defendant does not have an easement over his land, and to award damages against the Defendant for slander of title and tortious interference with contractual relations.

II. The Parties

2. Plaintiff Ephraim Hatfield resides in Casco.
3. Defendant William McCoy resides in Casco.

III. The Facts Concerning Plaintiffs' Land

4. On August 12, 1996, Mr. Hatfield Purchased from the Manatee Restaurant, Inc. four abutting parcels of property in Naples. A true and accurate copy of the Warranty Deed from Manatee Restaurant, Inc. to Mr. Hatfield is attached hereto as Exhibit A.

5. A true and accurate copy of a plan depicting the four abutting parcels of property Purchased by Mr. Hatfield is attached hereto as Exhibit B.

6. The four abutting parcels of property form one large piece of property which is at the corner of State Route 302 and State Route 11 in Naples.

7. At the time that Mr. Hatfield Purchased his property in Naples, he simultaneously gave a promissory note and a mortgage deed back to Manatee, Inc. A true and accurate copy of the promissory note and mortgage deed are attached hereto as Exhibits C and D, respectively.

8. The promissory note and mortgage from Mr. Hatfield to the Manatee Restaurant, Inc. are in the original principal amount of $77,500.

9. The promissory note, attached hereto as Exhibit C, provides that Mr. Hatfield must make certain monthly payments to the Manatee Restaurant, Inc., and then a balloon payment to it no later than January 1, 2009.

10. The balloon payment due to Manatee Restaurant, Inc. is in excess of $67,000.

11. On May 21, 2001, Mr. Hatfield entered into a Purchase and Sale Agreement to sell the Naples property at issue in this case to the ACME Company. A true and accurate copy of the contract entered into on May 21, 2001, is attached hereto as Exhibit E.

12. The Purchase and Sale Agreement attached hereto as Exhibit E provided that the closing shall take place on November 23, 2001.

13. This closing date preceded the date on which Mr. Hatfield owes a balloon payment to Manatee Restaurant, Inc.

14. Paragraph 25 of the Purchase and Sale Agreement, attached hereto as Exhibit E, provides that the contract is contingent upon the ACME Company obtaining "approval by the Town of Naples of a site plan review."

IV. The Facts Concerning Defendants' Land

15. Defendant William McCoy owns property abutting the land of Mr. Hatfield in Naples.

16. Defendant obtained the abutting property by deed, dated April 21, 1999, from his relatives, Robert F. McCoy and Eleanor L. McCoy. A true and accurate copy of this deed is attached hereto as Exhibit F.

17. Robert F. McCoy and Eleanor L. McCoy obtained the abutting property by deed, recorded June 28, 1995, from Marjorie D. McCoy. A true and accurate copy of this deed is attached hereto as Exhibit G.

18. Marjorie D. McCoy obtained much of the abutting property, as well as other surrounding property, by deed dated July 12, 1950, and corrective deed dated September 21, 1950. True and accurate copies of these deeds are attached hereto as Exhibits H and I, respectively.

19. On May 16, 1957, Marjorie D. McCoy sold a portion of her property, including her frontage on the State Route 302, to Plaintiff's predecessor in title. A true and accurate copy of this deed is attached hereto as Exhibit J.

20. Defendant claims that the May 16, 1957, sale creates an easement by necessity, for Margaret D. McCoy's remaining land, over Plaintiff's property.

21. On March 28, 1958, Marjorie D. McCoy Purchased another parcel of property which immediately adjoins her remaining property. A true and accurate copy of this deed is attached hereto as Exhibit K.

22. The property Purchased by Marjorie D. McCoy on March 28, 1958, has approximately seventy-five feet of road frontage on State Route 11.

23. The property Purchased by Marjorie D. McCoy on March 28, 1958, the deed to which is attached hereto as Exhibit K, enabled Marjorie McCoy to obtain direct access to and from State Route 11, a public way, to her remaining land without the need to trespass on the land of any third party.

24. On August 30, 1971, Marjorie D. McCoy sold to Plaintiff's predecessor in title the strip of her remaining land which was closest to State Route 302. A true and accurate copy of this deed is attached hereto as Exhibit L.

25. The August 30, 1971, deed, attached hereto as Exhibit L, reserved a ten-foot wide easement across the extreme southeasterly end of the strip.

26. The rest of Marjorie D. McCoy's property was ultimately conveyed to Defendant.

V. Defendant's Wrongful Conduct

27. Defendant has actively sought to derail the ACME Company's site plan review of the subject property and to scuttle Plaintiffs' sale of

their property by claiming that he has a twenty-foot-wide easement by necessity which runs through the middle of the land at issue.

28. After the Naples Planning Board finally granted site plan approval, Defendant tied up the approval by filing an appeal.

29. The Naples Planning Board site plan approval for the property is not final—and Mr. Hatfield has not yet been able to close on the Purchase and Sale Agreement—because of Defendant's wrongful claims. Defendant knows that his claims have no merit.

30. Upon information and belief, Defendant's meritless claims have been made in a fraudulent effort to cause Mr. Hatfield to pay him money in exchange for dropping the meritless claims.

31. By letter dated October 16, 2001, Defendant's attorney wrote a letter to Plaintiff's attorney claiming that Defendant has an easement which runs roughly through the middle of Plaintiff's property by virtue of an easement by necessity which was allegedly created when "Marjorie McCoy conveyed all of her road frontage on Route 302 and reserved no easement for access to the back land she retained. . . ." A true and accurate copy of the letter dated October 16, 2001 from Defendant's counsel to Plaintiff's counsel is attached hereto as Exhibit M.

32. The letter from Defendant's counsel to Plaintiff's counsel was copied to David R. Smith, counsel for the ACME Company.

33. The letter from Defendant's counsel to counsel for the ACME Company had the desired effect. As a result of the letter and Defendant's statements and actions at the Naples Planning Board, Mr. Hatfield has been unable to sell his property or to pay the lump sum payment to his mortgagee.

34. By letter dated October 17, 2001, counsel for the ACME Company informed the attorney for Mr. Hatfield that ACME "remains anxious to close on this Purchase" but that it considers Defendant's claim to be a title defect and that "the closing will have to be held in abeyance until the title issue is resolved." A true and accurate copy of the letter from counsel for ACME to counsel for Mr. Hatfield is attached hereto as Exhibit N.

35. In fact, Defendant does not have an easement by necessity over the property of Mr. Hatfield.

36. Although Defendant's relative and predecessor in title did sell property in 1957 which left her no road frontage on State Route 302, she subsequently bought another piece of property in 1958 which connected her remaining property to State Route 11.

37. An easement by necessity is an equitable easement which exists to the extent that there is a necessity to get access from a landlocked parcel of property to a road. The easement by necessity lasts only as long as the necessity itself.

38. The recognized rule in the State of Mind with respect to ways of necessity is that termination of the necessity extinguishes the easement.

39. Any easement by necessity, which Defendant's relative and predecessor in title may or may not have created in 1957, certainly ended when Defendant's relative and predecessor in title bought another parcel of property which connected the allegedly landlocked property to State Route 11.

40. The property, which Defendant's relative and predecessor in title allegedly landlocked in 1957, can be readily accessed from State Route 11 across Defendant's immediately abutting property (acquired in 1958), and there is no condition of the land or other impediment which would make such access impracticable.

41. There is also no evidence on the face of the earth which would suggest that Defendant has ever used an easement across the land of Mr. Hatfield.

42. Mr. Hatfield has never observed Defendant or his agents crossing his property.

43. Defendant's aforementioned conduct is either motivated by ill will toward Mr. Hatfield or is so outrageous that malice to Mr. Hatfield can be inferred. The aforementioned conduct represents a gross deviation from the standard of conduct that a reasonable person would follow.

COUNT I

Declaratory Judgment

44. The foregoing allegations set forth above in Paragraphs 1 through 43 of this Complaint are hereby repeated and realleged herein as if set forth in full.

45. There is a real and substantial controversy between the parties in that Mr. Hatfield cannot sell his property or make a balloon payment to his mortgagee because Defendant is claiming an easement by necessity over his land.

46. Mr. Hatfield has standing to raise this issue before this Court.

47. This Court has jurisdiction to determine the legal rights of the parties concerning the alleged easement pursuant to 14 M.R.S.A. §§ 5951 et seq.

WHEREFORE, Plaintiff Ephraim Hatfield respectfully requests that the Court declare that Defendant has no easement over his land; order the Defendant to cease interfering with the ACME Company's proposed project and efforts to Purchase the property; award Mr. Hatfield interest and costs; and grant such other and further relief as the Court deems just and appropriate.

COUNT II

Slander of Title

48. The foregoing allegations set forth above in Paragraphs 1 through 47 of this Complaint are hereby repeated and realleged herein as if set forth in full.

49. Defendant made statements to the ACME Company, to the Naples Planning Board, and to others which alleged that he had an easement by necessity over the land of Mr. Hatfield.

50. Defendant's aforementioned statements were false.

51. Defendant's false statements slandered and disparaged the Plaintiff's title.

52. Defendant's aforementioned statements were made and published with malice or with reckless disregard as to whether they were false or not.

53. Defendant's aforementioned statements have caused specific damages to Mr. Hatfield including, but not limited to, the fact that he has not been able to close his transaction with ACME, the fact that he is not able to make a balloon payment to his mortgagee, and the fact that he is having to expend considerable legal fees in rebutting the slander and addressing the cloud on the title to his property.

54. Defendant has acted outrageously by making the aforementioned false and slanderous statements.

55. Malice can be inferred from Defendant's outrageous behavior.

WHEREFORE, Plaintiff Ephraim Hatfield respectfully requests that the Court enter judgment in Plaintiff's favor and against Defendant in an amount consistent with the evidence in this case, together with punitive damages, interest, reasonable attorney's fees, costs, and such other and further relief as the Court deems just and appropriate.

COUNT III

Interference with Contract and/or Advantageous Relationship

56. The foregoing allegations set forth above in Paragraphs 1 through 55 of this Complaint are hereby repeated and realleged herein as if set forth in full.

57. Mr. Hatfield has a valid contract and/or prospective economic advantage with the ACME Company.

58. Defendant, through fraudulent statements, has prevented Mr. Hatfield from closing on his contract and/or advantageous relationship with the ACME Company.

59. But for the aforementioned fraudulent and inaccurate statements by Defendant, Mr. Hatfield would have been able to have closed on his contract and/or advantageous relationship with the ACME Company.

60. By their aforementioned fraudulent and inaccurate statements, Defendant has wrongfully interfered with the contracts between Plaintiff and the ACME Company.

61. Mr. Hatfield has suffered substantial damages as a result of Defendant's wrongful interference with his contract and/or advantageous relationship with the ACME Company.

WHEREFORE, Plaintiff Ephraim Hatfield respectfully requests that the Court enter judgment in Plaintiff's favor and against Defendant in an amount consistent with the evidence in this case, together with punitive damages, interest, reasonable attorney's fees, costs, and such other and further relief as the Court deems just and appropriate.

BLOCKING OF ACCESS/NUISANCE

STATE OF MIND SUPERIOR COURT

EPHRAIM M. HATFIELD, Plaintiff v. WILLIAM B. MCCOY, Defendant	))))))))	Civil Action No. ________

COMPLAINT FOR INJUNCTIVE RELIEF, DECLARATORY RELIEF, AND DAMAGES

(Title to Real Estate Is Involved)

Preliminary Statement

1. Plaintiff Ephraim M. Hatfield recently bought a home on Raccoon Road in Naples. Defendant William B. McCoy, however, has illegally and wrongfully blocked the legal access to his property. Mr. Hatfield asks this Court to enjoin Mr. McCoy from blocking access to his property and to compensate him for the damages caused by Defendant's wrongful actions.

The Parties

2. Plaintiff Ephraim Hatfield is a citizen of Exeter, New Hampshire. Mr. Hatfield is the owner of property on Raccoon Road in Naples.

3. Defendant William McCoy is a citizen of Braintree, Massachusetts. Mr. McCoy is the owner of property on Wiggin Road in Naples.

The Facts

Plaintiff Has an Easement Over Defendant's Land

4. Mr. Hatfield bought his home in Naples on March 15, 2002. A true and accurate copy of the deed to his new home is attached hereto as Exhibit A.

5. The deed to Mr. Hatfield states, among other things, the following:

> A certain lot or parcel of land situated in the Town of Naples, County and State aforesaid, on the easterly shore of Brandy Pond, so-called, therein, at its junction with the Songo River, and being Lot Number Three (#3) on Plan of Land of Robert Wiggin, by Earl C. Hotchkiss, Jr., Surveyor, dated July 30, 1970, and recorded in the Cumberland County Registry of Deeds, Plan Book 83, Page 17.
>
> Also conveying a right of common user in and to the camp roads as depicted on said Plan, as well as the Old Jackson Road, so-called, for ingress and egress from the property above set forth, in the Town way extending from Songo Locks to Route #302 in said Naples.

6. The property Purchased by Mr. Hatfield is shown as Lot 3 on the recorded Plan of Land, dated July 3, 1970, and recorded in the Cumberland County Registry of Deeds at Plan Book 83, Page 17. A true and accurate copy of the Plan is attached hereto as Exhibit B.

7. The six-lot subdivision shown on the Plan was created by Elmer Wiggin, Jr., in 1970. A true and accurate copy of the first deed from Elmer Wiggin, Jr., arising from the Plan—for Lot 3—is attached hereto as Exhibit C.

8. The April 27, 1971, deed for Lot 3 expressly states that it is "Also conveying a right of common user in and to the camp roads as depicted on said Plan, as well as the Old Jackson Road, so called, for ingress and egress from the property above set forth, to the Town way extending from Songo Locks to Route #302, in said Naples."

9. This same language appears in the deed into Mr. Hatfield, and is contained in every deed in the chain of title for Lot 3 from 1971 to present.

10. As also shown on the Plan, the "New Camp Road" leads to a road identified as Old Jackson Road. At the southerly end of Old Jackson Road, located on the land of "Wiggin"—today Wiggin Road—there is an arrow which points in a southerly direction and indicates "To Songo Lock Rd." This demonstrates that the owners of the subdivision lots (including Lot 3) have access over the property of Mr. Wiggin to Songo Lock Road.

11. The above-referenced property of Mr. Wiggin was recently purchased by Defendant William McCoy.

Defendant's Property Is Encumbered by Plaintiff's Easement

12. Defendant William McCoy bought his property on April 28, 2000, from Virginia D. Wiggin, widow and surviving joint tenant of Elmer H. Wiggin, Jr. A true and accurate copy of the deed from Virginia D. Wiggin to William McCoy is attached hereto as Exhibit D.

13. The deed from Ms. Wiggin to Defendant McCoy clearly sets forth the following: "being the premises conveyed by the Diamond Match Company to John Jackson by deed dated March 2, 1908, recorded in the Cumberland County Registry of Deeds, Book 820, Page 233, *subject* however, to exceptions and reservations as set forth therein and further excepting and reserving and *subject* to any and all parcels as conveyed away from the premises described in said deed *and any easements granted prior to date hereof.*" (emphasis added).

14. The deed from Mr. Wiggin to Lot 3—granting an easement over property now owned by Defendant McCoy—*precedes* the deed to Mr. McCoy.

15. The deed to Defendant McCoy, therefore, is subject to the easement now owned by Mr. Hatfield, the owners of Lot 3.

Name Changes

16. The camp road referenced in the 1970 Plan is known today as Raccoon Road.

17. The "Old Jackson Road" referenced in the 1970 Plan is known today as State Park Road.

18. The "Songo Lock Road" referenced in the 1970 Plan is known today as Songo School Road.

19. The road connecting State Park Road to Songo School Road, which travels through Defendant's property, is now known as Wiggin Road.

Plaintiffs Also Have Public and Private Rights Over Wiggin Road

20. Songo School Road is currently a public road in the Town of Naples.

21. What are now known as State Park Road and Wiggin Road were formerly town roads which have been discontinued pursuant to 23 M.R.S.A. § 3026(1) and/or abandoned for more than thirty years pursuant to 23 M.R.S.A § 3028(1).

22. Pursuant to 23 M.R.S.A. § 3026, there is a public easement over Wiggin Road.

23. In that Plaintiff's easement is part of a recorded subdivision which has been approved and signed by the members of the Naples Planning Board, Mr. Hatfield also has a right to use his easement pursuant to 23 M.R.S.A. § 3031.

Defendant's Wrongful Actions

24. Defendant McCoy has deliberately and intentionally placed a chain over the easement owned by Mr. Hatfield now known as Wiggin Road, and has, from time to time, also blocked the easement with vehicles.

25. Defendant McCoy has also refused to allow let Mr. Hatfield to pass through the easement to his new home.

26. Mr. Hatfield spoke to Mr. McCoy's son and asked him to allow Plaintiff to access his property via the easement. Mr. McCoy's son refused to allow Mr. Hatfield regular access along his deeded easement.

27. By letter dated June 13, 2002, counsel for Mr. Hatfield demanded that Mr. McCoy allow Plaintiff to use his easement. A true and accurate copy of the letter dated June 13, 2002 is attached hereto as Exhibit E.

28. Mr. McCoy has failed and/or refused to respond to the letter.

29. Despite demand, Defendant William McCoy has adamantly refused to unblock the easement or allow Mr. Hatfield access over his easement to his new home.

COUNT I

Declaratory Judgment

30. The foregoing allegations set forth above in Paragraphs 1 through 29 of this Complaint are hereby repeated and realleged herein as if set forth in full.

31. There is a real and substantial controversy between the parties in that Mr. Hatfield cannot access the easement to his property because it is being blocked by the Defendant.

32. Mr. Hatfield has standing to raise this issue before this Court.

33. This Court has jurisdiction to determine the legal rights of the parties concerning the easement over Wiggin Road pursuant to 14 M.R.S.A. §§ 5951, et seq.

WHEREFORE, Plaintiff Ephraim Hatfield respectfully requests that the Court declare that he has an easement over Defendant's property; order the Defendant to grant Plaintiff, his heirs, successors, and assigns, perpetual access over this easement (by either unblocking it or giving the Plaintiff a key to a gate); award Mr. Hatfield interest and costs; and grant such other and further relief as the Court deems just and appropriate.

COUNT II

Breach of Easement Contract

34. The foregoing allegations set forth above in Paragraphs 1 through 33 of this Complaint are hereby repeated and realleged herein as if set forth in full.

35. The easement of Mr. Hatfield to access his land over Defendant's property, and Defendant's reciprocal restriction relating to this easement, constitute an easement contract by and between the parties.

36. Defendant has breached the easement contract.

37. Mr. Hatfield has satisfied any and all conditions precedent to the easement contract.

38. Defendant's breach of the easement contract has proximately caused Mr. Hatfield to suffer substantial damages.

WHEREFORE, Plaintiff William Hatfield respectfully requests that the Court preliminarily and permanently enjoin Defendant from blocking access to his easement; order the Defendant to grant Plaintiff, his heirs, successors, and assigns, perpetual access over this easement (by either unblocking it or giving the Plaintiff a key to a gate); award Plaintiff damages in an amount consistent with the evidence in this case consistent with the evidence against Defendant; award him interest and costs; and grant such other and further relief as the Court deems just and appropriate.

COUNT III

Private Nuisance

39. The foregoing allegations set forth above in Paragraphs 1 through 38 of this Complaint are hereby repeated and realleged herein as if set forth in full.

40. Defendant's actions in obstructing or encumbering the easement and/or private way of Mr. Hatfield violates 17 M.R.S.A. § 2802 in

that it is a private nuisance which injures Plaintiff in his comfort, property, or enjoyment of his estate.

41. Defendant's blocking of the easement has proximately caused Mr. Hatfield to suffer substantial damages.

WHEREFORE, Plaintiff Ephraim Hatfield respectfully requests that the Court preliminarily and permanently enjoin Defendant from blocking access to his easement; order the Defendant to grant Plaintiff, his heirs, successors, and assigns, perpetual access over this easement (by either unblocking it or giving the Plaintiff a key to a gate); award Plaintiff damages in an amount consistent with the evidence in this case consistent with the evidence against Defendant; award him interest and costs; and grant such other and further relief as the Court deems just and appropriate.

ROAD ACCESS—PUBLIC OR PRIVATE PRESCRIPTIVE EASEMENT

STATE OF MIND SUPERIOR COURT

EPHRAIM M. HATFIELD,	)	
Plaintiff	)	
	)	
v.	)	
	)	Civil Action No. ________
WILLIAM B. MCCOY,	)	
Defendant	)	
	)	

COMPLAINT FOR DECLARATORY RELIEF

(Title to Real Estate Is Involved)

Plaintiff Ephraim M. Hatfield, by his undersigned counsel, states the following as his Complaint against Defendant William B. McCoy:

Preliminary Statement

1. Mr. Hatfield brings this action to secure his continued right to gain access from Stetson Road, via Hatfield Road, to the Hatfield home. For a continuous period of well over 20 years, Hatfield—and his predecessor in title—have used and relied upon Hatfield Road as their sole means of access to their property on Sebasticook Lake. Mr. Hatfield, in fact, has been relying on Hatfield Road to reach the Hatfield Home for more than seventy years. Three subdivisions have been granted approval by the Town of Newport since July 9, 1974, and all property owners within those subdivisions—including Hatfield—rely solely on Hatfield Road for access. In 1954, the Town of Newport accepted Hatfield Road for summer maintenance as a Town road—and for many years, up to and including 1998—received road maintenance subsidies from the State. Defendant, however, wrongfully claims that he owns that portion of Hatfield Road situated on his property. Mr. Hatfield asks the Court to declare that he has the right to access his home on Hatfield Road via a public and/or prescriptive easement.

The Parties

2. Plaintiff Ephraim M. Hatfield resides in Newport.
3. Defendant William B. McCoy resides in Newport.

The Facts

4. Mr. Hatfield owns two lots or parcels of land located in Newport, more accurately described (a) in a deed from H. Madeline Hatfield, George L. Hatfield, Cora E. Hatfield, Michael A. Hatfield, Jon Hatfield, George Louis Hatfield, II, and Pamela A. Howe to Malcolm M. Hatfield and Beverly E. Hatfield, dated December 23, 1991, and recorded in the Penobscot County Registry of Deeds in Book 4977, Page 313 ("Hatfield Lot A"); and (b) in a deed dated July 24, 1996, from George L. Hatfield, Cora E. Hatfield, Michael A. Hatfield, Jon A. Hatfield, George L. Hatfield, II, and Pamela A. Howe to Malcolm M. Hatfield, Jr. and Beverly E. Hatfield and recorded in the Penobscot County Registry of Deeds in Book 6213, Page 201 ("Hatfield Lot B"), Hatfield Lot A and Hatfield Lot B are referred to collectively hereinafter as the "Hatfield Home."

5. A true and accurate copy of the deed to Hatfield Lot A is attached hereto as Exhibit A.

6. A true and accurate copy of the deed to Hatfield Lot B is attached hereto as Exhibit B.

7. Hatfield Lot A and Hatfield Lot B are more accurately depicted on a certain Town of Newport Tax Map 5, dated 1975 and prepared by James W. Sewall Company, as Lot 8-13 and 8-14, respectively.

8. A true and accurate copy of Newport Tax Map 5 is attached hereto as Exhibit C.

9. Defendant William McCoy owns a lot or parcel of land located in Newport, more accurately described in a deed from Parker L. Argent and Lila C. Argent to Carl M. McCoy and Sara J. McCoy, dated September 20, 1971, and recorded in the Penobscot County Registry of Deeds in Book 2227, page 113 (the "McCoy Lot").

10. A true and accurate copy of the deed to the McCoy Lot is attached hereto as Exhibit D.

11. The McCoy Lot is more accurately depicted on a certain Town of Newport Tax Map 3, dated 1975 and prepared by James W. Sewall Company, as Lot 11.

12. A true and accurate copy of Tax Map 3 is attached hereto as Exhibit E.

Hatfield Road

13. Hatfield Road, in Newport, is a road more accurately depicted on Newport Tax Maps 2, 3, and 5.

14. Hatfield Road terminates at its southernmost end where it meets Stetson Road.

15. From its southern terminus at Stetson Road, Hatfield Road continues north, then northwest, until it becomes Old County Road.

16. From its southern terminus at Stetson Road to the point where it changes from a northerly to a northwesterly direction, Hatfield Road is abutted to the west and east by the McCoy Lot.

17. Hatfield Road has been in the location depicted in Town of Newport Tax Maps 2, 3, and 5 since at least 1931, as depicted on a United States Geological Survey Map dated 1935, based on survey work completed in 1930 and 1931.

The Subdivisions

18. The Birch Hollow Subdivision was approved by the town of Newport on July 9, 1974, and is more accurately depicted on a certain Plan entitled Birch Hollow Property and recorded in the Penobscot County Registry of Deeds in Map File No. 364 (the "Birch Hollow Plan").

19. A true and accurate copy of the Birch Hollow Plan is attached hereto as Exhibit F.

20. The Point of View Subdivision was approved by the Town of Newport on October 2, 1987, and is more accurately depicted on a certain Plan entitled Point of View Subdivision, dated October 13, 1987, and recorded in the Penobscot County Registry of Deeds in Plan Book 87, Page D112 (the "Point of View Plan").

21. A true and accurate copy of the Point of View Plan is attached hereto as Exhibit G.

22. The Lots of Hatfield's Subdivision (the "Hatfield Subdivision") was approved by the Town of Newport on September 10, 1991, and is more accurately depicted on a certain Plan recorded in the Penobscot County Registry of Deeds in Plan Book 91, Page C99 (the "Hatfield Subdivision Plan").

23. A true and accurate copy of the Hatfield Subdivision Plan is attached hereto as Exhibit H.

24. Lot owners in the Birch Hollow Subdivision, the Point of View Subdivision, and the Hatfield Subdivision have at all times used and continue to use Hatfield Road as their only means of access to their lots from Stetson Road.

25. The Birch Hollow Subdivision, the Point of View Subdivision, and the Hatfield Subdivision are all subdivisions approved by the Town of Newport.

26. The Hatfield Home is located in the Hatfield Subdivision.

27. Mr. Hatfield has at all times used, and continues to use, Hatfield Road as his only means of access to the Hatfield Home from Stetson Road.

28. In fact, Mr. Hatfield has used Hatfield Road to access the Hatfield Home for more than seventy years.

29. The predecessors in title to Mr. Hatfield continuously used, for more than 20 years, Hatfield Road, and continue to use it as their only means of access to the land now comprising the Hatfield Home from Stetson Road.

Hatfield Road as a Public Way

30. Hatfield Road has, at all times relevant to this action, provided access from Stetson Road to the Hatfield Home.

31. Hatfield Road has, at all times relevant to this action, provided access from Stetson Road to the Birch Hollow Subdivision, the Point of View Subdivision, and the Hatfield Subdivision.

32. Hatfield Road was accepted by the Town of Newport for "summer maintenance as a town way" by means of warrant article 27 in the 1954–1955 Newport Annual Report.

33. A true and accurate copy of warrant article 27 is attached hereto as Exhibit I.

34. The Town of Newport consistently included Hatfield Road on its inventory of town roads in its annual appeal for local road assistance from the State of Mind.

35. As recently as 1998, the State provided local road assistance subsidies to Newport Mind for the maintenance of town roads, including Hatfield Road.

36. From its southerly terminus at Stetson Road to its junction with Old County Road, Hatfield Road is a Public Road.

37. From its southerly terminus at Stetson Road to its junction with Old County Road, Hatfield Road is a Public Easement.

COUNT I

Declaratory Judgment for Legal Access by Public or Prescriptive Easement

38. Mr. Hatfield repeats and realleges herein each and every allegation set forth in the preceding Paragraphs.

39. Mr. Hatfield—and his predecessors in title—have continuously, under a claim of right adverse to the McCoys—and with his knowledge and acquiescence, or with use so open, visible, and uninterrupted that knowledge and acquiescence will be presumed—used Hatfield Road to access their homes for more than 20 years.

40. In addition, the public generally has continuously, under a claim of right adverse to Mr. McCoy—and with his knowledge and acquiescence, or with use so open, visible, and uninterrupted that knowledge and acquiescence will be presumed—used Hatfield Road for more than 20 years.

41. To the extent that Hatfield Road has been abandoned or discontinued by the Town of Newport, there remains in place a public easement pursuant to 23 M.R.S.A. § 3026.

42. Mr. Hatfield has no other means of accessing his home other than by Hatfield Road.

43. Since July 9, 1974, the Town of Newport has approved at least three subdivisions that rely on Hatfield Road as their only means of access to Stetson Road.

44. Mr. Hatfield has a permanent easement by prescription to access his home by Hatfield Road.

45. The Hatfields and Rices have a permanent public easement by prescription to access their homes by Hatfield Road.

46. This Court has jurisdiction to determine the legal rights of the parties concerning the continued existence of the ROW pursuant to 14 M.R.S.A. §§ 5951 et seq.

WHEREFORE, Plaintiff Ephraim Hatfield respectfully requests that the Court declare that a public easement exists over that portion of Hatfield Road, between the Defendant's property, currently used by him to access his home or, in the alternative, that a prescriptive easement or public prescriptive easement, appurtenant to the Hatfield Home, exists such that Mr. Hatfield has and shall continue to have the right to cross that portion of Hatfield Road currently used in order to gain access to his property from the Stetson Road in Newport; declare that Mr. McCoy, and his respective successors in title, are and shall forever be enjoined from interfering with that access in any way; order that Mr. Hatfield be awarded interest and costs; and grant such other and further relief as the Court deems just and appropriate.

BREACH OF MORTGAGE / DISCHARGE OF MORTGAGE/EQUITABLE SUBROGATION

STATE OF MIND SUPERIOR COURT

EPHRAIM M. HATFIELD,	)	
Plaintiff	)	
	)	
v.	)	
	)	Civil Action No. ________
WILLIAM B. MCCOY and	)	
MIND BANK & TRUST,	)	
Defendants	)	
	)	

COMPLAINT FOR FORECLOSURE BY CIVIL ACTION, DECLARATORY JUDGMENT, AND DAMAGES

(Title to Real Estate Is Involved)

COUNT I

Breach of Promissory Note and Foreclosure Against Mr. McCoy

1. On September 23, 2004, Defendant William McCoy executed and delivered to Ephraim Hatfield an Adjustable Rate Note and Adjustable Rate Rider in the principal amount of $600,000.00, a true copy of which Adjustable Rate Note and Adjustable Rate Rider are attached hereto as Exhibit A.

2. To secure the above Adjustable Rate Note and Adjustable Rate Rider, Defendant William McCoy executed and delivered a real estate mortgage deed covering certain real property located on 64 Country Lane in the Town of North Yarmouth (the "Property"), in favor of Ephraim Hatfield, which mortgage is recorded in the Cumberland County Registry of Deeds in Book 21831, Page 192. A true copy of this mortgage deed is attached hereto as Exhibit B.

3. The Defendant has defaulted upon said Adjustable Rate Note and Adjustable Rate Rider including by his failure to pay the installments when due thereunder and, therefore, has breached the conditions set forth in the mortgage referred to in Paragraph 2 of this Complaint.

4. As of April 24, 2007, the amount due to Ephraim Hatfield under the terms of the mortgage, Adjustable Rate Note and Adjustable Rate Rider was: principal balance of $582,940.80, plus accrued interest in the amount of $15,331.31 and late charges in the amount of $851.65, for a total of $599,123.76, with interest accruing on the principal balance at the rate of $87.28 per day. Defendant William McCoy is further liable to Ephraim Hatfield for all costs and expenses, including but not limited to, reasonable attorney's fees, and any funds advanced to protect his collateral by way of real estate taxes paid, incurred and to be incurred in regard to said Adjustable Rate Note and Adjustable Rate Rider and mortgage.

COUNT II

Breach of Promissory Note and Foreclosure Against McCoy

5. Plaintiff repeats and realleges herein each and every allegation set forth above in Paragraphs 1 through 4.

6. On September 22, 2004, Defendant William McCoy executed and delivered to Ephraim Hatfield a Home Equity Line of Credit Agreement in the principal amount of $228,750.00, a true copy of which Home Equity Line of Credit Agreement is attached hereto as Exhibit C.

7. To secure the above Home Equity Line of Credit Agreement, Defendant William McCoy executed and delivered a real estate mortgage deed covering certain real property located on 64 Country Lane in the Town of North Yarmouth, in favor of Ephraim Hatfield, which mortgage is recorded in the Cumberland County Registry of Deeds in Book 21872, Page 54. A true copy of this mortgage deed is attached hereto as Exhibit D.

8. The Defendant has defaulted upon said Home Equity Line of Credit Agreement including by his failure to pay the installments when due thereunder and, therefore, has breached the conditions set forth in the mortgage referred to in Paragraph 6 of this Complaint.

9. As of April 24, 2007, the amount due to Ephraim Hatfield under the terms of the mortgage and Home Equity Line of Credit Agreement was: principal balance of $228,211.29, plus accrued interest in the amount of $8,703.28, for a total of $236,914.57, with interest accruing on the principal balance at the rate of $50.02 per day. Defendant William McCoy is further liable to Ephraim Hatfield for all costs and expenses, including but not limited to, reasonable attorney's fees, and

any funds advanced to protect his collateral by way of real estate taxes paid, incurred and to be incurred in regard to said Home Equity Line of Credit Agreement and mortgage.

10. By virtue of Defendant's breach of condition, Ephraim Hatfield hereby demands a Foreclosure and Sale of the real estate covered by said mortgages.

WHEREFORE, Plaintiff Ephraim Hatfield requests that this Honorable Court:

a. Determine that there has been a breach of the condition of Ephraim Hatfield's mortgages referred to in Paragraph 2 and Paragraph 6 of this Complaint;

b. Determine the amount due on Ephraim Hatfield's mortgages including principal, interest, accrued interest, reasonable attorney's fees, and costs of enforcement through the civil action and protection of his mortgages' interest in the collateral;

c. Determine the order of priority of all of the Parties in interest as may appear herein, together with the amount due such parties;

d. Order exclusive possession of the real estate to Ephraim Hatfield upon expiration of the statutory ninety (90) day redemption period, and order Defendant to vacate the real estate at that time, if Defendant has not by that date redeemed the real estate;

e. Issue a Judgment of Sale and Foreclosure of Ephraim Hatfield's mortgages referred to in Paragraph 2 and Paragraph 6 in conformity with 14 M.R.S.A. §§ 6321 et seq.;

f. Find the Defendant liable for any deficiency balance remaining owing to Ephraim Hatfield after sale of the real estate and application of the proceeds of sale;

g. Grant such other and further relief as the Court may deem proper.

COUNT III

Neglect to Discharge Mortgage Against Mind Bank & Trust

11. Plaintiff repeats and realleges herein each and every allegation set forth above in Paragraphs 1 through 10.

12. The funds from the $600,000 and $228,750 loans from Ephraim Hatfield, referenced above, were used to pay off two preexisting mortgages on the Property, as well as to make general improvements to the Property.

13. Prior to the closing of the refinancing with Ephraim Hatfield, the property was encumbered by a mortgage to First National Trust Company (the "First Mortgage"), in the initial principal amount of $533,000, and a mortgage to Mind Bank & Trust (the "Second Mortgage") in the initial principal amount of $165,000.

14. Mind Bank & Trust is a subsidiary or affiliate of First National Trust Company.

15. Rainbow Title Company was the closing agent for the Ephraim Hatfield refinancing of the Property.

16. Rainbow Title Company requested pay off quotes from both First National Trust Company and from Mind Bank & Trust.

17. A true and accurate copy of the Payoff Quote from First National Trust Company is attached hereto as Exhibit E.

18. The First National Payoff Quote for the Property has an effective date of September 29, 2004 and a total payoff of $521,862.01.

19. A true and accurate copy of the "Loan Payoff Inquiry" from Mind Bank & Trust is attached hereto as Exhibit F.

20. The Mind Bank & Trust Payoff Quote for the Property has an effective date of September 29, 2004 and a total payoff of $150,623.03.

21. On September 29, 2004, Rainbow Title Company sent First National Trust Company a payoff letter and a check in the amount of $521,862.01. A true and accurate copy of the payoff letter and check is attached hereto as Exhibit G.

22. The September 29, 2004 letter and check was to pay off the First National Trust Company loan on the Property.

23. The funds for the payoff came from the refinancing with Ephraim Hatfield.

24. First National Bank accepted the payoff letter and check, and discharged its First Mortgage on the Property.

25. On September 28, 2004, Rainbow Title hand delivered to Mind Bank & Trust both a payoff letter and a check in the amount of $150,623.03. A true and accurate copy of Rainbow Title Company's payoff letter, and check are attached hereto as Exhibits H and I.

26. The September 28, 2004 hand delivery to Mind Bank & Trust was to pay off the Mind Bank & Trust loan on the Property

27. The funds for the payoff came from the refinancing with Ephraim Hatfield.

28. The letter from Rainbow Title Company to Mind Bank & Trust makes reference to a mortgage from Mind Bank & Trust to William

McCoy in the original principal amount of $165,000.00, dated January 24, 2001, and recorded in the Cumberland County Registry of Deeds at Book 15990, Page 28.

29. The letter from Rainbow Title Company to Mind Bank & Trust is also signed by William McCoy.

30. The letter from Rainbow Title Company to Mind Bank & Trust further states the following: "Enclosed please find a check in the amount of $150,623.03 representing the mortgage payoff in the above-referenced loan."

31. In addition, the payoff letter states the following—in bold—immediately prior to the signature of William McCoy: "**Please close out and cancel the above-referenced account and discharge the mortgage that secures it.**"

32. The check accompanying the payoff letter is made to Mind Bank & Trust in the amount of $150,623.03.

33. The accompanying check references "McCoy Loan # 2039982 Payoff."

34. Mind Bank & Trust Loan No. 2039982 is the Mind Bank & Trust loan which it secured by the Second Mortgage on the Property.

35. Mind Bank & Trust promptly accepted, cashed, and negotiated the check attached hereto as Exhibit I.

36. Mind Bank & Trust, however, has never issued a discharge of its mortgage on the Property.

37. On or about March 13, 2007, Rainbow Title Company wrote a letter to Mind Bank & Trust referencing the payoff letter hand delivered on September 28, 2004, and requested that Mind Bank & Trust promptly discharge its mortgage. A true and accurate copy of the letter dated March 13, 2007, is attached hereto as Exhibit J.

38. On or about March 15, 2007, counsel for Ephraim Hatfield wrote a letter to the President and Chief Executive Officer of Mind Bank & Trust again requesting that its mortgage be discharged or subrogated. A true and accurate copy of the letter dated March 15, 2007, is attached hereto as Exhibit K.

39. On or about March 23, 2007, counsel for Ephraim Hatfield again wrote a letter to Mind Bank & Trust requesting that its mortgage on the Property be discharged. A true and accurate copy of the letter dated March 23, 2007, is attached hereto as Exhibit L.

40. On or about April 20, 2007, counsel for Ephraim Hatfield sent yet another letter to Mind Bank & Trust requesting that it discharge its

mortgage on the Property. A true and accurate copy of the letter dated April 20, 2007, is attached hereto as Exhibit M.

41. In addition, Rainbow Title Company sent multiple letters to Mind Bank & Trust, and its affiliates, on April 26, 2007, requesting that the mortgage on the Property be discharged. True and accurate copies of the letters from Rainbow Title Company are attached hereto as Exhibits N, O, P, Q, R, S, and T.

42. Despite all of these letters, Mind Bank & Trust has failed and refused to discharge its mortgage on the Property.

43. Mind law, 33 M.R.S.A. § 551, requires Mind Bank & Trust to discharge its mortgage on the Property.

44. Mind Bank & Trust violated Mind law by failing to promptly discharge its mortgage on the Property.

45. Mind Bank & Trust is liable to Plaintiff for actual damages, exemplary damages, court costs, and reasonable attorney's fees as a result of its violation of Mind law in failing to discharge the aforementioned mortgage.

WHEREFORE, Plaintiff Ephraim Hatfield respectfully requests that the Court enter judgment against Defendant Mind Bank & Trust (a) declaring that its mortgage on the Property is hereby fully discharged; (b) entering an award in favor of Plaintiff, against Defendant Mind Bank & Trust, in the amount of the Plaintiff's actual damages; (c) awarding Plaintiff exemplary damages; (d) awarding Plaintiff his interest and costs; (e) awarding Plaintiff reimbursement of his reasonable attorney's fees; and (f) and granting such other and further relief as the Court deems just and appropriate.

COUNT IV

Equitable Subrogation Against Mind Bank & Trust

46. Plaintiff repeats and realleges herein each and every allegation set forth above in Paragraphs 1 through 46.

47. Equitable subrogation is a device adopted by equity to compel the ultimate discharge of an obligation by one who, in good conscience, ought to pay it.

48. Ephraim Hatfield advanced money to McCoy with which to discharge the First National Trust Company mortgage and the Mind Bank & Trust mortgage.

49. It is proper to apply the doctrine of equitable subrogation to subrogate Ephraim Hatfield to the mortgages of First National Trust Company and Mind Bank & Trust.

50. Applying the doctrine of equitable subrogation in this case will prevent injustice.

WHEREFORE, Plaintiff Ephraim Hatfield respectfully requests that the Court declare that he is equitably subrogated to the prior loans on the Property by First National Trust Company and Mind Bank & Trust; declare that the Mind Bank & Trust mortgage on the Property is fully discharged; award Plaintiff his interest and costs; and grant such other and further relief as the Court deems just and appropriate.

COUNT V

Slander of Title Against Mind Bank & Trust

51. Plaintiff repeats and realleges herein each and every allegation set forth above in Paragraphs 1 through 51.

52. The Mind Bank & Trust loan, secured by its mortgage on the Property, has been paid in full.

53. Despite repeated requests, Mind Bank & Trust has failed and refused to discharge its mortgage on the Property.

54. Mind Bank & Trust's actions are wrongful and/or fraudulent.

55. Mind Bank & Trust's wrongful and fraudulent actions, in failing to discharge its mortgage on the Property, have disparaged the title to the Property.

56. Mind Bank & Trust's aforementioned actions were done with malice or with reckless disregard of its actions.

57. Mind Bank & Trust's wrongful actions have proximately caused damage to Ephraim Hatfield.

58. Mind Bank & Trust has acted outrageously in refusing to discharge the mortgage on the Property.

WHEREFORE, Plaintiff Ephraim Hatfield respectfully requests that the Court enter judgment in his favor and against Defendant Mind Bank & Trust, in an amount consistent with the evidence in this case, together with punitive damages, interest, costs, reasonable attorney's fees, and such other and further relief as the Court deems just and appropriate.

ABANDONMENT OF PUBLIC ROAD/DECLARATORY JUDGMENT REGARDING PRESCRIPTIVE RIGHTS

STATE OF MIND SUPERIOR COURT

EPHRAIM M. HATFIELD,)
Plaintiff)
)
v.)
) Civil Action No. ________
WILLIAM B. MCCOY and)
CITY OF PLEASANTVILLE,)
Defendants)
)

COMPLAINT FOR DECLARATORY JUDGMENT AND DAMAGES

(Title to Real Estate Is Involved)

Plaintiff Ephraim M. Hatfield, by his undersigned counsel, states the following as his Complaint against Defendant William B. McCoy and the City of Pleasantville:

Preliminary Statement

1. Plaintiff Ephraim Hatfield wants to build a new home on his land in Pleasantville. The Defendants, however, have opposed Mr. Hatfield's efforts to get a building permit by claiming that the proposed home does not meet setback requirements from an ancient, colonial pathway known as the "Old King's Highway." Mr. Hatfield requests that this Court declare that, to the extent that the Old King's Highway crossed Mr. Hatfield's land in colonial times, it has long since been abandoned and that no public or private easements exist over that portion of the ancient pathway.

The Parties

2. Plaintiff Ephraim Hatfield is a citizen of Vancouver, British Columbia, Canada. Mr. Hatfield is the record owner of a certain property located in that portion of Pleasantville known as Fortunes Rocks,

more fully described in a deed from Edmund S. Kazan, Trustee of the Edmund S. Kazan Living Trust, dated January 15, 2002, and recorded in the York County Registry of Deeds in Book 10396, Page 314.

3. Defendant the City of Pleasantville (hereinafter "Pleasantville") is a municipal corporation duly organized under the laws of the State of Mind.

4. Defendant William McCoy is, upon information and belief, a resident of the City of Pleasantville, and the record owner of a certain property located at 15 Old King's Highway, Pleasantville, Mind, which is also identified on the City of Pleasantville's Tax Map 66, as Lot 20, and is further described in a deed from Marion H. Smith to Polly S. Warren, dated August 9, 1984, and recorded in the York County Registry of Deeds in Book 3374, Page 352.

The Facts

The Old King's Highway

5. In colonial times, there was a common trail, or bridle path, along the shore above high-water mark, from Portland to Portsmouth and Boston, known as the Old King's Highway.

6. This exceedingly ancient pathway, which meandered along the shoreline, dates back to 1672 and was the first land access into the Province of Mind.

7. The Old King's Highway followed beaches and the coast generally, forded rivers, and was, by all reports, casually created.

8. In many areas, its exact location cannot be found because it was either relocated or lost during the course of erosion along the coast.

9. Since it "just grew," there are very few deeds or grants actually creating sections of the Old King's Highway.

10. There are no records formally incorporating it as a public way on the property owned today by Mr. Hatfield.

11. To the extent that an ancient trail or bridle path went over Mr. Hatfield's property, its use by the public was abandoned when better, year-round roads, with bridges, were created farther inland more than 200 years ago.

12. Furthermore, Mr. Hatfield and his predecessors in title have occupied the property at issue continuously, openly, notoriously, and exclusively, in such a manner as to have adverse possession of any public or private easements once held in connection with the ancient trail.

13. In 1979, by a vote of its City Council, Pleasantville acknowledged the existence of public ways within its boundaries "because of usage and maintenance by the City of Pleasantville for many years." A true copy of a portion of what is described as the "Street List Acceptance" is attached hereto and incorporated herein as Exhibit A.

14. Within the list of streets accepted by the City Council in November of 1979 is Old King's Highway, which is described as running "from Fortunes Rocks Road Southwesterly 800' ± to dead end."

15. The easterly sideline of Mr. Hatfield's property is at the end of what appears to be the terminus of a graveled roadway, which is located approximately 924 feet from the Fortunes Rocks Road, and is well beyond the 800 feet recognized by the City of Pleasantville in its vote of November 1979.

16. Pleasantville has no other public records that evidence any public use, maintenance, or activity on the Old King's Highway as it extends from Fortunes Rocks Road to Mr. Hatfield's property.

17. If there was ever a public road that existed prior to 1979, which extended beyond the easterly sideline of Mr. Hatfield's property, then that portion of Old King's Highway, to the extent that it ever existed, has been abandoned by the City of Pleasantville, without any further public rights or easements.

The Granting of the Building Permit

18. Mr. Hatfield, after purchasing his property, developed plans to demolish the existing structure on its land and to construct a new home on the property.

19. On August 27, 2008, this proposal for new construction was presented to the Pleasantville Coastal Area Committee (hereinafter "Committee"), which, by the authority of Pleasantville's Zoning Ordinance, is authorized to do the following:

> Section 2-308(1)—Review and provide recommendations to the Code Enforcement Officer applications submitted to the City by owners of property or representatives thereof within the Coastal Residential (CR) Zone that would result in new structures or additions and/or a change in use.

20. On the day of the hearing, the Committee voted to approve the application as submitted by a unanimous vote.

21. On September 10, 2008, Mr. Hatfield obtained a demolition permit on the existing structure.

22. On September 13, 2008, the Committee, through Defendant William McCoy, filed an appeal of the granting of the demolition permit to the Zoning Board of Appeals.

23. Upon information and belief, there was never a vote of the Committee to file such an appeal as it appears that this was done at the initiative of the three members identified on the appeal.

24. On September 24, 2008, a letter was written from Donna J. Labbe, Mayor of Pleasantville, to the Committee. A true copy of this letter is attached hereto and incorporated herein as Exhibit B.

25. The letter from Mayor Labbe informed the Committee that they had no authority to appeal this demolition permit to the Town's Zoning Board of Appeals, and also contained the following passage:

> Your major concern seems to lie on the location of the Old King's Highway. Research as far back as 1991 demonstrates that it has not been used for a public highway for approximately 200 years. The first 800 feet (southwesterly from the Fortunes Rocks Road) of the Old King's Highway was addressed on November 20, 1979, as being the only portion that was going to be taken and maintained by the City. Based on a state law, 23 M.R.S.A. § 3031, any remaining reference to the Old King's Highway—beyond the 800 feet—have clearly not been accepted. Therefore the Old King's Highway will terminate and pass to the abutting property owners.

26. On April 26, 2009, Mr. Hatfield was issued a building permit for the construction of a new residence on the property. A true copy of the sketch plan that was submitted to the Code Enforcement Officer is attached hereto and incorporated herein as Exhibit C (with the locations of the existing structures highlighted).

27. On or about May 23, 2009, an appeal of this building permit was filed with the Zoning Board of Appeals (hereinafter "ZBA") by Defendant William McCoy, who, as noted earlier, attempted to file an appeal on behalf of the Committee, seeking to overturn the building permit on the basis that the site plan for the Hatfield property failed to recognize Old King's Highway running through Mr. Hatfield's property, and therefore failed to provide for an adequate setback from the Old King's Highway as a public road.

28. In his response to the appeal filed by the abutters, Mr. Hatfield submitted a picture of his property (a true copy of which is included here for illustrative purposes as Exhibit D, attached hereto and incorporated herein), which shows the existing King's Highway, and the area

leading up to the Hatfield property line, and also illustrates the location of the existing Hatfield residence.

29. On July 10, 2009, a hearing was held by the ZBA on the appeal of the building permit on the Mr. Hatfield property.

30. During the course of the hearing conducted by the ZBA, several of the appellants asserted that the appellants had both public and private rights to pass through the Hatfield property as access to the ocean and beach.

31. During the course of the ZBA hearing, the Mayor of Pleasantville addressed the ZBA and expressed her opinion that the Old King's Highway did in fact go through the Mr. Hatfield property and should be treated as any road requiring a proper setback, notwithstanding that this was in direct contradiction to the letter that she had previously provided to the Committee.

32. The evidence before the ZBA clearly established that, to the extent that a portion of the Old King's Highway was a Town road, the area beyond the Hatfield property line has long since been abandoned and, even if any residual public rights did exist (which they do not) that would not in and of itself require a setback of twenty feet distance from the structure to this area.

33. The evidence before the ZBA also established that the Hatfield property line was over 900 feet from the Fortunes Rocks Road.

34. The ZBA voted to uphold the appeal, and remanded the case back to the Code Enforcement Officer, with the requirement that some setback be recognized by the applicant to the Old King's Highway. A true copy of the ZBA decision is attached hereto and incorporated herein as Exhibit E.

35. Upon information and belief, the decision of the ZBA (Exhibit E), and its incorporated findings of fact, were never formally adopted or voted on by the ZBA, as the decision itself was drafted by the Code Enforcement Officer and, after a review by the City's Solicitor, it was signed by the ZBA Chairman.

COUNT I

Declaratory Judgment for Abandonment of Road v. City of Pleasantville

36. The foregoing allegations set forth above in Paragraphs 1 through 35 are hereby repeated and realleged as if set forth in full.

37. There is a real and substantial controversy between the parties concerning the status of the Old King's Highway as it may exist at or near the Hatfield property.

38. This Court has jurisdiction to determine the legal rights of the parties concerning the public rights in the Old King's Highway pursuant to 14 M.R.S.A. § 5951 et seq.

WHEREFORE, Plaintiff Ephraim Hatfield respectfully requests that the Court declare that any ancient trail that may have existed over his property has been long since abandoned, without public easement; declare that the use of the property by Mr. Hatfield and his predecessors has, by prescriptive use, eliminated any such ancient rights; award Mr. Hatfield interest and costs; and grant such other and further relief as the Court deems just and appropriate.

COUNT II

Declaratory Judgment on Prescriptive Rights v. William McCoy

39. The foregoing allegations set forth above in Paragraphs 1 through 38 of this Complaint are hereby repeated and realleged herein as if set forth in full.

40. During the course of the ZBA appeal in this matter, Mr. McCoy has asserted both public and private rights to what he claims was the Old King's Highway passing through Mr. Hatfield's property.

41. Prior to the ZBA appeal, Mr. McCoy has asserted private rights to pass through the Hatfield property, by a claim that they have established prescriptive rights through periods of use or other rights to pass through Mr. Hatfield's property along the alleged Old King's Highway to access to the ocean and the beach.

42. Mr. Hatfield and his predecessors in title have denied such access as a matter of right, and for many years there was a "no trespassing" sign that stood at the terminus of the graveled road along the boundary of the Hatfield property.

43. Any use of such a pathway through the Hatfield property by Mr. McCoy has been by permission only.

44. There is a real and substantial controversy between the parties concerning the status of the Old King's Highway as it may exist at or near the Hatfield property.

45. This Court has jurisdiction to determine the legal rights of the parties concerning the public rights in the Old King's Highway pursuant to 14 M.R.S.A. § 5951 et seq.

WHEREFORE, Plaintiff Ephraim Hatfield respectfully requests that the Court declare that any ancient trail or Old King's Highway that may have existed over his property has been long since abandoned, without public easement; declare Mr. McCoy has no rights over any ancient or other pathway on Mr. Hatfield's property; declare that the use of the property by Mr. Hatfield and his predecessors has, by prescriptive use, eliminated any such ancient rights; award Mr. Hatfield interest and costs; and grant such other and further relief as the Court deems just and appropriate.

COUNT III

Declaratory Judgment on Beach Access v. Defendant William McCoy

46. The foregoing allegations set forth above in Paragraphs 1 through 45 of this Complaint are hereby repeated and realleged herein as if set forth in full.

47. The parcel of land acquired by Mr. Hatfield in his deed from Edmund S. Kazan, Trustee, referenced above, conveyed a parcel of land that included land to the Atlantic Ocean, including its tidal flats.

48. This ocean frontage owned by Mr. Hatfield is depicted on a plan prepared for Edmund S. Kazan by Nelson and Coulombe, Inc. dated March 15, 1999, a true and reduced copy of which is attached hereto as Exhibit F.

49. This area of ocean frontage, depicted on Exhibit F, is exclusive in nature, and in the absence of a grant of right, cannot be used by Defendant William McCoy in this matter except for the public's right to fish, fowl, and navigate.

50. While Mr. Hatfield's predecessors in title did grant certain rights to properties on Seal Lane to utilize a certain right-of-way, which included a grant of use of the beach, Mr. McCoy was not granted such a right.

51. Over the course of many years, without it rising to level of establishing prescriptive use or any adverse claim, Mr. McCoy has from time to time gone upon the beach area of the Hatfield property.

52. There is a real and substantial controversy between Mr. Hatfield and Mr. McCoy concerning the use of the beach area along the ocean frontage of the Hatfield property.

53. This Court has jurisdiction to determine the legal rights of the parties concerning the use of this beach area, pursuant to 14 M.R.S.A. § 5951 et. seq.

WHEREFORE, Plaintiff Ephraim Hatfield respectfully requests that this Honorable Court declare that Defendant William McCoy has no right to utilize the beach and shore frontage along the Hatfield property; declare that any prior use of this beach area was either by permission, or has not risen to the level of an adverse claim of use; award Mr. Hatfield interest and costs; and grant such other further relief as the Court may deem just and appropriate.

BREACH OF WARRANTY/EASEMENT BY NECESSITY

STATE OF MIND SUPERIOR COURT

EPHRAIM M. HATFIELD,	)	
Plaintiff	)	
	)	
v.	)	
	)	Civil Action No. ________
WILLIAM B. MCCOY and	)	
BERT DAVIS,	)	
Defendants	)	
	)	

COMPLAINT FOR DECLARATORY JUDGMENT AND DAMAGES

Plaintiff Ephraim M. Hatfield, by his undersigned counsel, states the following Complaint against Defendants William B. McCoy and Bert Davis:

Preliminary Statement

1. Despite his claim, Defendant William McCoy does *not* have an easement by necessity over the property of Ephraim Hatfield (1) because Mr. McCoy has other ways of accessing his property and (2) because—if the other access routes are not viable—Mr. McCoy's predecessor land-locked himself.

The Parties

2. Plaintiff Ephraim Hatfield resides on 74 Katahdin Road in South Berwick.

3. Defendant William McCoy lives in Falmouth.

The Facts

4. Mr. Hatfield has a small lot with approximately 210 feet of frontage on Katahdin Road in South Berwick, Mind. Mr. Hatfield's land is depicted on South Berwick Tax Map 29, Lot 2, a true copy of which is attached hereto as Exhibit A-1.

5. Mr. McCoy owns approximately eight acres of land which is to the rear of the Hatfield property. Mr. McCoy's land is depicted on Tax Map 11, Lot 23, a true copy of which is attached hereto as Exhibit A-2.

6. As shown on the aforementioned Tax Map, Mr. McCoy's property is bordered easterly by a way leading to Katahdin Road. Katahdin Road is a public way in South Berwick, Mind.

7. The South Berwick tax map, attached hereto as Exhibit A-2, also shows another way leading to the southwesterly corner of the McCoy property.

8. There are also other subdivision roads and ways, on the face of the earth, in a subdivision plan, and in recorded deeds which go from the McCoy property to a public road.

9. At one time, the property of both of the parties was owned by Defendant Bert Davis.

10. On October 16, 1968, Bert Davis sold what is today the Hatfield lot to Defendant William McCoy.

11. The aforementioned deed from Bert Davis to William McCoy is recorded in the York County Registry of Deeds at Book 1823, Page 482, and a true copy of which is attached hereto as Exhibit B.

12. The deed from Bert Davis to Mr. McCoy contains a description of the property which includes the following:

> A certain lot or parcel of land situated in South Berwick, and bounded Northerly by Katahdin Road and by land formerly of Helen Lambert; Easterly by said Lambert land and by the S.P. Huntress Road, so-called . . .

13. The McCoy property is currently bordered by the so-called S.P. Huntress Road.

14. Mr. McCoy claims that Bert Davis landlocked himself when he sold a portion of his property to William McCoy on October 16, 1968.

15. In the event that this sale did create a landlocked parcel, it is the grantor that landlocked himself.

16. At the time that Mr. McCoy bought the aforementioned property, he knew that there was a claim that the property was landlocked.

17. At the time that Mr. McCoy bought the aforementioned property, he knew that all of Mr. Davis's road frontage on Katahdin Road had previously been sold.

COUNT I

Declaratory Judgment

18. The foregoing allegations set forth above in Paragraphs 1 through 17 of this Complaint are hereby repeated and realleged herein as if set forth in full.

19. There is a real and substantial controversy between the parties in that Mr. McCoy is claiming that he has an easement by necessity over the property of Mr. Hatfield.

20. Mr. Hatfield vigorously contests this assertion and maintains that Mr. McCoy has no interest in his property.

21. Mr. Hatfield has standing to raise this issue before this Court.

22. This Court has jurisdiction to determine the legal rights of the parties concerning the lack of any such easement pursuant to 14 M.R.S.A. §§ 5951 et seq.

WHEREFORE, Plaintiff Ephraim Hatfield respectfully requests that the Court declare that Defendant William McCoy has no easement over the Hatfield land; award Mr. Hatfield his interest and costs; and grant such other and further relief as the Court deems just and appropriate.

ADDITIONAL COMPLAINT

Plaintiff Ephraim Hatfield, by his undersigned counsel, states the following as his Complaint against Defendant Bert Davis:

Preliminary Statement

1. Mr. Hatfield maintains that Bert Davis does not have an easement by necessity or any other easement over his property. In the unlikely event that Mr. McCoy is able to prove that he has some interest over the Hatfield property, then Mr. Hatfield brings this action against his predecessor in title for breach of warranty covenants.

The Parties

2. Plaintiff Ephraim Hatfield is a resident of South Berwick.

3. Defendant Bert Davis is a resident of Elliot.

The Facts

4. Bert Davis sold what is today the Hatfield lot to Ephraim Hatfield on October 16, 1968, via Warranty Deed.

5. A true copy of the Warranty Deed from Bert Davis to Mr. Hatfield is recorded in the York County Registry of Deeds at Book 1823, Page 482, and a true copy is attached hereto as Exhibit B.

6. There is nothing in the aforementioned Warranty Deed from Bert Davis to Mr. Hatfield which references or takes an exception for an

easement, across their remaining property, benefiting the lot currently owned by Mr. McCoy.

COUNT I

Breach of Warranty Covenant

7. The foregoing allegations as set forth above in Paragraphs 1 through 6 are realleged herein as if set forth in full.

8. If William McCoy prevails in his Complaint against Ephraim Hatfield, it will be because Defendant Bert Davis was not seized and possessed of the entire premises in fee simple and did not have the right to convey the entire property. In such case, the aforementioned conveyances were wrongful.

9. If Mr. McCoy prevails in his action against Mr. Hatfield, Mr. Hatfield will sustain damages, including damages in defending against Mr. McCoy's claims, as a direct and proximate result of the failure of title by the Defendant Bert Davis.

10. Defendant Bert Davis is liable to Mr. Hatfield for any such damages, including damages in defending against Mr. McCoy's claims, because he warranted title to the premises.

WHEREFORE, Plaintiff Ephraim Hatfield demands judgment against Defendant Bert Davis for amounts reasonable under the circumstances, together with costs, interest, reasonable attorney's fees, and such other and further relief as the Court deems just and appropriate.

COUNT II

Breach of Covenant of Seizen

11. The foregoing allegations set forth above in Paragraphs 1 through 10 of the Complaint are hereby repeated and realleged herein as if set forth in full.

12. If Mr. McCoy prevails on his Complaint against Mr. Hatfield, it will be because Defendant Bert Davis was not seized and possessed of the entire premises in fee simple absolute, and did not have the right to convey same to a purchaser in the manner conveyed. In such case, the aforementioned conveyances were wrongful and the breach of the covenant of seizen.

13. If Mr. McCoy prevails in his action against Mr. Hatfield, Mr. Hatfield will sustain damages, including the cost of defending against Mr. McCoy's claims, as a direct and proximate result of the breach of the covenant of seizen by Defendant Bert Davis.

14. Defendant Bert Davis is liable to Mr. Hatfield for any such damages.

WHEREFORE, Plaintiff Ephraim Hatfield demands judgment against Defendant Bert Davis for amounts reasonable under the circumstances, together with costs, interest, reasonable attorney's fees, and any further relief that the Court deems just and appropriate.

BREACH OF WARRANTY/FRAUDULENT TRANSFER

STATE OF MIND SUPERIOR COURT

GARY A. ARBUCKLE and	)	
MARILYN J. ARBUCKLE,	)	
Plaintiffs	)	
	)	
v.	)	
	)	Civil Action No. ________
JASON I. MCCAIN, MELISSA A.	)	
MCCAIN, ROBERT J. SYMINGTON,	)	
and CECILIA SYMINGTON,	)	
Defendants	)	
	)	

COMPLAINT

Plaintiffs Gary A. Arbuckle and Marilyn J. Arbuckle, by their undersigned counsel, state the following as their Complaint against Defendants Jason I. McCain, Melissa A. McCain, Robert J. Symington, and Cecelia Symington:

Introductory Statement

1. Defendants Jason I. McCain and Melissa A. McCain sold a home and sent a portion of their sale proceeds to their banks to pay off the pending mortgage and the pending home equity line of credit ("HELOC"). Instead of ensuring that the HELOC mortgage was discharged, however, the McCains fraudulently ran up the line of credit again—after the closing—to $208,346.98. Plaintiffs Gary A. Arbuckle and Marilyn J. Arbuckle, who are the current owners of the property, are now saddled and encumbered with a $208,346.98 mortgage which the McCains were obligated to discharge. Instead of meeting their obligations to discharge the HELOC mortgage, the McCains are selling other properties and transferring assets into the names of their relatives. Accordingly, the Arbuckles bring this action for fraud, fraudulent transfer, breach of warranty, breach of contract, and conversion.

The Parties

2. Plaintiffs Gary A. Arbuckle and Marilyn J. Arbuckle are a married couple who reside in China.

3. Defendants Jason I. McCain and Melissa A. McCain (formerly Melissa A. Symington) are a married couple who reside in South China.

4. Defendants Robert J. Symington and Cecilia Symington are a married couple who reside in Spring Hill, Florida.

The Facts

5. The McCains—as Jason I. McCain and Melissa A. Symington—took title to a certain lot or parcel of land located in South China, Mind, and more accurately described in a deed dated May 24, 2004, and recorded in the Kennebec County Registry of Deeds in Book 7955, Page 22 (the "Property").

6. A true and accurate copy of the deed transferring the Property to the McCains is attached hereto as Exhibit A.

7. The McCains' Purchase of the Property was financed with a first mortgage on the property.

8. After purchasing the Property, the McCains obtained a home equity line of credit (the "HELOC") secured by the Property.

9. During the course of their ownership of the Property, the McCains incurred approximately $166,184.81 in debt against the HELOC.

10. The McCains transferred the Property to Christopher T. Choate and Kelly M. Choate (the "Choates") by warranty deed dated October 8, 2005, and recorded in the Kennebec County Registry of Deeds in Book 8643, Page 0135.

11. A true and accurate copy of the deed transferring the Property from the McCains to the Choates is attached hereto as Exhibit B.

12. At the closing, the McCains represented that the Property was being sold free and clear of the mortgages.

13. As a condition of the closing, a portion of the proceeds from the sale of the Property from the McCains to the Choates were used to discharge and close the first mortgage.

14. As a condition of the closing, a portion of the remaining proceeds, totaling $166,184.81, were used to pay off the HELOC mortgage encumbering the Property, held by Bank of Mind.

15. Following the closing, Kennebec Title Company forwarded a check to Bank of Mind in the amount of $166,184.81 accompanied by a cover letter dated October 13, 2005 (the "Cover Letter").

16. The Cover Letter, which references Jason I. McCain, the Loan Number, and the Property Address, states: "Enclosed please find our firm check in the amount of $166,184.81 which represents payoff of the above-referenced loan pursuant to your payoff letter."

17. In a receipt dated October 14, 2005, Bank of Mind acknowledged receipt of a payment of $166,174.81 against a line of credit with an account number ending in 1299 (the "Receipt").

18. A true and accurate copy of the Cover Letter and Receipt are attached hereto as Exhibit C.

19. As a condition of the Closing, the McCains executed a document entitled "Shortfall Agreement" (the "Shortfall Agreement"), which read, in part, "we ask that you sign this agreement to reconfirm your commitment to pay your lender whatever is legally required to secure a discharge of the mortgage."

20. A true and accurate copy of the Shortfall Agreement is attached hereto as Exhibit D.

21. At the time of the closing, the McCains never intended to keep their representations, warranties, or contractual commitments.

22. Despite their representations, warranties, and execution of the Shortfall Agreement, the McCains—after the closing of the Property—proceeded to once again draw down the funds under the HELOC.

23. Following the closing on the Property, and the paying off of the HELOC, the McCains were aware that the HELOC was secured by property they no longer owned.

24. As indicated by the Shortfall Agreement, the McCains understood it was their legal obligation to pay those lenders whose interests were secured by the Property, including the Bank of Mind HELOC.

25. Despite this knowledge, the McCains intentionally, deliberately, and fraudulently drew down nearly $200,000.00 against the HELOC, then ceased payments to Bank of Mind.

26. As of September 17, 2008, the HELOC was more than 600 days overdue, and the payoff amount was $208,346.98.

The McCain Subdivision

27. After the closing, the McCains, by deed dated August 1, 2007, and recorded in the Kennebec County Registry of Deeds in Book 9447,

Page 0229, took title to a certain lot or parcel of land located in China, Mind (the "McCain Subdivision").

28. A true and accurate copy of the deed for the McCain Subdivision is attached hereto as Exhibit D.

29. The McCains fraudulently used the money from the HELOC to develop and improve the Subdivision.

30. In a deed dated May 30, 2008, and recorded in the Kennebec County Registry of Deeds in Book 9745, Page 0194, the McCains sold a portion of the McCain Subdivision to Jason K. Fredette and Jessica L. Fredette (the "Fredettes").

31. A true and accurate copy of the deed from the McCains to the Fredettes is attached hereto as Exhibit E.

32. Despite this sale, the McCains failed to pay off or discharge the HELOC.

33. Following the sale of a portion of the McCain Subdivision, the McCains applied to the Town of China for approval to create an additional lot within the Meadows Subdivision, as more accurately depicted on China Tax Map 8, Lot 12-3, from the portion of the McCain Subdivision to which they retained title.

34. A true and accurate copy of China Tax Map 8 is attached hereto as Exhibit F.

35. During the September 9, 2008, meeting of the Planning Board for the Town of China, the McCains obtained approval to create an additional lot from the portion of the McCain Subdivision to which they still held title.

36. The McCains plan to sell one or both lots within the McCain Subdivision, and have retained a real estate broker to list one or both properties for sale.

37. The McCains know that they owe over $208,000 to Bank of Mind, secured by a HELOC mortgage on the Property.

38. In a deed dated September 15, 2008, and recorded in the Kennebec County Registry of Deeds in Book 9856, Page 2, the McCains conveyed a 7/10 undivided interest in their remaining portion of the McCain Subdivision to Robert J. Symington and Cecilia Symington.

39. A true and accurate copy of that deed is attached hereto as Exhibit G.

40. The Symingtons are relatives of the McCains.

41. The Symingtons did not pay fair value for this transfer.

42. The purpose of the transfer was to avoid creditors.

The HELOC—Encumbered Property

43. In a Foreclosure Judgment dated January 15, 2008, and recorded in the Kennebec County Registry of Deeds in Book 9683, Page 258, First National Bank foreclosed on the Property, taking title from the Choates.

44. A true and accurate copy of that Foreclosure Judgment is attached hereto as Exhibit H.

45. In a Foreclosure Deed dated May 27, 2008, and recorded in the Kennebec County Registry of Deeds in Book 9778, Page 135, First National Bank took title to the Property.

46. A true and accurate copy of that Foreclosure Deed is attached hereto as Exhibit I.

47. In Special Warranty Deed dated July 28, 2008, and recorded in the Kennebec County Registry of Deeds in Book 9847, Page 29, First National Bank conveyed the Property to Plaintiffs Gary A. Arbuckle and Marilyn J. Arbuckle.

48. A true and accurate copy of that Special Warranty Deed is attached hereto as Exhibit J.

49. The Plaintiffs' property is, unfortunately, saddled and encumbered with the McCains' HELOC mortgage.

The McCains' Wrongful Conduct

50. The McCains sold the Property to the Choates and delivered title by Warranty Deed.

51. At the time they sold the Property to the Choates, the McCains knew they were obligated to discharge and close the HELOC.

52. The McCains' knowledge is demonstrated by their execution of the Shortfall Agreement.

53. Despite their knowledge, the McCains proceeded to draw down the HELOC following the payment of $166,184.81 made by check from Rainbow Title Company, Inc., received by the Bank of Mind on October 14, 2005.

54. After drawing down the HELOC, the McCains ceased payments, and have not made payments on the HELOC for more than 600 days, resulting in an outstanding balance in excess of $208,000.00.

55. The Property remains encumbered by the HELOC.

56. Despite their outstanding debt, the McCains Purchased the McCain Subdivision in China.

57. There are no liens or encumbrances on the McCain Subdivision.

58. The McCains sold a portion of the McCain Subdivision to the Fredettes.

59. The McCains did not apply the proceeds from that sale to satisfy the HELOC.

60. The McCains have applied to the Town of China to obtain approval to subdivide the McCain Subdivision and create an additional lot.

61. If successful in obtaining town approval, the McCains plan to create two lots out of their remaining portion of the McCain Subdivision.

62. The McCains plan to sell one or both of the two lots they plan to create out of their remaining portion of the McCain Subdivision.

63. The McCains are aware that one or more parties are investigating the status of the HELOC burdening the Property.

64. In a deed dated September 15, 2008 (attached hereto as Exhibit G), the McCains wrongfully transferred an undivided 7/10 interest in the remaining portion of the McCain Subdivision to Robert J. Symington and Cecilia Symington (the "Symingtons").

65. Melissa A. McCain is directly related to the Symingtons.

66. Jason I. McCain is related to the Symingtons by marriage.

COUNT I

Fraud

67. Plaintiffs Gary A. Arbuckle and Marilyn J. Arbuckle repeat and allege herein each and every allegation set forth above in the preceding Paragraphs.

68. The McCains falsely represented that they were granting title to the Property free and clear of any encumbrances.

69. The McCains further represented that they would pay lenders any sums legally necessary to secure discharge of any mortgages encumbering the Property at the time of the sale.

70. The McCains never satisfied their obligation to discharge and close the HELOC after the sale of the Property to the Choates.

71. At the time of their representations, the McCains never intended to satisfy their obligation to discharge the HELOC encumbering the property.

72. Their representation was, at all times, material and false.

73. Despite their representation that they would deliver title to the Choates free and clear of any encumbrances, the McCains knowingly drew down funds against the HELOC after the sale of the Property to the Choates.

74. The McCains' aforementioned representations—to deliver unencumbered title to the Property—are material misstatements of fact.

75. At the time the McCains made the false representations, they knew or should have known that their misrepresentations of fact were false.

76. As a result of the McCains' fraud, the Arbuckles have suffered substantial damages.

WHEREFORE, Plaintiffs Gary A. Arbuckle and Marilyn J. Arbuckle respectfully request that the Court award damages in their favor, against Defendants Jason I. McCain and Melissa A. McCain, jointly and severally, in the amount consistent with the evidence in this case, together with interest, costs, attorney's fees, punitive damages, and such other and further relief as the Court deems just and appropriate.

COUNT II

Breach of Warranty

77. Plaintiffs repeat and reallege herein each and every allegation set forth in the preceding Paragraphs.

78. By way of the Warranty Deed conveying the Property to the Choates, the McCains warranted to the Choates and their successors in title, including the Arbuckles, that title to the Property was free and clear of all encumbrances.

79. By their actions to draw down the HELOC secured by the Property after the sale of the Property was complete, the McCains delivered title that was, in fact, encumbered.

80. The McCains' failure to deliver title to the Property free and clear of all encumbrances constitutes breach of warranty.

81. Because the HELOC continues to encumber the Property, the McCains have breached their warranty to Arbuckles.

82. The Choates and their successors in title, the Arbuckles, have satisfied any conditions required to maintain the warranty.

83. As a result of the McCains' breach of warranty, the Arbuckles have suffered, and continue to suffer, substantial damages.

WHEREFORE, Plaintiffs Gary A. Arbuckle and Marilyn J. Arbuckle respectfully request that the Court award damages in their favor, against Defendants Jason I. McCain and Melissa A. McCain, jointly and severally, in an amount consistent with the evidence in this case, together with interest, costs, and such other and further relief as the Court deems just and appropriate.

COUNT III

Conversion

84. Plaintiffs repeat and reallege herein each and every allegation set forth above in the preceding Paragraphs.

85. The Arbuckles had a right to have the McCains' prior mortgage on the Property discharged as part of the McCains' sale of the Property to the Choates on October 8, 2005.

86. The Arbuckles had a right to own the Property free and clear of any encumbrances at the time of their July 28, 2008, closing on the Property.

87. The McCains wrongfully converted the funds they drew down against the HELOC by failing to pay off, and close, the loan secured by the Property.

88. Despite demand, the McCains have failed and/or refused to pay off the HELOC.

89. As a direct result of the McCains' conversion, the Arbuckles have suffered substantial damages.

WHEREFORE, Plaintiffs Gary A. Arbuckle and Marilyn J. Arbuckle respectfully requests that the Court award damages in their favor, against Defendants Jason I. McCain and Melissa A. McCain, jointly and severally, in an amount consistent with the evidence in this case, together with interest, costs, attorney's fees, punitive damages, and such other and further relief as the Court deems just and appropriate.

COUNT IV

Breach of Contract

90. Plaintiffs repeat and reallege herein each and every allegation set forth in the preceding Paragraphs.

91. The McCains had a contractual obligation to deliver clear title to the Choates (and correspondingly, to their successors in title, the Arbuckles) at the time of the sale of the Property on May 24, 2004.

92. The McCains are in privity of contract with the Arbuckles.

93. The McCains breached that contract by failing to discharge and close the HELOC encumbering the Property.

94. The McCains have further breached their contractual obligations by drawing down against the HELOC after the sale of the Property to the Choates, and by failing and/or refusing to remove the encumbrance on the Property.

95. The Choates and their successors in title, the Arbuckles, have satisfied all conditions precedent involving their contractual obligations to the McCains.

96. As a result of the McCains' breach of contract, the Arbuckles have suffered substantial damages.

WHEREFORE, Plaintiffs Gary A. Arbuckle and Marilyn J. Arbuckle respectfully request that the Court award damages in their favor, against Defendants Jason I. McCain and Melissa A. McCain, jointly and severally, in an the amount consistent with the evidence in this case, together with interest, costs, and such other and further relief as the Court deems just and appropriate.

COUNT V

Fraudulent Transfer

97. Plaintiffs repeat and reallege herein each and every allegation set forth in the preceding Paragraphs.

98. The McCains held all interest in the title to the remaining portion of the McCain Subdivision free and clear of encumbrances.

99. The McCains were aware that interested parties, including Bank of Mind and the Arbuckles, were considering action to compel discharge of the HELOC encumbering the Property.

100. By Deed dated September 15, 2008, the McCains conveyed an undivided 7/10 interest in the remaining portion of the McCain Subdivision to the Symingtons.

101. The McCains and the Symingtons made the transfer with actual intent to hinder, delay, and defraud the McCains' creditors, including the Arbuckles.

102. As a result of the McCains' and the Symingtons' fraudulent transfer, the Arbuckles have suffered substantial damages.

WHEREFORE, Plaintiffs Gary A. Arbuckle and Marilyn J. Arbuckle respectfully request that the Court (1) avoid the transfer of the McCain Subdivision; (2) enjoin any further disposition of the McCain Subdivision by either the McCains or the Symingtons; (3) appoint a receiver to take charge of the McCain Subdivision or other property of the McCains and Symingtons; (4) award damages in an amount not to exceed double the value of the property transferred or concealed; and (5) award any other relief the circumstances may require, and such other and further relief as the Court deems just and appropriate.

SPECIFIC PERFORMANCE OF CONTRACT

STATE OF MIND SUPERIOR COURT

ACME, INC.,	)	
Plaintiff	)	
	)	
v.	)	
	)	Civil Action No. ________
JOSEPH A. HUNTINGTON and	)	
STAR, L.L.C.,	)	
Defendants	)	
	)	
MIND SAVINGS BANK,	)	
Party in Interest	)	
	)	

COMPLAINT FOR SPECIFIC PERFORMANCE AND DAMAGES

(Title to Real Estate Is Involved)

Plaintiff Acme, Inc. ("Acme"), by its undersigned counsel, states the following as its Complaint against Defendants Joseph A. Huntington ("Huntington") and Star, L.L.C. ("Star"):

Preliminary Statement

1. Defendants Huntington and Star have violated their Purchase and Sale Agreement with Acme by: (a) failing to obtain and deliver all of the licenses, permits, and approvals necessary for the construction and operation of an Acme convenience store and gas station in Pleasantville, and (b) failing to act consistently with their fiduciary obligations of good faith and fair dealing with Acme. Additionally, Huntington and Star induced Acme into the aforementioned agreement by intentionally and/or negligently misrepresenting their skills and abilities as real estate developers. The parties' agreement dated March 4, 2005, requires Huntington and Star to obtain and deliver to Acme all of the necessary licenses and permits—and precludes the Defendants from agreeing to any conditions on such licenses and permits without Acme's approval. Despite this, Huntington and Star have failed to pursue certain licenses

and permits, have failed to deliver to Acme other licenses and approvals which they claim to have obtained, and have further violated the agreement and their fiduciary duties by agreeing to certain conditions without the approval of Acme. Acme requests that this Court order Huntington and Star to specifically and fully perform all of their obligations under the agreement, and also award damages for the Defendants' wrongful conduct.

The Parties

2. Plaintiff Acme is a Delaware corporation with the principal place of business in Canton, Massachusetts.

3. Defendant Huntington is a citizen of Yarmouth.

4. Defendant Star is a Mind limited liability company with a principal place of business in Yarmouth.

5. Defendant Huntington is the Managing Member of Defendant Star.

6. Party in Interest Mind Savings Bank is a Mind bank corporation with a principal place of business in Mind.

The Facts

7. Huntington is the owner of a parcel of property located at 100 Alfred Street in Pleasantville (the "Property"). The property is described in a deed to Huntington dated October 31, 2005, and recorded in the York County Registry of Deeds at Book 14663, Page 71. A true and accurate copy of the deed for the Property is attached hereto as Exhibit A.

8. Mind Savings Bank has an interest in the Property by virtue of a Mortgage Deed, dated October 31, 2005, and recorded in the York County Registry of Deeds at Book 14663, Page 73.

9. On March 4, 2004, Huntington, both individually and in his capacity as the Managing Member of Star, entered into a Purchase and Sale Agreement (the "Agreement") with Acme. A true and accurate copy of the Agreement is attached hereto as Exhibit B.

10. Pursuant to the Agreement, Huntington and Star agreed to sell the Property to Acme. They also agreed, among other things, to secure "all federal, state and local licenses, permits and approvals, including but not limited to any approvals from the appropriate local zoning

board and any building or other permits . . . necessary for the construction and operation of a convenience store with self-service gasoline and fast food facility in a configuration deemed appropriate by [Acme] in its sole discretion. . . ."

11. In addition, Paragraph 10 of the Agreement provides as follows: "[It is] specifically acknowledged and agreed that [Acme] will provide [Huntington and Star] with the plans to secure the Approvals and that [Huntington and Star have] no right or authorization to modify such plans or enter into any agreements with the permitting officials for any concessions or modifications without the express written consent of [Acme]."

Defendants' Wrongful Conduct

12. When the parties were negotiating the terms of the Agreement, Huntington insisted upon controlling the process of obtaining all of the required licenses, permits, and approvals, and he assured Acme that he and Star were ready, willing, and able to act as Acme's agents in this regard and that he and Star had the requisite experience and skill to obtain the required licenses, permits, and approvals in the time frame set forth in the Agreement.

13. In reliance upon Huntington's representations regarding his motivation and ability to obtain all of the required licenses, permits, and approvals, Acme agreed to allow Huntington and Star to act as its agents in this regard and also agreed to pay Huntington and Star $35,000 for costs associated with this work.

14. Pursuant to the terms of the Agreement, Huntington and Star had one year from the execution of the Agreement on March 4, 2005, to obtain the required licenses, permits, and approvals.

15. That deadline was subsequently extended to August 26, 2006, and then extended again to September 8, 2006.

16. Despite numerous requests, Huntington and Star have failed to secure a wide variety of required licenses, permits, and approvals, including permits from the Town and permits from the Mind Department of Transportation.

17. Furthermore, Huntington and Star have failed—despite repeated requests—to provide Acme with copies of the permits and permit applications which they are pursuing and to inform Acme of their discussions concerning permits and permit conditions.

18. In addition, Huntington and Star also have agreed to certain conditions associated with some of the required permits without first

obtaining consent of Acme—despite an express provision in the Agreement which precludes them from doing so without the written approval of Acme. For example, after the Pleasantville Planning Board required third-party easements as a condition for its approval, Huntington and Star refused—in bad faith—to allow any input from Acme in its discussions with the third parties, in direct contravention of Defendants' agreement.

19. On March 30, 2006, Acme wrote a letter to counsel for Huntington and Star detailing all of these aforementioned concerns. A true and accurate copy of the letter dated March 30, 2006, from Acme is attached hereto as Exhibit C.

20. Despite this letter—and many communications since that time in which Defendants provided Acme with assurances that they were actively engaged in the process of obtaining the required licenses, permits, and approvals and that those licenses, permits, and approvals would be forthcoming—Huntington and Star have failed to perform their obligations pursuant to the Agreement.

21. Defendants' failure to perform their obligations pursuant to the Agreement has deprived Acme of the benefit of its bargain with Defendants and prevented Acme from moving ahead with the construction and operation of its planned convenience store and gas station in Pleasantville.

COUNT I

Breach of Contract

22. Acme repeats and realleges herein each and every allegation set forth in the preceding Paragraphs.

23. The Agreement constitutes a binding and enforceable contract between Acme and the Defendants.

24. Acme has satisfied all conditions precedent to its ability to enforce the Agreement.

25. The Defendants have breached the Agreement by failing to secure the required licenses, permits, and approvals and by agreeing with permitting officials to certain concessions and modifications of the plans, provided by Acme, without the express written consent of Acme.

26. Acme has suffered damages as a result of Defendants' breach of the Agreement.

27. The Agreement expressly provides in Paragraph 21 that "[n]otwithstanding any provisions to the contrary herein, [Acme] shall have the right to obtain specific performance of this Agreement as well as to the benefit of any other rights or remedies provided herein or by applicable law . . ."

28. Due to the unique nature of the real estate involved in this case, money damages alone would not be adequate to compensate Acme for Defendants' breach of their contractual obligations.

WHEREFORE, Plaintiff Acme, Inc. respectfully requests that the Court order specific performance of the Defendants' obligations under the Agreement and award compensatory damages in its favor, and against the Defendants jointly and severally, in an amount consistent with the evidence, together with, interest, reasonable attorney's fees, costs, and such other and further relief as the Court deems just and appropriate.

COUNT II

Breach of Fiduciary Duty

29. Acme repeats and realleges herein each and every allegation set forth in the preceding Paragraphs.

30. As agents of Acme with respect to the securing of all federal, state, and local licenses, permits, and approvals necessary for the construction and operation of a convenience store and gasoline station in Pleasantville, Defendants acted as fiduciaries.

31. As fiduciaries, Defendants owed Acme duties of loyalty and diligence.

32. Defendants have breached those duties by failing to make a good faith effort to secure the required licenses, permits, and approvals, by failing and refusing upon demand by Acme to provide Acme with copies of the permits and applications that they claim to have been pursuing, and by agreeing with permitting officials to certain concessions and modifications of the plans provided by Acme without the express written consent of Acme.

33. Defendants have willfully disregarded their fiduciary duties and have acted with malice or, alternatively, their willful disregard of their fiduciary duties is so outrageous that malice may be implied.

WHEREFORE, Plaintiff Acme, Inc. respectfully requests that the Court award compensatory damages in their favor, and against the

Defendants jointly and severally, in an amount consistent with the evidence, together with punitive damages, interest, reasonable attorney's fees, costs, and such other and further relief as the Court deems just and appropriate.

COUNT III

Negligent Misrepresentation

34. Acme repeats and realleges herein each and every allegation set forth in the preceding Paragraphs.

35. Defendants supplied false information to Acme regarding their motivation and ability to secure all federal, state, and local licenses, permits, and approvals, necessary for the construction and operation of a convenience store and gasoline station in Pleasantville, Mind.

36. This information was provided in the course of Defendants' business, profession, or employment and/or in the course of a transaction in which they had a pecuniary interest.

37. This information was provided for the guidance of Acme in its business transactions and was justifiably relied upon by Acme.

38. Defendants failed to exercise reasonable care or competence in obtaining and/or communicating this information.

39. Acme has suffered damages as a result of its justifiable reliance upon the false information that was negligently provided by Defendants.

WHEREFORE, Plaintiff Acme, Inc. respectfully requests that the Court award compensatory damages in their favor and against the Defendants jointly and severally, in an amount consistent with the evidence, together with interest, reasonable attorney's fees, costs, and such other and further relief as the Court deems just and appropriate.

COUNT IV

Intentional Misrepresentation

40. Acme repeats and realleges herein each and every allegation set forth in the preceding Paragraphs.

41. Defendants made false representations of a material fact to Acme regarding their motivation and ability to secure all federal, state, and local licenses, permits, and approvals, necessary for the

construction and operation of a convenience store and gasoline station in Pleasantville.

42. These representations were made with knowledge of their falsity or in reckless disregard of whether they were true or false.

43. These representations were made for the purpose of inducing Acme to rely upon them.

44. Defendants made these false representations willfully and with malice or, alternatively, their conduct is so outrageous that malice may be implied.

45. Acme has suffered damages as a result of its justifiable reliance upon the Defendants' false representations.

WHEREFORE, Plaintiff Acme, Inc. respectfully requests that the Court award compensatory damages in their favor, and against the Defendants jointly and severally, in an amount consistent with the evidence, together with punitive damages, interest, reasonable attorney's fees, costs, and such other and further relief as the Court deems just and appropriate.

PARTITION

STATE OF MIND SUPERIOR COURT

PETER H. SAMUELSON, Individually and as Personal Representative of the Estate of Betsy H. Samuelson,	)	
ELIZABETH F. TALBOT, Individually and as Personal Representative of the Estate of Betsy H. Samuelson, and	)	Civil Action No. ________
JOHN A. SAMUELSON, Plaintiffs	)	
v.	)	
ARNOLD SAMUELSON, Defendant	)	

COMPLAINT

(Title to Real Estate Is Involved)

Plaintiffs Peter H. Samuelson, Elizabeth F. Talbot, and John A. Samuelson, by their respective undersigned counsel, state the following as their Complaint against Defendant Arnold Samuelson:

I. Preliminary Statement

1. Peter H. Samuelson and Elizabeth F. Talbot, in their capacity as Co-Personal Representatives of the Estate of their mother, Betsy H. Samuelson, hold legal title to a fractional ownership interest in real estate located in Kennebunkport. Peter H. Samuelson, Elizabeth F. Talbot, John A. Samuelson, and Arnold Samuelson (individually)—the children of Betsy H. Samuelson—own properties in Kennebunkport, as tenants in common by virtue of deeds from their mother (the Co-Personal Representatives and the four Samuelson children individually

are collectively referred to as "the parties"). The parties have been unable to agree on how to divide these properties among them. The Plaintiffs request that the Court appoint Commissioners to divide the properties or, in the alternative, request that the Court use its equitable powers to order the sale of all or a portion of the properties and—after using the proceeds to pay Plaintiffs' full expenses for this action—to equally divide the proceeds among the parties in their individual capacities.

II. The Parties

2. Plaintiff Peter H. Samuelson brings this action in his individual capacity and in his capacity as Co-Personal Representative of the Estate of Betsy H. Samuelson. Mr. Samuelson is a resident of Kennebunkport.

3. Plaintiff Elizabeth F. Talbot brings this action in her individual capacity and as Co-Personal Representative of the Estate of Betsy H. Samuelson. Ms. Talbot is a resident of Kennebunkport.

4. Plaintiff John A. Samuelson is a resident of Wilmington, Delaware.

5. Defendant Arnold Samuelson is a resident of Westford, Massachusetts.

III. The Kennebunkport Properties

6. The parties own Lots 5 and 21 shown on Tax Map 12 of the Kennebunkport Tax Maps (the "Kennebunkport Properties"), as tenants in common by virtue of deeds and by virtue of the Will of Betsy H. Samuelson. A true and accurate copy of Kennebunkport Tax Map 12 is attached hereto as Exhibit A.

7. The Estate of Betsy H. Samuelson owns, in fee simple, a portion of the property as described on Kennebunkport Tax Map 12, Lot 5. The Kennebunkport Tax Map lists this property as containing 25.1 acres. Pursuant to the Will of Betsy H. Samuelson, the Estate's portion of this property is devised in equal shares as tenants-in-common to Peter H. Samuelson, Elizabeth F. Talbot, John A. Samuelson, and Arnold Samuelson. The Estate's historic title to this property, as well as other properties no longer owned by the Estate, is described in the Affidavit of Betsy Huke Samuelson, dated July 20, 1993, and recorded in the York County Registry of Deeds at Book 6635, Page 351. A true and accurate copy of the Affidavit of Betsy Huke Samuelson is attached hereto as Exhibit B.

A true and accurate copy of the Certificate and Abstract of the Will of Betsy H. Samuelson, recorded in the York County Registry of Deeds at Book 9988, Page 231, is attached hereto as Exhibit C.

8. In their individual capacities, Peter H. Samuelson, Elizabeth Talbot, John A. Samuelson, and Arnold Samuelson, each owns, in fee simple and as tenants in common, an undivided one-fourth interest in the remaining portion of the land shown on Kennebunkport Tax Map 12, Lot 5, and all of the property shown on Kennebunkport Tax Map 12, Lot 21. The Kennebunkport Tax Map lists Lot 21 of Map 12 as containing 90.4 acres.

9. The individual parties' title to a portion of the property shown in Kennebunkport Tax Map 12, Lot 5 is by virtue of a deed dated December 30, 1988, and recorded in the York County Registry of Deeds at Book 4957, Page 312 (one-eighth interest of part of Lot 5 to Peter Hill Samuelson); by deed dated December 30, 1988, and recorded in the York County Registry of Deeds at Book 4957, Page 316 (one-eighth interest of part of Lot 5 to Elizabeth Talbot); by deed dated December 30, 1988 and recorded in the York County Registry of Deeds at Book 4957, Page 320 (one-eighth interest of part of Lot 5 to John Allen Samuelson); by deed dated October 20, 1997, and recorded in the York County Registry of Deeds at Book 8939, Page 324 (one-eighth interest of part of Lot 5 to Arnold Samuelson); by deed dated October 16, 1990, and recorded in the York County Registry of Deeds at Book 5547, Page 226 (three-twentieths interest of a portion of Lot 5 to each of the individual parties); and by deed dated May 9, 1991 and recorded in the York County Registry of Deeds at Book 5700, Page 290 (two-twentieths interest in a portion of Lot 5 to each of the individual parties). True and accurate copies of these deeds are attached hereto as Exhibits D-1, D-2, D-3, D-4, D-5, and D-6.

10. The individual parties' title to the property shown on Kennebunkport Tax Map 12, Lot 21 is by virtue of a deed dated December 30, 1988, and recorded in the York County Registry of Deeds at Book 4957, Page 308 (one-fourth interest to Arnold Samuelson); by deed dated December 30, 1988, and recorded in the York County Registry of Deeds at Book 4957, Page 312 (one-fourth interest to Peter Hill Samuelson); by deed dated December 30, 1988, and recorded in the York County Registry of Deeds at Book 4957, Page 316 (one-fourth interest to Elizabeth Talbot); and by deed dated December 30, 1988, and recorded in the York County Registry of Deeds at Book 4957, Page 320 (one-fourth interest to

John Allen Samuelson). True copies of these deeds are attached hereto as Exhibits E-1, E-2, E-3, and E-4.

11. By Agreement for the Transfer of Real Estate, dated October 25, 1992 (the "Transfer Agreement"), Peter H. Samuelson, John A. Samuelson, and Arnold Samuelson, each agreed to convey to Elizabeth F. Talbot his interest in a one-acre lot that had previously been part of Lot 21 of Kennebunkport Tax Map 12 (the "Woodlot Property"). In exchange, Ms. Talbot agreed to convey to each of her three brothers a one-quarter undivided interest in a one-acre lot from the Woodlot Property at such time as each of them requested in writing that she do so. A true copy of the Transfer Agreement is attached hereto as Exhibit F.

12. None of Ms. Talbot's brothers has, to date, exercised his rights under the Transfer Agreement.

IV. The Dispute

13. Arnold Samuelson is unable to agree with his brothers, his sister, or the Personal Representatives of the Estate concerning the division, distribution, improvement, maintenance, upkeep, surveying, or appraising of the Kennebunkport Properties.

14. Plaintiffs Peter H. Samuelson, Elizabeth Talbot, and John A. Samuelson, in their individual capacities, have contributed funds to improve, repair, and maintain a portion of the Kennebunkport Properties and to remove a leasehold encumbrance.

15. Defendant Arnold Samuelson has not contributed any funds for the improvement, repair, or maintenance of the Kennebunkport properties, and has not contributed any funds to have the leasehold encumbrance removed.

COUNT I

Physical Partition

16. Plaintiffs repeat and reallege herein each and every allegation set forth above in Paragraphs 1 through 15.

17. The Estate of Betsy H. Samuelson and Peter H. Samuelson, Elizabeth Talbot, John A. Samuelson, and Arnold Samuelson, individually, are owners in fee simple of the Kennebunkport Properties, as tenants in

common, by virtue of the aforementioned deeds by virtue of the Will of Betsy H. Samuelson.

18. Peter H. Samuelson and Elizabeth F. Talbot, individually and on behalf of the Estate, and John A. Samuelson request that the Kennebunkport Properties be partitioned.

WHEREFORE, Plaintiffs Peter H. Samuelson and Elizabeth F. Talbot, individually and as Personal Representatives of the Estate of Betsy H. Samuelson, and John A. Samuelson respectfully request that the Court grant the following relief:

a. Enter a judgment of physical partition for the Kennebunkport Properties;

b. Enter an Order, pursuant to 14 M.R.S.A. § 6511, appointing three disinterested persons as Commissioners to make partition of the Kennebunkport Properties, to set off three one-acre lots from Lot 21 for each of the Samuelson brothers, and to then set off an equal share of the Kennebunkport Properties for each party in his or her individual capacity, all of which shall be expressed in a warrant issued by the Commissioners.

c. Order that the Commissioners shall consider improvements, repairs, and maintenance made to the Kennebunkport Properties by the Plaintiffs, as well as other contributions paid on behalf of the properties, when deciding how to divide the Kennebunkport Properties;

d. Order that the Kennebunkport Properties be divided pursuant to the warrant issued by the Commissioners;

e. As contemplated by 18-A M.R.S.A. § 1-601, order that the Estate of Betsy H. Samuelson may advance to Plaintiffs all funds for paying the fees and expenses of their attorneys and experts, as well as the Court-appointed Commissioners.

f. Award Plaintiffs costs pursuant to 14 M.R.S.A. § 6508 and as otherwise prescribed by law;

g. Order an apportionment of expenses pursuant to 14 M.R.S.A. § 6516;

h. Award Plaintiffs their reasonable attorney's fees in prosecution of this action for the common benefit of the parties hereto; and

i. Grant such other and further relief as the Court deems just and appropriate.

COUNT II

Equitable Partition

19. Plaintiffs repeat and reallege herein each and every allegation set forth above in Paragraphs 1 through 18.

20. In the alternative, Plaintiffs state that all or a portion of the Kennebunkport Properties cannot be physically divided without materially injuring one or more of the parties and that physical division of all or a portion of the Kennebunkport Properties is impractical.

WHEREFORE, Plaintiffs Peter H. Samuelson and Elizabeth F. Talbot, individually and as Personal Representatives of the Estate of Betsy H. Samuelson, and John A. Samuelson respectfully request that the Court grant the following relief:

a. Enter an Order granting an equitable partition of all or part of the Kennebunkport Properties pursuant to 14 M.R.S.A. § 6051(7);

b. Order a judicial sale of all or a portion of the Kennebunkport Properties, provided that the parties, in their individual capacities, shall first have the opportunity to buy all or a portion of the properties for fair market value (or, if more than one party is willing to pay full value, to the highest bidder);

c. Order that the proceeds from the sale shall first be used to pay all expenses associated with this action and to reimburse the Plaintiffs for their improvements and repairs to the Kennebunkport Properties, as well as for other expenditures made on behalf of the properties, such as removing the leasehold encumbrance;

d. Order that the remaining proceeds of the judicial sale shall be divided equally by and among Peter H. Samuelson, Elizabeth Talbot, John A. Samuelson, and Arnold Samuelson, in their individual capacities.

e. Award Plaintiffs their costs of suit;

f. Enter an Order equitably apportioning expenses pursuant to 14 M.R.S.A. § 6516;

g. Award Plaintiffs their reasonable attorney's fees in prosecution of this action for the common benefit of the parties hereto; and

h. Grant such other and further relief as this Court finds just and appropriate.

COUNT III

Unjust Enrichment

21. Plaintiffs repeat and reallege herein each and every allegation set forth above in Paragraphs 1 through 20.

22. Arnold Samuelson has been unjustly enriched by the benefits conferred upon him by the Plaintiffs in that Arnold Samuelson has failed and refused to pay for his share of those benefits.

23. It would be inequitable for Arnold Samuelson to retain the benefit conferred upon him by the Plaintiffs without compensating the Plaintiffs for the value of that benefit.

24. Arnold Samuelson received and accepted the benefit of Plaintiffs' improvements, repairs, contributions, and payments on behalf of the Kennebunkport Properties with the knowledge and understanding that he was obligated to pay his pro rata share of these benefits.

WHEREFORE, Plaintiffs respectfully request judgment against Defendant Arnold Samuelson, in an amount that is reasonable under the circumstances, plus interest, costs of suit, and such other and further relief as the Court may deem just and appropriate.

COUNT IV

Quantum Meruit

25. Plaintiffs repeat and reallege herein each and every allegation set forth above in Paragraphs 1 through 24.

26. The improvements, repairs, contributions, and payments made or performed by the Plaintiffs were provided under circumstances that clearly establish Plaintiffs' reasonable expectation that they would be compensated by Arnold Samuelson for his pro rata share of such improvements, repairs, contributions, and payments.

27. Arnold Samuelson benefited from the improvements, repairs, contributions, and payments, but has not reimbursed Plaintiffs for his share of the improvements, repairs, contributions, and payments.

28. Arnold Samuelson is liable to Plaintiffs in quantum meruit for the reasonable value of the improvements, repairs, contributions, and payments made, performed, and/or provided.

WHEREFORE, Plaintiffs respectfully request judgment against Defendant Arnold Samuelson in an amount that is reasonable under the circumstances, plus interest, costs of suit, and such other and further relief as the Court may deems just and appropriate.

CHAPTER 7

Responsive Pleadings

If we desire to avoid insult, we must be able to repel it.
—George Washington

There are two ways to respond to a Complaint: by Answer or by a motion to dismiss. An Answer, of course, serves to admit or rebut the assertions in the Complaint, and to list all affirmative defenses. A motion to dismiss, on the other hand, is a full frontal attack on any of the plaintiff's claims.

THE ANSWER

The Answer is a response to each and every one of the allegations in the Complaint, a thorough listing of affirmative defenses, and all Counterclaims and Third Party Complaints.

An Answer, as with every pleading in real estate litigation, deserves a lot of thought. Do not undertake it until you have reviewed the title in dispute, viewed the property, and interviewed the client and the principal accessible witnesses. Read all of the referenced deeds and review all of the plans and surveys. Research the elements of the counts and the defenses to each claim.

Avoid the temptation of filing a "down and dirty" Answer. Take a moment to review the Complaint and to understand—and fully appreciate—the theories it espouses. Carefully explore the factual allegations with your client.

Most jurisdictions require the Answer to specifically address each and every allegation in the Complaint. There is nothing wrong with admitting assertions that are plainly correct. Denying accurate statements is not cost effective or professional. A lot of needless expense and momentum is lost by inappropriately denying every allegation. There is no point in denying facts that your documents and witnesses will eventually admit.

However, you should absolutely deny those portions of an allegation that are not fully correct or are misleading. Consider the allegation: "The Dawsons have a pedestrian easement, over the Rosenbergs' land, to the shore for swimming, fishing, and the placement of a dock." If you acknowledge the pedestrian easement—but challenge the scope—be straight about your position: "The Rosenbergs deny the allegations set forth in Paragraph 3 of Plaintiff's Complaint, but admit that the Dawsons have a pedestrian easement over their land."

Your admissions must be narrowly tailored to what is accurate. Admit only those portions of an allegation that are correct—and firmly deny the rest. For example, if the plaintiff claims "that the deed from Akari to Baker, dated August 12, 2009, creates an easement over the Defendant's property" and you challenge only the characterization of the deed, your response to this allegation should state: "Defendant admits that he entered into a deed with Plaintiff Baker dated August 12, 2009. The rest of the allegations in Paragraph 8 of the Plaintiff's Complaint are denied."

Where part of an allegation is true and part is not, deny the allegation and except out the admission. Doing the opposite may result in the admission being broader than intended. Accordingly, the allegation should be denied in its entirety, and a specifically excepted statement should be made encompassing the narrow admission. The narrow admission should be in your words and limited to exactly what is unambiguously admitted.

Before filing the Answer, review all of your admissions one last time to ensure that the admissions are accurate and not overbroad. It is difficult to change an admission after it is made.

There will also be assertions that, despite investigation, cannot be admitted or denied. Pursuant to Rule 8(b)(5) of the Federal Rules of Civil Procedure, you are entitled to state words to the following effect: "The Rosenbergs are without knowledge or information sufficient to form a belief as to the truth of the allegations set forth in Paragraph 1 of

Plaintiff's Complaint and therefore deny same and demand strict proof thereof."

After responding to all of the allegations in the Complaint, the Answer must set forth each and every affirmative defense on which you intend to rely. This is very important. The failure to list an affirmative defense *prevents* its use at trial.

If you are unsure as to whether your defense is an *affirmative* defense, be safe and list it. Typical affirmative defenses in real estate litigation are the following:

1. Plaintiff's Complaint fails to state a cause of action upon which relief can be granted.
2. Plaintiff's claims are barred by the doctrine of waiver.
3. Plaintiff's claims are barred by the doctrine of estoppel.
4. Plaintiff's claims are barred by the doctrine of laches.

Rule 12(b) lists certain required defenses. One basic defense waived at trial if not listed—arises from Rule 12(b)(6): "Plaintiff's Complaint fails to state a claim upon which relief can be granted."

A nonexclusive list of other affirmative defenses is set forth in Rule 8(c)(1) of the Rules of Civil Procedure. Common affirmative defenses in real estate actions are estoppel, laches, license, statute of frauds, statute of limitations, and waiver.

Estoppel and waiver are similar affirmative defenses in property cases. "Waiver" applies where a party voluntarily and knowingly gives up a right. If a condominium sues a unit owner for using a common area, the unit owner can rely on the doctrine of waiver where the condominium has never enforced common area rights. A bank may waive foreclosure rights where it accepts monthly mortgage payments. A party to a purchase and sale agreement waives the arbitration provision by filing a complaint.

"Estoppel," on the other hand, precludes a party from asserting rights against a person who, in good faith, has relied on the first party's conduct. An example is a new neighbor who asks for the location of a mutual boundary line. Where the old neighbor incorrectly identifies the boundary line—and watches the new neighbor build a driveway on the old neighbor's land—the old neighbor is estopped from subsequently preventing the new neighbor from using the driveway. Similarly, where a seller divides his land and gives the buyer a parcel bordered by a pre-existing right-of-way to the new parcel, the seller is estopped from precluding the buyer from using the right-of-way.

Thus, "waiver" is the voluntary and knowing relinquishing of a right. "Estoppel" is the relinquishment of a right where a party relies, in good faith, on the other party's conduct or actions. One or the other of these affirmative defenses is very often present in property disputes.

Two other similar defenses are statute of limitations and laches. The statute of limitations is, of course, the deadline for filing a dispute in the jurisdiction at issue. Many jurisdictions have specific statutes of limitations in real property actions. Statutes of limitations in real estate actions are usually lengthy. However, if a deadline for filing suit has been missed, make sure you assert that the claims are barred by the statute of limitations. Many a case has been lost by the failure to assert this defense at the appropriate time. Thus, a claim such as for breach of an easement or violation of a restrictive covenant must be filed and/or served within that designated time frame set forth by state statute or common law.

"Laches" is an equitable defense that is available where the plaintiff has waited an unreasonable time to file the claim, and the other side is prejudiced by this unreasonable delay. An example of a common laches issue is where the plaintiff sues to enforce a purchase and sale agreement to buy property but has waited for so long to seek specific performance that the defendant has already closed on the deal with a third party.

"License" is an often forgotten affirmative defense against adverse possession or prescriptive easement claims. These claims are neutralized by permission or "license." "License" negates a claim for trespass since the basis of a trespass claim—unauthorized use of another's land—is negated by a lease, permission, or other license to use it.

The "statute of frauds" defense, while full of exceptions, can also be very powerful. The general rule is that an oral agreement related to real estate cannot be enforced. Real estate contracts, agreements, and deeds must be in writing and signed by the party against whom the agreement is being asserted. Most jurisdictions, however, recognize numerous exceptions to the statute of frauds, including where one party has partially performed the agreement with the other side's knowledge.

The list of Rule 8 affirmative defenses is not exclusive. Look to the elements and defenses of each count alleged in the Complaint. Make sure that the Answer lists all pertinent affirmative defenses related to each alleged count.

Most judges will allow poorly drafted affirmative defenses to stand as long as it puts the other side no notice of your defense. Therefore, it is good practice to add a few affirmative defenses that summarize your position, such as:

1. The boundary between the parties' property is plainly set forth in the deed dated August 12, 2009, and the survey recorded on that same date.
2. Defendant did not trespass on Plaintiff's land because he has an easement by necessity to travel across it.

You should set forth all of your defenses in a clearly written statement. Given that the failure to list an affirmative defense precludes its use, the prudent real estate litigator should include all significant defenses. This puts the other side on notice of these defenses and ensures that they can be raised at trial.

For example, if the Complaint states that you have wrongfully blocked access to the plaintiff's home, the affirmative defenses in your Answer should include the following:

- Plaintiff's driveway is on land wholly owned by the Defendant.
- Plaintiff has no easement, license, or other right to traverse Defendant's property.
- Any easement held by Plaintiff, to traverse Defendant's land, has been abandoned or taken by adverse possession.

By adding defenses in clear English, after listing the more traditional affirmative defenses, you ensure that nothing is waived.

At the conclusion of the Answer, you must also state the relief you are requesting: "Defendant Thomas Rosenberg respectfully requests that Plaintiff's Complaint be denied with prejudice, that Defendant be awarded his interest and costs, and that the Court grant such other and further relief as it deems just and appropriate." If there is a contractual and statutory basis, you should also request the reimbursement of reasonable attorney's fees.

After setting forth your affirmative defenses and "wherefore" clause, you are expected by most jurisdictions to make all Counterclaims and Third-Party Complaints. This is especially true with *mandatory* Counterclaims. The strategy for the Counterclaim is identical to that for the Complaint. Make sure that the Counterclaim contains an independent claim for declaratory judgment, if that is an issue in the case. In other words, if the Complaint seeks a declaratory judgment stating that the plaintiff has an easement over the defendant's land, the defendant should file a Counterclaim asking the court to declare that the plaintiff does *not* have an easement over his land. This ensures that, if the defendant wins, he can obtain a final judgment for filing in the local Registry of Deeds. The judgment, recorded for posterity, would state that the judgment is entered in favor of the counterclaimant and the plaintiff, his heirs and assigns, does not have an easement over the property of the defendant/counterclaim plaintiff.

The Third-Party Complaint is simply a Complaint against parties not yet in the case (a Cross-Claim is against co-defendants). In a disputed boundary case, the plaintiff must file a Complaint against defendant Neighbor and all parties with an interest in defendant Neighbor's property, such as Neighbor's bank. Defendant Neighbor must then file a Counterclaim against the plaintiff—asking the court to declare that his version of the boundary is correct—and a Third-Party Complaint against the plaintiff's bank. The Answer should also contain a Third-Party Complaint against anyone else with an interest in the litigation: other neighbors, predecessors in title, tenants, or lien holders.

The Counterclaim and Third-Party Complaint follow the same format and strategies as the Complaint, *infra*. Exemplars of Answers begin on the next page.

STATE OF MIND SUPERIOR COURT

YORK, ss.

MIND REALTY, INC.,	)	
Plaintiff	)	
	)	
v.	)	CIVIL ACTION
	)	DOCKET NO. RE-04-40
WILLIAM JACKSON, *et al.*,	)	
Defendants	)	
	)	

ANSWER

Defendant William Jackson, by his undersigned counsel, states the following as his Answer to Plaintiff's Complaint:

1. Mr. Jackson is without knowledge or information sufficient to form a belief as to the truth of the allegations set forth in Paragraph 1 of Plaintiff's Complaint, and therefore denies same and demands strict proof thereof.

2. Mr. Jackson is without knowledge or information sufficient to form a belief as to the truth of the allegations set forth in Paragraph 2 of Plaintiff's Complaint, and therefore denies same and demands strict proof thereof.

3. Mr. Jackson denies the allegations set forth in Paragraph 3 of Plaintiff's Complaint.

4. Mr. Jackson is without knowledge or information sufficient to form a belief as to the truth of the allegations set forth in Paragraph 4 of Plaintiff's Complaint, and therefore denies same and demands strict proof thereof.

5. Mr. Jackson is without knowledge or information sufficient to form a belief as to the truth of the allegations set forth in Paragraph 5 of Plaintiff's Complaint, and therefore denies same and demands strict proof thereof.

6. Mr. Jackson is without knowledge or information sufficient to form a belief as to the truth of the allegations set forth in Paragraph 6 of Plaintiff's Complaint, and therefore denies same and demands strict proof thereof.

7. Mr. Jackson is without knowledge or information sufficient to form a belief as to the truth of the allegations set forth in Paragraph 7 of Plaintiff's Complaint, and therefore denies same and demands strict proof thereof.

8. Mr. Jackson is without knowledge or information sufficient to form a belief as to the truth of the allegations set forth in Paragraph 8 of Plaintiff's Complaint, and therefore denies same and demands strict proof thereof.

9. Mr. Jackson denies the allegations set forth in Paragraph 9 of Plaintiff's Complaint.

10. Mr. Jackson denies the allegations set forth in Paragraph 10 of Plaintiff's Complaint.

11. Mr. Jackson repeats and realleges the response to allegations set forth in Paragraphs 1 through 10 above as if fully set forth herein.

12. Mr. Jackson is without knowledge or information sufficient to form a belief as to the truth of the allegations set forth in Paragraph 12 of Plaintiff's Complaint, and therefore denies same and demands strict proof thereof.

13. Mr. Jackson admits the allegations set forth in Paragraph 13 of the Plaintiff's Complaint.

14. Mr. Jackson is without knowledge or information sufficient to form a belief as to the truth of the allegations set forth in Paragraph 14 of Plaintiff's Complaint, and therefore denies same and demands strict proof thereof.

15. Mr. Jackson admits that he purchased the property on or about March 24, 2004.

16. Mr. Jackson is without knowledge or information sufficient to form a belief as to the truth of the allegations set forth in Paragraph 16 of Plaintiff's Complaint, and therefore denies same and demands strict proof thereof.

17. Mr. Jackson repeats and realleges the response to allegations set forth in Paragraphs 1 through 16 above as if fully set forth herein.

18. Mr. Jackson is without knowledge or information sufficient to form a belief as to the truth of the allegations set forth in Paragraph 18 of Plaintiff's Complaint, and therefore denies same and demands strict proof thereof.

19. Mr. Jackson is without knowledge or information sufficient to form a belief as to the truth of the allegations set forth in Paragraph 19

of Plaintiff's Complaint, and therefore denies same and demands strict proof thereof.

20. Mr. Jackson is without knowledge or information sufficient to form a belief as to the truth of the allegations set forth in Paragraph 20 of Plaintiff's Complaint, and therefore denies same and demands strict proof thereof.

Affirmative and Other Defenses

First Defense

Plaintiff's Complaint against Defendant William C. Jackson fails to state a claim upon which relief can be granted.

Second Defense

Plaintiff's claims are barred by the doctrines of waiver and estoppel.

Third Defense

Plaintiff is not in privity of contract with Defendant William Jackson.

Fourth Defense

Plaintiff failed to perfect its mechanic's lien.

Fifth Defense

Plaintiff's mechanic's lien is defective.

Sixth Defense

Plaintiff's second mechanic's lien does not list its last day of work.

Seventh Defense

Plaintiff never provided Defendant William Jackson with advance notice of the mechanic's lien attached to the Complaint as Exhibit A.

Eighth Defense

Defendant William Jackson is a bona fide purchaser who knew nothing about the mechanic's lien, attached to Plaintiff's Complaint as Exhibit A, at the time he purchased the property at issue.

WHEREFORE, Defendant William Jackson respectfully requests that Plaintiff's Complaint be denied with prejudice; that he be awarded interest and costs; and that the Court grant such other and further relief as it deems just and appropriate.

STATE OF MIND SUPERIOR COURT

YORK, ss.

VALERIE A. ATCOTT,	)	
Plaintiff	)	
	)	
v.	)	CIVIL ACTION
	)	DOCKET NO. RE-05-108
JERRY D. SIMONS, *et al.*,	)	
Defendants	)	
	)	

DEFENDANT WANDA WINSTON'S ANSWER TO PLAINTIFF'S FIRST AMENDED COMPLAINT AND DEFENDANT'S COUNTERCLAIM

Defendant Wanda Winston, by her undersigned counsel, states the following as her Answer to Plaintiff's Complaint:

1. Ms. Winston admits the allegations set forth in Paragraph 1 of Plaintiff's First Amended Complaint.

2. Ms. Winston admits the allegations set forth in Paragraph 2 of Plaintiff's First Amended Complaint.

3. Ms. Winston admits the allegations set forth in Paragraph 3 of Plaintiff's First Amended Complaint.

4. Ms. Winston admits the allegations set forth in Paragraph 4 of Plaintiff's First Amended Complaint.

5. Ms. Winston admits the allegations set forth in Paragraph 5 of Plaintiff's First Amended Complaint.

6. Ms. Winston admits the allegations set forth in Paragraph 6 of Plaintiff's First Amended Complaint.

7. Ms. Winston admits the allegations set forth in Paragraph 7 of Plaintiff's First Amended Complaint.

8. Ms. Winston admits the allegations set forth in Paragraph 8 of Plaintiff's First Amended Complaint.

9. Ms. Winston is without knowledge or information sufficient to form a belief as to the truth of the allegations set forth in Paragraph 9 of Plaintiff's First Amended Complaint, and therefore denies same and demands strict proof thereof.

10. Ms. Winston denies the allegations set forth in Paragraph 10 of Plaintiff's First Amended Complaint.

11. Ms. Winston denies the allegations set forth in Paragraph 11 of Plaintiff's First Amended Complaint.

12. Ms. Winston denies the allegations set forth in Paragraph 12 of Plaintiff's First Amended Complaint.

13. Ms. Winston denies the allegations set forth in Paragraph 13 of Plaintiff's First Amended Complaint.

14. Ms. Winston denies the allegations set forth in Paragraph 14 of Plaintiff's First Amended Complaint.

15. Ms. Winston is without knowledge or information sufficient to form a belief as to the truth of the allegations set forth in Paragraph 15 of Plaintiff's First Amended Complaint, and therefore denies same and demands strict proof thereof.

16. Ms. Winston is without knowledge or information sufficient to form a belief as to the truth of the allegations set forth in Paragraph 16 of Plaintiff's First Amended Complaint, and therefore denies same and demands strict proof thereof.

17. Ms. Winston denies the allegations set forth in Paragraph 17 of Plaintiff's First Amended Complaint, except that she admits that Exhibit C is a true copy of a document sent by her attorney and states that the document speaks for itself.

18. Ms. Winston denies the allegations set forth in Paragraph 18 of Plaintiff's First Amended Complaint.

19. Ms. Winston is without knowledge or information sufficient to form a belief as to the truth of the allegations set forth in Paragraph 19 of Plaintiff's First Amended Complaint, and therefore denies same and demands strict proof thereof.

20. Ms. Winston repeats and realleges herein each and every allegation set forth above in Paragraphs 1 through 19.

21. Ms. Winston denies the allegations set forth in Paragraph 20 of Plaintiff's First Amended Complaint.

22. Ms. Winston denies the allegations set forth in Paragraph 21 of Plaintiff's First Amended Complaint. Ms. Winston repeats and realleges herein each and every allegation set forth above in Paragraphs 1 through 21.

23. Ms. Winston denies the allegations set forth in Paragraph 23 of Plaintiff's First Amended Complaint.

24. Ms. Winston repeats and realleges herein each and every allegation set forth above in Paragraphs 1 through 23.

25. Ms. Winston denies the allegations set forth in Paragraph 25 of Plaintiff's First Amended Complaint.

26. Ms. Winston repeats and realleges herein each and every allegation set forth above in Paragraphs 1 through 25.

27. Ms. Winston denies the allegations set forth in Paragraph 27 of Plaintiff's First Amended Complaint.

28. Ms. Winston repeats and realleges herein each and every allegation set forth above in Paragraphs 1 through 27.

29. Ms. Winston denies the allegations set forth in Paragraph 29 of Plaintiff's First Amended Complaint.

30. Ms. Winston repeats and realleges herein each and every allegation set forth above in Paragraphs 1 through 29.

31. Ms. Winston denies the allegations set forth in Paragraph 31 of Plaintiff's First Amended Complaint.

32. Ms. Winston repeats and realleges herein each and every allegation set forth above in Paragraphs 1 through 31.

33. Ms. Winston denies the allegations set forth in Paragraph 33 of Plaintiff's First Amended Complaint.

34. Ms. Winston repeats and realleges herein each and every allegation set forth above in Paragraphs 1 through 33.

35. Ms. Winston denies the allegations set forth in Paragraph 35 of Plaintiff's First Amended Complaint.

36. Ms. Winston repeats and realleges herein each and every allegation set forth above in Paragraphs 1 through 35.

37. Ms. Winston denies the allegations set forth in Paragraph 37 of Plaintiff's First Amended Complaint.

38. Ms. Winston repeats and realleges herein each and every allegation set forth above in Paragraphs 1 through 37.

39. Ms. Winston denies the allegations set forth in Paragraph 39 of Plaintiff's First Amended Complaint.

Affirmative and Other Defenses

First Defense

Plaintiff's Complaint fails to state a claim against Defendant Wanda Winston.

Second Defense

Plaintiff's tort damages are barred, in whole or in part, by contributory and/or comparative negligence.

Third Defense

Plaintiff has an express deeded easement, over a third party's property, to a public road.

Fourth Defense

Plaintiff's sewer line is neither open nor notorious.

Fifth Defense

Plaintiff does not have a recorded or express easement over Ms. Winston's property.

Sixth Defense

Plaintiff's distress is not manifested by objective symptomatology.

Seventh Defense

Plaintiff has failed to mitigate her damages.

Eighth Defense

Ms. Winston's conduct has not been extreme or outrageous.

WHEREFORE, Defendant Wanda Winston respectfully requests that Plaintiff's claims against her be dismissed with prejudice; that Ms. Winston be reimbursed for her costs, interest, and reasonable attorney's fees; and that the Court grant such other relief as is just and appropriate.

STATE OF MIND SUPERIOR COURT

Oxford, ss.

VICTOR BITWORTH, *et al.*,	)	
Plaintiffs	)	
	)	
v.	)	CIVIL ACTION
	)	DOCKET NO. RE-05-32
SHERI L. WEISBURG, *et al.*,	)	
Defendants	)	
	)	

ANSWER TO AMENDED COMPLAINT,
AND COUNTERCLAIM

Defendants Sheri L. Weisburg and Michael A. Peters, by their undersigned counsel, state the following as their Answer to Plaintiffs' Amended Complaint:

1. Ms. Weisburg and Mr. Peters are without knowledge and information sufficient to form a belief as to the truth of the allegations set forth in Paragraph 1 of Plaintiffs' Complaint, and therefore deny same and demand strict proof thereof.

2. Ms. Weisburg and Mr. Peters are without knowledge and information sufficient to form a belief as to the truth of the allegations set forth in Paragraph 2 of Plaintiffs' Complaint, and therefore deny same, except that Ms. Weisburg and Mr. Peters admit that Estelle Betty Bitworth acquired the property by deed dated August 25, 1969, and recorded in the Oxford County (Western District) Registry of Deeds at Book 198, Page 596.

3. Ms. Weisburg and Mr. Peters are without knowledge and information sufficient to form a belief as to the truth of the allegations set forth in Paragraph 3 of Plaintiffs' Complaint, and therefore deny same and demand strict proof thereof, except that Ms. Weisburg and Mr. Peters admit that Mr. Lavoie is a resident of Hiram and that his property was conveyed to him by deed dated July 3, 2002, and recorded in the Oxford County (Western District) Registry of Deeds at Book 437, Page 187.

4. Ms. Weisburg and Mr. Peters are without knowledge and information sufficient to form a belief as to the truth of the allegations set forth in Paragraph 4 of Plaintiffs' Complaint, and therefore deny same and demand strict proof thereof, except that Ms. Weisburg and Mr. Peters admit that Mr. and Mrs. Danforth are residents of Hiram, Mind, and that they acquired their property by deed dated April 23, 2002, and recorded in the Oxford County (Western District) Registry of Deeds at Book 433, Page 815.

5. Ms. Weisburg and Mr. Peters are without knowledge and information sufficient to form a belief as to the truth of the allegations set forth in Paragraph 5 of Plaintiffs' Complaint, and therefore deny same and demand strict proof thereof, except Ms. Weisburg and Mr. Peters admit that Michael L. Twist and Susan J. Twist obtained their property by deed dated August 16, 1990, and recorded in the Oxford County (Western District) Registry of Deeds at Book 313, Page 497.

6. Ms. Weisburg and Mr. Peters are without knowledge or information sufficient to form a belief as to the truth of the allegations set forth in Paragraph 6 of Plaintiff's Complaint, and therefore deny same and demand strict proof thereof.

7. Ms. Weisburg and Mr. Peters admit the allegations set forth in Paragraph 7 of Plaintiffs' Complaint.

8. Ms. Weisburg and Mr. Peters admit the allegations set forth in Paragraph 8 of Plaintiffs' Complaint.

9. Ms. Weisburg and Mr. Peters are without knowledge or information sufficient to form a belief as to the allegations set forth in Paragraph 9 of Plaintiffs' Complaint, and therefore deny same and demand strict proof thereof, except that they admit that the Town of Hiram discontinued the portion of Bray Road at issue.

10. Ms. Weisburg and Mr. Peters deny the allegations set forth in Paragraph 10 of Plaintiffs' Complaint.

11. Ms. Weisburg and Mr. Peters are without knowledge or information sufficient to form a belief as to the allegations set forth in Paragraph 11 of Plaintiffs' Complaint, and therefore deny same and demand strict proof thereof, except that they admit that a way known as Bray Ridge Road goes through a portion of their property.

12. Ms. Weisburg and Mr. Peters deny the allegations set forth in Paragraph 12 of Plaintiffs' Complaint.

13. Ms. Weisburg and Mr. Peters deny the allegations set forth in Paragraph 13 of Plaintiffs' Complaint.

14. Ms. Weisburg and Mr. Peters deny the allegations set forth in Paragraph 14 of Plaintiffs' Complaint.

15. Ms. Weisburg and Mr. Peters deny the allegations set forth in Paragraph 15 of Plaintiffs' Complaint, except that Ms. Weisburg and Mr. Peters admit that Plaintiffs do not have an easement across Bray Road.

16. Ms. Weisburg and Mr. Peters repeat and reallege the response to the allegations set forth in Paragraphs 1 through 15 above as if fully set forth herein.

17. Ms. Weisburg and Mr. Peters deny the allegations set forth in Paragraph 17 of Plaintiffs' Complaint.

Affirmative and Other Defenses

First Defense

Plaintiffs' Complaint fails to state a cause of action against Ms. Weisburg and Mr. Peters upon which relief can be granted.

Second Defense

Plaintiffs' claims are barred, in whole, or in part by the doctrine of estoppel.

Third Defense

Plaintiffs' Complaint is barred by laches.

Fourth Defense

Plaintiff's Complaint is barred by the doctrine of waiver.

Fifth Defense

Any use of Bray Road by any of the Plaintiffs has been with the permission of the Defendants or their predecessors-in-interest.

Sixth Defense

None of the Plaintiffs or their predecessors-in-interest has continuously used Bray Road for 20 years.

Seventh Defense

Any prescriptive easement over Bray Road is limited to pedestrian use to an undeveloped lot, without any utilities.

Eighth Defense

The discontinuance of Bray Road did not create any public easement.

Ninth Defense

Plaintiffs' use of Bray Road has not been adverse or hostile.

WHEREFORE, Defendants Sheri L. Weisburg and Michael A. Peters respectfully request that Plaintiffs' Complaint be dismissed; that they be awarded interest and costs; and that the Court grant such other and further relief as it deems just and appropriate.

Tenth Defense

Plaintiffs' claims are barred by collateral estoppel and/or res judicata as a result of prior litigation.

Eleventh Defense

The Plaintiffs all have alternative means to access their properties.

WHEREFORE, Defendants Sheri L. Weisburg and Michael A. Peters respectfully request Plaintiff's Complaint be denied with prejudice; that they be awarded interest and costs; and that the Court grant such other and further relief as it deems just and appropriate.

MOTIONS TO DISMISS

Motions to Dismiss are rarely used for real estate causes of action. In general, real estate cases are too fact intensive and the factual contentions, at the very least, need to be threshed out in discovery. They should only be considered in four narrow situations:

1. **Failure to state a cause of action**. The best way to challenge a real estate cause of action, as a matter of law, is to take discovery and prove that the undisputed facts all point in your direction. In very rare cases, this is apparent based on the Complaint itself. Assume, for example, that a realtor seeks to enforce a mechanic's lien for failure to pay a leasing commission. Most jurisdictions do not allow real estate brokers to file a mechanic's lien to collect a lease commission. Accordingly, this is one of the few situations where a motion to dismiss makes sense.

   A motion to dismiss also makes sense where the allegations in the Complaint are simply not supported by concrete facts raising a reasonable expectation that the plaintiff has a meritorious case. The U.S. Supreme Court's decisions in *Bell Atlantic Corp. v. Twombley*, 550 U.S. 544 (2007) and *Ashcroft v. Igbal*, 129 S. Ct. 1937 (2009) have made it clear that a "bare bones" Complaint, or simply reciting elements or conclusory statements, is not enough. These federal holdings have been adopted, in whole or in part, in other jurisdictions, as well.
2. **Lack of standing**. Determine whether the plaintiff has the standing to seek the requested relief. A plaintiff cannot bring a partition action unless he owns a fee interest in the property. A boundary action cannot be brought unless the plaintiff owns one of the abutting properties.
3. **Failure to include all necessary parties**. A motion to dismiss can be made when the plaintiff has failed to join all necessary parties to the action. Depending on the type of real estate action involved, you need to check to see if all heirs, abutters, lenders, or other stakeholders are named in the litigation. The court, however, may give the plaintiff more time to add these parties, rather than dismiss the case.
4. **No actual controversy**. A declaratory judgment action must meet the standards of ripeness, mootness, and justiciability. There must be an actual dispute.

CHAPTER 8

Notice of Claim

So long as the great majority of men are not deprived of either property or honor, they are satisfied.
—Niccolò Machiavelli

One of the mightiest tools in the real estate trial lawyer's arsenal is the ability to tie up the property at issue in the case. Most states allow the claimant to record a Notice of Claim, Clerk's Certificate, or Lis Pendens at the local Registry of Deeds, putting the world on notice that the property is subject to litigation. Anyone who buys property, subject to the Notice of Claim, takes the property subject to litigation.

The practical effect of a Notice of Claim is that the owner of the real estate at issue cannot readily sell or mortgage any portion of the property until the litigation is complete. This gives the plaintiff tremendous leverage.

Typically, the plaintiff files the Complaint with the court, and then requests a certificate from the clerk or court identifying the litigation and describing the property at issue. This Clerk's Certificate is promptly recorded, with a copy to all other parties. The certificate, which is within the property's chain of title, acts as a notification that someone is claiming a problem or defect with the land or its title. If a third party buys the property or uses it to secure a mortgage, he is subject to the ruling of the court if the purchase or mortgage comes after (or with constructive notice of) the Notice of Claim. This risk persists as long as the court case is pending or unresolved.

The defendant, of course, can challenge the Notice of Claim, but such challenges are generally useless if the facts in the Notice of Claim are true. In other words, the court will not (and generally cannot) interfere with a Notice of Claim that simply, and accurately, states that the property is subject to a dispute in litigation.

The defendant, under certain circumstances, may consider a Counterclaim alleging slander of title, abuse of process, or malicious prosecution. However, all of these claims are very hard to prove.

Slander of title generally involves the making of false and/or malicious representations about the title of the opponent's property title with the intent to injure the opponent. The claimant must show that the Notice of Claim is not only wrong, but essentially fraudulent.

Similarly, abuse of process is often synonymous with wrongdoing by a party or an attorney in the deliberate misuse of a court process—unjustified by the underlying legal action—in the filing of a court process (such as a Notice of Claim). An example would be filing a Notice of Claim where the underlying action is clearly frivolous and intended to impose harm.

Malicious prosecution is another tort involving misuse of the court process. In most jurisdictions, it cannot be brought until the conclusion of the underlying litigation.

Note: The preferred format for a Notice of Claim is a Clerk's Certificate signed by a court clerk. This cannot be a perversion of the court system because it is simply a statement, signed by a court clerk, factually attesting that litigation over the property has been filed. Obviously, the underlying litigation must be brought in good faith. An example of a Clerk's Certificate is the following:

CLERK'S CERTIFICATE

STATE OF MIND
Cumberland, ss.

I, ____________, Clerk of the Cumberland County Superior Court for the State of Mind, do hereby certify that **Eugene L. Aslin** and **Patricia D. Aslin**, residents of Cape Coral, County of Lee and State of Florida, have filed in this office of the Clerk of this Court a Complaint against **Cynthia D. Roundhill,** an individual residing in Hampton, County of Rockingham and the State of New Hampshire.

Said Complaint affects title to land and buildings owned by said Eugene L. Aslin and Patricia D. Aslin located at 12 Hio Ridge Shores North in the Town of Bridgton, County of Cumberland and State of Mind. Said property of Eugene L. Normand and Patricia D. Aslin is also known as Map 8, Block 19, Lot 10 on the tax map of the Town of Bridgton. The property is further described by a deed, dated July 1, 2008, for William Smith and Samantha Smith to Eugene L. Aslin and Patricia D. Aslin, and recorded in the Cumberland County Registry of Deeds at Book 5941, Page 36.

The Complaint, Docket No. RE-05-91, is dated July 26, 2010, and was filed in this Clerk's office on or about July 26, 2010.

IN TESTIMONY WHEREOF, I have hereunto set my hand and affixed the seal of said Court this _____ day of August, 2010.

____
Name:
Clerk, Cumberland County
Superior Court

As shown above, put the owners of the property in bold or take other precautions to ensure that the Clerk's Certificate is properly indexed at the Registry of Deeds. Do enough title work to confirm that you have the exact name of the owners and that the property is correctly and thoroughly described. The Clerk's Certificate is not effective if a reasonable person cannot determine which land is subject to the dispute or litigation.

Some attorneys simply record their personal affidavit identifying the property and attesting to the nature of the dispute. You need to be careful about recording an affidavit because of the risks of slander of title and the other causes of action set forth above. Any affidavit recorded in the Registry of Deeds—and effecting title—should be limited to the bare bones and plain facts of a good-faith dispute. File the Complaint first and limit the affidavit to the fact of the filing and the description of the property. This limits the slander of title risk for the plaintiff and his agents and attorneys.

Where Notices of Claim are not readily available, some lawyers will seek to obtain a prejudgment attachment of the property. This is risky. The standards for prejudgment attachment are often higher or more complicated than the standard for winning at trial. In such cases, there is a significant chance of not winning the attachment—and losing the critical momentum on which successful cases are based. As attachment motions are often brought at the very beginning of a case, this is a very troubling point at which to be losing momentum. An example of an attachment motion is the following:

STATE OF MIND SUPERIOR COURT

GARY A. ARNOLD and MARILYN J. ARNOLD, Plaintiffs v. JASON I. TIMPTON, MELISSA A. TIMPTON, ROBERT J. SAMUELS and CECILIA SAMUELS, Defendants	)))))))))))	Action No. _________

PLAINTIFFS' EX PARTE MOTION FOR ATTACHMENT AND TRUSTEE PROCESS

(Memorandum Incorporated)

Defendants Jason I. Timpton and Melissa A. Timpton sold a home and sent a portion of their sale proceeds to their banks to pay off the pending mortgage and the pending home equity line of credit ("HELOC"). Instead of ensuring that the HELOC mortgage was discharged, however, the Timptons fraudulently ran up the line of credit again—after the closing—to $208,346.98. Plaintiffs Gary A. Arnold and Marilyn J. Arnold, who are the current owners of the property, are now saddled and encumbered with a $208,346.98 mortgage which the Timptons were obligated to discharge. Instead of meeting their obligations to discharge the HELOC mortgage, the Timptons are selling other properties and transferring assets into the names of their relatives. The Arnolds, by their undersigned counsel, hereby move this Court to order that an attachment, including an attachment on trustee process, be made against the property of the Timptons and the Samuelses in the amount of $208,346.98 pursuant to M.R.Civ.P. 4A and 4B.

This Motion is based upon the grounds that: (1) it is more likely than not that the Arnolds will recover judgment, including interest and costs, in an amount equal to or greater than $208,346.98, and there is no liability insurance, bond, or other security, in any property attached by other writ of attachment or trustee process by the Arnolds; and (2) there is a clear and present danger that the Timptons and the Samuelses, if notified in advance of this Motion for Attachment, will conceal or remove their property, assets, or bank accounts, and other property to be attached, or otherwise will take steps to make their assets unavailable to satisfy any judgment of the Arnolds. In support of this Motion, the Arnolds submit the accompanying Affidavits of Loraine L. Litz and Daniel J. Pickard and the below Memorandum of Law.

The Facts

On May 20, 2004, Defendants Jason I. Timpton and Melissa A. Samuels (now Melissa A. Timpton) obtained title to property located at 78 South Road in China, Mind (the "Property"). *Affidavit of Daniel J. Pickard ¶ 4* (hereafter "*Pickard Affidavit*"). After purchasing the property, Jason I. Timpton and Melissa A. Timpton (the "Timptons") obtained a home equity line of credit (the "HELOC") secured by the Property. *Pickard Affidavit ¶ 5.* The HELOC was serviced by Bank of Mind. *Id.*

On October 8, 2005, the Timptons sold the Property to Christopher T. Choate and Kelley M. Choate (the "Choates"). *Affidavit of Loraine Litz ¶ 7* (hereafter "*Litz Affidavit*"); *Pickard Affidavit ¶ 5.* The Timptons transferred the property to the Choates by warranty deed, promising title free and clear of any encumbrances. *Pickard Affidavit ¶ 5; Litz Affidavit ¶ 11.* During the closing, the Timptons executed a "Shortfall Agreement," which provided, in part, that the Timptons agreed to pay their lenders "whatever is legally required to secure a discharge of mortgage." *Pickard Affidavit ¶ 6.* As a condition of the closing, the Timptons also agreed that some proceeds of the sale of the Property to the Choates would be used to discharge both their first mortgage and the HELOC encumbering the Property. *Pickard Affidavit ¶ 5.* To comply with those terms and discharge the HELOC, Rainbow Title Company, the closing agent on the Timpton/Choate transaction, sent a check to Bank of Mind in the amount of $166,184.81. *Litz Affidavit ¶ 8.* The check was sent to Bank of Mind with a cover letter that recited the HELOC's account number and read as follows: "Enclosed please find our firm check in the amount of $166,184.81 which represents payoff of the above-referenced loan pursuant to your payoff letter." *Id.* Bank of Mind received the payment, and credited it to the HELOC account. *Id.*

The Timptons were aware that Bank of Mind had not discharged the HELOC. *Pickard Affidavit ¶ 7.* Subsequent to the closing of the sale to the Choates, the Timptons began to draw down substantial sums of money from the HELOC—which still encumbered the Property—despite the fact that the Timptons no longer owned the Property. *Id*; *Litz Affidavit ¶ 9.* Despite their knowledge that the HELOC still encumbered the Property, they did not take steps to discharge the HELOC and remove the encumbrance from the Property. *Pickard Affidavit ¶ 7.* Instead, the Timptons drew down more than $200,000.00 on the HELOC. *Pickard Affidavit ¶ 8.* In fact, as of September 17, 2008, the Timptons owed $208,346.98 on the HELOC. *Id.* As of that date, more than 600 days had passed since the Timptons' last payment on the HELOC. *Id.*

Despite their unresolved debt encumbering the Property, the Timptons obtained title to another parcel of property identified as Lot 4 in the Meadows Subdivision in China, Mind (the "Timpton Property"). *Pickard Affidavit ¶ 9.* When they acquired the Timpton Property, the Timptons did not pay off the HELOC or move the HELOC to the Timpton Property. *Pickard Affidavit ¶ 12.* In fact, there are no liens or encumbrances on the Timpton Property. *Pickard Affidavit ¶ 10.*

Shortly after purchasing the Timpton Property, the Timptons sold a parcel to Jason K. Fredette and Jessica L. Fredette (the "Fredettes"). *Pickard Affidavit ¶ 13.* The funds obtained through the sale to the Fredettes were not used to discharge the HELOC. *Pickard Affidavit ¶ 14.*

Following the sale to the Fredettes, the Timptons applied to the Town of China for permission to subdivide the remaining portion of the Timpton Property. *Id.* If successful in obtaining Town approval, the Timptons intend to sell one or more lots from their remaining portion of the Timpton Property. *Id.* At this point, the Town of China, Mind considers the Timptons' subdivision application complete. *Pickard Affidavit ¶ 15.* The Town of China deferred their final approval of the Timptons' subdivision application until September 23, 2008. *Id.*

On September 15, 2008, The Timptons, despite their outstanding indebtedness, transferred a 7/10 undivided interest in their title to the Timpton Subdivision to Robert J. Samuels and Cecelia Samuels. *Pickard Affidavit ¶ 16.* "Samuels" is the maiden name of Defendant Melissa A. Timpton. *Pickard Affidavit ¶ 17.* Despite transferring most of their interest in the Timpton Subdivision to relatives, the Timptons have not paid or discharged the HELOC.

On July 28, 2008, Gary A. Arnold and Marilyn J. Arnold purchased the Property from successors to the Choates' title. *Pickard Affidavit ¶ 20.* The HELOC still encumbers the Property. *Pickard Affidavit ¶ 21.*

Argument

I. Legal Standard

Rules 4A and 4B of the Mind Rules of Civil Procedure allow attachment and trustee process to be ordered on a finding by the Court that:

> [I]t is more likely than not that the plaintiff will recover judgment, including interest and costs, in an amount equal to or greater than the aggregate sum of the attachment and any liability insurance, bond, or other security, and any property of credits attached by other writ of attachment or by trustee process shown by the defendant to be available to satisfy the judgment.

In order to meet its burden on this attachment motion, the Arnolds must convince the Court, by a preponderance of the evidence that it is probable that it will recover an amount equal to or greater than $208,346.98, which is the amount it seeks to attach. *Cirrincione v. Pratt Chevrolet*, 275 F.Supp. 2d 26, 28 (D. Me. 2003), see also *Wilson v. DelPapa*, 634 A.2d, 1252, 1255 (Me. 1993). Further, to obtain an *ex parte* attachment, the Arnolds must convince the Court that "there is a clear danger that the defendant, if notified in advance of the attachment of the property will conceal it or otherwise make it unavailable to satisfy a judgment." *Rules of Civil Procedure 4A(g).*

II. The Arnolds Have Shown a Likelihood of Success on the Merits

The Complaint and the Affidavits of Ms. Litz and Mr. Pickard are more than sufficient to demonstrate a likelihood of success on the merits. It is clear from the facts that the Timptons have defrauded the Arnolds, converted funds, and breached the promises they made to convey the Property free and clear of all encumbrances. It is equally clear that the Timptons and the Samuelses have engaged in a fraudulent transfer of the Timpton Subdivision in an effort to conceal the Timptons' assets from their creditors.

As is amply demonstrated and documented, the Timptons knew, in order to deliver title to the Choates free and clear of encumbrances, that they were obligated to discharge the HELOC as a condition of that sale. That knowledge is evidenced by the Shortfall Agreement the Timptons executed during the closing for that transaction, acknowledging their obligation to take whatever steps necessary to satisfy the mortgages encumbering the Property. Despite their promise to deliver clear title, and their promise to discharge any mortgages encumbering the Property, the Timptons proceeded to draw down against the HELOC—knowing that by doing so, they were violating the very promises they made.

Following the closing on the Property, the Timptons proceeded to purchase the Timpton Subdivision—which remains unencumbered and to sell a portion of their newly acquired land to the Fredettes. Then, rather than using the proceeds of that sale to discharge the HELOC, the Timptons pursued a plan to further subdivide—and presumably sell—additional lots.

When the Timptons learned that one or more parties were attempting to resolve the encumbrance on the Property, they transferred a 7/10 share of the Timpton Subdivision to the Samuelses—shielding their assets with relatives in a clear effort to avoid attachment.

As of September 17, 2008, the Timptons owe $208,346.98 on the HELOC. They have made no payments in more than 600 days. The Arnolds now own property that was deeded by the Timptons to the Arnolds' predecessors-in-title with the promise of clear, unencumbered title. In order for the Arnolds to obtain the clear title to the Property they purchased, the Timptons must discharge the HELOC.

III. The Arnolds are Entitled to an Ex Parte Attachment

The Affidavits of Ms. Litz and Mr. Pickard establish the "clear danger that the Defendant, if notified in advance of attachment of the property, will conceal it or otherwise make it unavailable to satisfy a judgment." There is *every* reason to believe that, if notified in advance of this attachment, the Timptons and the Samuelses will sell property, refinance property, or move monies outside the jurisdiction of this court.

As all of the foregoing facts demonstrate, the Timptons and the Samuelses have violated their promises to deliver clear title and discharge the HELOC. They will presumably do whatever is necessary to escape their obligations, and would likely hide or encumber their assets if they were notified that a motion for attachment has been filed. Furthermore, the Timptons have already transferred property to the

Samuelses in an attempt to protect it from attachment, and they are fast approaching the Town approval necessary to sell one or more lots out of the Timpton Subdivision.

Despite their promises, the Timptons have repaired none of the outstanding balance of the HELOC, despite having sold property since incurring that debt. With history as our guide, we believe it is likely that any future sales by the Timptons—and now the Samuelses—will not result in any effort by the Timptons to discharge the HELOC unless Ex Parte Attachment is granted.

Conclusion

For all of the foregoing reasons, we respectfully request that the Court issue an Order of Attachment and Trustee Process in the form attached hereto.

CHAPTER 9

Injunctions

Whatever your hand finds to do, do it with all your might . . .
—Ecclesiastes 9:10

Injunctive relief is another powerful sword in the possession of the real estate litigator. The common law has held—for ages—that property is "unique" and that "extraordinary" remedies such as equitable and injunctive relief are welcome. The extraordinary remedy of an injunction is granted where a court finds that such an action is essential to justice, or to prohibit an act that is contrary to good conscience. In the real estate context, the court can use the equitable remedy to force a party to do something, such as to remove a building from the property, or to force a person to refrain from doing something, such as blocking access to land. The violation of an injunction can lead to civil penalties and sanctions, including imprisonment.

Most jurisdictions afford emergency injunctive relief in the form of temporary restraining orders, interim injunctive relief in the form of preliminary injunctions, and permanent injunctive relief as part of the trial verdict. A temporary restraining order is an emergency action that is generally heard immediately by the court. The court will sometimes make a ruling *ex parte*—without notice to the other side—where there is a danger that notice will cause harm to the moving party. *Ex parte* motions are rare in real estate litigation, except where there is a claim for monetary damages and there is evidence suggesting that funds will be hidden if the other side has notice. Advance notice to the other side, before filing a motion for temporary restraining order in a real estate case, is strongly preferred. The temporary restraining order, or TRO, only lasts until the court can hold a hearing on a motion for a preliminary injunction. It is not a conclusive determination of the right of the parties. The TRO serves to protect against the alleged wrong or injustice until the court can render its ultimate decision.

Similarly, a preliminary injunction is a more thorough attempt to address the threatened irreparable injury. It is not an ultimate ruling—although *any* decision creates momentum that is, practically speaking, hard to overturn.

The hearing on a motion for preliminary injunction is generally a more formal procedure. It usually involves live testimony from both sides and cross-examination. A preliminary injunction, if issued by the court, lasts until the conclusion of trial.

Injunctions issued at trial are permanent. Where the ruling involves the title to property, or the location or use of boundaries or easements, the injunction should be recorded in the appropriate Registry of Deeds.

The object of injunctive relief is to make a person "whole" where a legal remedy, such as an award of damages, cannot fairly achieve this end. Many rules of court require the passing of a fourfold test in order to obtain preliminary injunctive relief: (1) a likelihood of success on the merits; (2) irreparable harm; (3) a balancing of the relative benefits and harms that weigh in favor of the injunctive relief; and (4) an analysis of the public interest.

The U.S. Supreme Court, interpreting the Federal Rules of Civil Procedure, has recently required that the movant demonstrate that irreparable injury is "likely," *Winter v. Natural Resources Defense Council, Inc.*, 129 S. Ct. 365, 375 (2009). An example of an injury considered "irreparable" is when it cannot be adequately compensated by monetary damages. Thus, injunctive relief is generally denied where "dollar damages" affords a sufficient remedy, regardless of the other party's ability to pay such damages. Loss of profits, regardless of the amount, cannot be remedied with an injunction. The potential destruction of property, however, *is* generally considered irreparable.

Real estate litigation, because of the uniqueness of property and because of inadequacy of calculating monetary damages, is fertile ground for injunctive relief. Typical cases involving real estate injunctions are where a building is placed on another person's property, where a structure violates scenic or other easements, or where access to property is blocked. Injunctive relief also makes sense where a trespasser is continually violating a property boundary and where the owner cannot be made whole with mere dollars.

An example of where an injunction is typically granted involves a property owner blocking access to a property, claiming that the access to the property is on his land. Dollar or "legal" damages are not sufficient because a trial could be years away—and your client has no access to his property. The loss of the property to the client, in such circumstances, is irreparable.

Similarly, equitable relief makes sense where a neighbor believes that the beautiful trees screening your client's home are on the neighbor's property—and the neighbor is planning to cut them down for firewood. Your client arguably cannot be made whole by monetary damages, as the value of the mature tree screen is irreparable and incalculable.

Courts have awarded injunctive relief in some situations even where dollar damages *were* calculable. For example, where a structure is intentionally placed on the wrong land injunctive relief may be granted, even though it would be less expensive for the tortfeasor to pay for the land under the building. Experienced real estate trial lawyers will tell you that, in cases where a neighbor is warned in advance that a home will block a view easement, it is common for the court to order that the offending portion of the home be removed.

Seeking preliminary injunctive relief tends to be expensive. The moving party must assemble all of the motion papers and a plethora of affidavits supporting his position. Live testimony at a hearing, as mentioned above, is required by many jurisdictions.

One possible method for reducing the expenses of injunctive relief, if appropriate based on the nature of the emergency, is to consolidate the request for preliminary and permanent relief. This often has the outcome of extending the date for a hearing on a preliminary injunction—but, practically speaking, advancing the date of a trial on the merits. This is because many courts—when faced with a motion to consolidate various stages of a request for injunctive relief—simply advance the trial date and hear everything at once.

The risk to the real estate litigator for a request for injunctive relief is that (1) obtaining it involves a higher standard than winning at trial and (2) losing a motion for injunctive relief will strike a serious blow to the momentum of the moving party's case. Given the fact that most judges will not grant injunctive relief where a case is essentially about dollar damages, a motion for injunctive relief is generally not favored among real estate litigators involved in a battle over commercial real estate or business property.

The ideal use for a motion for injunctive relief, as set forth above, is where the plaintiff has been denied access to his home. Courts are loath to deny injunctive relief where the result of such a denial would preclude a party from going home. In such cases, the irreparable injury is readily apparent and the harm to the plaintiff is not genuinely capable of being measured in dollars and cents. The granting of injunctive relief, in such cases, is so powerful that it often strikes a mortal blow to the opposing side. Injunctions are a truly powerful weapon that, because they are not liberally granted, should not be used in weak cases where the momentum can backfire on your case.

Following is an example of a motion for injunctive relief.

STATE OF MIND SUPERIOR COURT

CHRISTOPHER ANDREWS and	)	
MELINDA J. ROSENBERG,	)	
Plaintiff	)	
	)	
v.	)	
	)	Action No. _________
JOHN F. CHANDLER,	)	
Defendant	)	
	)	

PLAINTIFF'S MOTION FOR TEMPORARY RESTRAINING ORDER AND PRELIMINARY INJUNCTION

(Memorandum Incorporated)

Plaintiffs Christopher Andrews and Melinda J. Rosenberg hereby apply, pursuant to Rule 65 of the Rules of Civil Procedure, for the entry of a Temporary Restraining Order and a Preliminary Injunction enjoining Defendant from blocking their easement and legal access to their newly Purchased house and property on Raccoon Road in Naples. Mr. Andrews and Ms. Rosenberg do not have any other legal or sufficient access to their property. Defendant's deliberate and wrongful blocking of the easement is in direct violation of the law.

The Facts

Plaintiffs Have an Easement Over Defendant's Land

Mr. Andrews and Ms. Rosenberg bought their home in Naples, on March 15, 2008. *Affidavit of Christopher Andrews, the original of which is being simultaneously filed herewith (the "Andrews Affidavit") ¶ 2; Affidavit of Karen Gauthier, the original of which is being simultaneously filed herewith (the "Gauthier Affidavit") ¶ 4.* The deed to Mr. Andrews and Ms. Rosenberg states, among other things, the following:

> A certain lot or parcel of land situated in the Town of Naples, County and State aforesaid, on the easterly shore of Brandy Pond, so-called, therein, at its junction with the Songo River, and being Lot Number Three (#3) on Plan of Land of Robert Wiggin, by Earl

> C. Hotchkiss, Jr., Surveyor, dated July 30, 1970, and recorded in the Cumberland County Registry of Deeds, Plan Book 83, Page 17.
>
> Also conveying a right of common user in and to the camp roads as depicted on said Plan, as well as the Old Jackson Road, so-called, for ingress and egress from the property above set forth, in the Town way extending from Songo Locks to Route #302 in said Naples.

Andrews Affidavit ¶ 3; Gauthier Affidavit ¶ 5. The property Purchased by Mr. Andrews and Ms. Rosenberg is shown as Lot 3 on the recorded Plan of Land, dated July 3, 1970, and recorded in the Cumberland County Registry of Deeds at Plan Book 83, Page 17. *Gauthier Affidavit ¶ 6.* A true and accurate copy of the Plan is attached to the Complaint as Exhibit B. *Gauthier Affidavit ¶ 6.*

The six-lot subdivision shown on the Plan was created by Elmer R. Wiggin, Jr., in 1970. *Gauthier Affidavit ¶ 7.* The April 27, 1971, deed for Lot 3 expressly states that it is "Also conveying a right of common user in and to the camp roads as depicted on said Plan, as well as the Old Jackson Road, so called, for ingress and egress from the property above set forth, to the Town way extending from Songo Locks to Route #302, in said Naples." *Gauthier Affidavit ¶¶ 7–8.* This same language appears in the deed into Mr. Andrews and Ms. Rosenberg, and is contained in every deed in the chain of title for Lot 3 from 1971 to present. *Gauthier Affidavit ¶ 9.*

Thus, the deed for Lot 3 (which Mr. Andrews and Ms. Rosenberg now own) grants an express easement over all Wiggin land to Songo Lock Road. The deeds to Lot 2 contain identical language.

This express easement is made ever clearer by an examination of the deeds to Lots 1, 4, 5, and 6. The first deed from the Wiggin subdivision—Lot 6 on the Plan—was sold in 1970 with the following express easement: "Also conveying a right of common user in and to the camp roads *as now situate on land of Elmer R. Wiggin, Jr.* for ingress and egress to the town way extending to Route #302 in said Naples." *Gauthier Affidavit ¶¶ 10–11 (emphasis added).* Similar language also appears in the first deeds from Mr. Wiggin conveying Lots 1, 4, and 5. *Gauthier Affidavit ¶ 12.* Accordingly, all of the lots on the Plan have easements and over the subdivision roads and over the Wiggin property to get to the town road.

In addition, the Plan shows the "New Camp Road," which leads to a road identified as "Old Jackson Road." *Gauthier Affidavit ¶ 13.* At the southerly end of Old Jackson Road, located on the land of "Wiggin," there is an arrow which points in a southerly direction and indicates "To Songo Lock Road." *Gauthier Affidavit ¶ 13.* The above-referenced property of Mr. Wiggin was recently acquired by Defendant John F. Chandler. *Gauthier Affidavit ¶ 14.*

Defendant's Property Is Encumbered by Plaintiffs' Easement

Defendant John F. Chandler bought his property on April 28, 2000, from Virginia D. Wiggin, widow and surviving joint tenant of Elmer H. Wiggin, Jr. *Gauthier Affidavit ¶ 14.* The deed from Ms. Wiggin to Defendant Chandler clearly sets forth the following: "being the premises conveyed by the Diamond Match Company to John Jackson by deed dated March 2, 1908, recorded in the Cumberland County Registry of Deeds, Book 820, Page 233, *subject* however, to exceptions and reservations as set forth therein and further excepting and reserving and *subject* to any and all parcels as conveyed away from the premises described in said deed *and any easements granted prior to date hereof.*" *Gauthier Affidavit ¶ 15 (emphasis added).*

The deed from Mr. Wiggin to Lot 3, granting an easement over property now owned by Defendant Chandler, *precedes* the deed to Mr. Chandler. *Gauthier Affidavit ¶ 16.*

The deed to Defendant Chandler, therefore, is subject to the easement now owned by Mr. Andrews and Ms. Rosenberg, the owners of Lot 3. *Gauthier Affidavit ¶ 16.*

Name Changes

The camp road referenced in the 1970 Plan is known today as Raccoon Road. *Andrews Affidavit ¶ 5.* The "Old Jackson Road" referenced in the 1970 Plan is known today as State Park Road. *Andrews Affidavit ¶ 5.* The "Songo Lock Road" referenced in the 1970 Plan is known today as Songo School Road. *Andrews Affidavit ¶ 5.* The road connecting State Park Road to Songo School Road, which travels through Defendant's property, is now known as Wiggin Road. *Andrews Affidavit ¶ 6.* Wiggin Road, over which Mr. Andrews and Ms. Rosenberg have an easement, is referenced on the 1970 Wiggin subdivision (the Plan) as the land of "Wiggin." *Andrews Affidavit ¶ 7.* The relevant portion of the land is owned today by Defendant. *Andrews Affidavit ¶ 7.*

Defendant's Wrongful Actions

Defendant Chandler has deliberately and intentionally placed a permanent chain over the easement owned by Mr. Andrews and Ms. Rosenberg, now known as Wiggin Road, and has, from time to time, also blocked the easement with vehicles. *Andrews Affidavit ¶ 8.* Defendant Chandler has also refused to allow Mr. Andrews and Ms. Rosenberg to pass through the easement to their new home. *Andrews Affidavit ¶ 9.* Mr. Andrews spoke to Mr. Chandler's son and asked him to allow Plaintiffs to access their property via the easement. *Andrews Affidavit ¶ 9.* Mr. Chandler's son refused to allow Mr. Andrews and Ms. Rosenberg regular access along their deeded easement. *Andrews Affidavit ¶ 9.* By letter dated June 13, 2002, counsel for Mr. Andrews and Ms. Rosenberg demanded that Mr. Chandler allow Plaintiffs to use their easement. *Andrews Affidavit ¶ 10.* Mr. Chandler has failed and/or refused to respond to the letter. *Andrews Affidavit ¶ 11.* Despite demand, Defendant John Chandler has adamantly refused to unblock the easement or allow Mr. Andrews and Ms. Rosenberg access over their easement to their new home. *Andrews Affidavit ¶¶ 9–11.*

I. The Law

In considering an application for a temporary restraining order or preliminary injunctive relief, a Court must weigh (1) the likelihood of success on the merits; (2) the potential for irreparable harm to the person seeking relief; (3) the balance of hardship if relief is denied versus the other party's hardship if relief is granted; and (4) the effect of the decision on the public interest. *Coburn v. Chitwood,* 145 F. Supp. 2d 92, 95–96 (D. Me. 2001); *Ingraham v. University of Mind,* 441 A.2d, 691, 693 (Me. 1982).

II. Plaintiffs Have Demonstrated a Likelihood of Success on the Merits

As set forth above, the Wiggin subdivision was created in 1970. The subdivision included a number of country roads, which are known today as Wiggin Road, State Park Road, and Raccoon Road. The setup for the subdivision was that the lot owners would have access to the town road, now known as Songo School Road, over the subdivision country roads.

One of the first lots to be sold was Lot 3, which is now owned by Plaintiffs Christopher Andrews and Melinda J. Rosenberg. The 1971 deed to Lot 3 expressly gave the lot owners an easement over all of the subdivision roads to get to Songo School Road. The deeds to Lots 1, 4, 5, and 6 expressly state that the easement crosses the land of "Wiggin." The Subdivision Plan even includes an arrow which shows lot owners which way they should travel on Old Jackson Road (now State Park Road) to get out to Wiggin Road and then Songo School Road (the Town Road).

The easement afforded to the predecessors of Mr. Andrews and Ms. Rosenberg could not be clearer.

In 2000, Defendant John F. Chandler bought the land of Wiggin shown on the Plan and referenced by the deeds. Defendant's deed is expressly made *subject* to all conveyances and easements in the subdivision which pre-date him. The 1971 sale of Lot 3, which was given an easement over the Wiggin land and all of the subdivision roads, predates Chandler's deed by almost thirty years. Thus, Chandler's land is expressly subject to an easement whereby the owners of Lot 3 can drive over Wiggin Road to access their property.

Mr. Chandler has seen fit to unilaterally block this easement. His unilateral closing of the easement deprives Mr. Andrews and Ms. Rosenberg of their only legal and sufficient access to their newly Pur chased house—in express and direct violation of the easement clearly burdening his property.

III. Defendant's Blocking of the Easement Has Irreparably Harmed the Plaintiffs

Mr. Andrews and Ms. Rosenberg's only legal and sufficient access to their property is over the easement which passes through Mr. Chandler's property. *Andrews Affidavit ¶ 13.* While there is an old road, through a different subdivision, which can theoretically be used to access Plaintiffs' property, this access is unsatisfactory and insufficient. First, the alternative access road is a very poor quality road over a much longer route. *Andrews Affidavit ¶ 13.* Second, Mr. Andrews hauls a boat to and from his property, and the alternate access is too narrow and too poorly maintained to be used by vehicles hauling boat trailers. *Andrews Affidavit ¶ 13.* Third, the alternative access is unsuitable for fuel delivery trucks and other larger vehicles that need to service the property of Mr. Andrews and Ms. Rosenberg. *Andrews Affidavit ¶ 13.* Fourth, and perhaps most importantly, neither Mr. Andrews nor Ms. Rosenberg have any deeded access over the alternate access road to which Defendant Chandler is unilaterally demanding they travel. *Andrews Affidavit ¶ 13.*

IV. The Balance of Hardships Clearly Cuts in Plaintiffs' Favor

Granting injunctive relief presents irreparable harm to Mr. Andrews and Ms. Rosenberg and creates no harm to Mr. Chandler. Specifically, Mr. Chandler will suffer no harm whatsoever by granting the requested relief because the easement already goes over an existing road. *Andrews Affidavit ¶ 14.* Plaintiffs are not asking, in this action, that Mr. Chandler build or maintain the road—just that he unblock it so that Mr. Andrews and Ms. Rosenberg can get to their house. *Andrews Affidavit ¶ 14.*

V. The Public Interest Strongly Favors Granting the Injunction

There is a strong public interest in the law that property owners not be landlocked and that roads and easements not be blocked. In fact, it is a crime to obstruct a public way. 17-A M.R.S.A. § 505. Similarly, it is a legal nuisance to obstruct or encumber a private way or street. 17 M.R.S.A. § 2802.

Conclusion

For the reasons set forth above, Plaintiffs Christopher Andrews and Melinda J. Rosenberg respectfully request that the Court enjoin Defendant John F. Chandler from obstructing, in any way, their easement access over Wiggin Road to their house and property on Raccoon Road in Naples, Mind. Alternatively, if the Court believes that a gate is appropriate, Mr. Andrews and Ms. Rosenberg respectfully request that the Court order Mr. Chandler to provide them with a key for opening and closing a gate so that they can access their property.

CHAPTER 10

Written Discovery Requests

We do not believe in ourselves until someone reveals that deep inside us something is valuable, worth listening to, worthy of our trust, sacred to our touch. Once we believe in ourselves we can risk curiosity, wonder, spontaneous delight or any experience that reveals the human spirit.
—e.e. cummings

To win in real estate litigation, you must delve and explore. You must turn over every material rock.

You must be thorough. However, your discovery strategy must also be focused and cost effective. The purpose of discovery is (1) to learn facts unknown to you which are pertinent to the parties' claims and defenses; (2) to "lock in" a party's position so that it cannot be changed at trial; and (3) to gather undisputed facts necessary for a motion for summary judgment.

Start by analyzing the elements of the story. What are the facts that must be proven to vindicate the claims of either party? What facts must be shown to prove the defenses? Before drafting the discovery requests, determine exactly what facts you need to know, what facts you need to challenge, and what facts need to be pinned down.

There are three primary written discovery requests for use in real estate litigation: requests for documents, interrogatories, and requests for admissions. All of these discovery requests are indispensable.

In most cases, it would be a big mistake to walk into either a deposition or a trial without having an advance opportunity to review and analyze written discovery responses. There are a very few cases where, due to the inexperience of opposing counsel or the arrogance of an opposing party, you can successfully move quickly to depose an opponent and obtain valuable answers from that party before he has a sufficient opportunity to think through the case or prepare. This, however, is *not* the general rule, and counting on such incompetence is likely to be a major error.

DOCUMENT REQUESTS

Accordingly, the greatly preferred approach in real estate litigation is to file discovery requests, make sure that the other side answers completely—and *then* go forward with depositions, motions, and/or trial.

In real estate litigation, documents are critical. Whether it is a deed, a plan, a letter, an e-mail, or a photograph—virtually every real estate case depends on exhibits. These documents should be gathered from the outset of the case. In jurisdictions that allow it, it is a good practice to send out the requests for documents with the Complaint.

Note: Some jurisdictions provide that written discovery requests cannot be sent out until after an initial conference with the court. This, obviously, does not prevent you from gathering documents from the client, Registry of Deeds, surveyors, historical societies, neighbors, and depositories of aerial photographs. Jurisdictions that allow a request for production of documents to be filed at the outset of a case often give the opposing party an extra few weeks to respond. Practically speaking, this is not a good reason to wait before serving document requests. A request for an extension of time in responding to document requests is typical, and giving a little bit of extra time to the other side to gather documents will not have materially adverse consequences.

Think through the document request carefully before filing it, and tailor it to the facts of the case and your story. You want it to be broad enough to encompass all needed documents, but not so burdensome as to be objectionable or to lead to unnecessary discovery fights. Accordingly, the document requests must be clear and limited to relevant properties, transactions, and time frames.

Ask for all relevant deeds. While deeds should all be public records at the Registry, the other side may have or be relying upon unrecorded deeds, deeds that have not been properly indexed, or deeds that you or your title searcher considered irrelevant. You need to make sure that the other side is not relying on an important deed that is not in your collection.

Most cases also involve survey exhibits. Unlike deeds, many surveys are not recorded or in any public depository. Even where the deeds are part of a public record, the public record is unlikely to contain the surveyor's notes and calculations.

Note: The opposing party is also unlikely to have the surveyor's notes in his possession. Subpoena all opposing surveyors. If the surveyor is an independent witness, he may voluntarily agree to share work product with you.

You should also always demand all letters, e-mails, memoranda, notes, and other evidence of communications that the other side has written or exchanged with your client, with government officials, with neighbors, with surveyors, and with any other third parties conceivably involved in the relevant aspects of the case. Perhaps the opposing side communicated with a surveyor and received information and/or a plan that was adverse to your opponent's case. Assuming that this was done before the threat of litigation and that no work product privileges are involved, this would be tremendous evidence in support of your case. E-mails with neighbors may also provide the identity of witnesses who have tangled with the opposing side in the past, and would be great witnesses in this case. The opportunity for positive "smoking guns" in communications, especially e-mails, is unlimited.

Furthermore, you should request, if relevant, all closing documents related to the purchase or sale of the land in question. Closing binders contain valuable damage-related materials such as HUD statements, promissory notes, and appraisals.

In addition, photographs are an often overlooked source of documentary evidence. Assuming that the opponent owns or has owned the subject property, it is likely that he has historical or current photographs depicting relevant physical or man-made features or structures on the property that might be pertinent to your case.

Clearly, many of the documents that you receive from the other side will be harmful to your case. However, you need to see all of these documents as soon as possible so that you can appropriately tailor your story to the facts. If you believe that a document from the other side is not accurate, getting it as quickly as possible will give you a full opportunity to counter or object to it. Examples of Requests for Production of Documents follow.

STATE OF MIND SUPERIOR COURT

JAMES M. COHEN AND MICHELE F.	)	
COHEN, TRUSTEES OF THE EIGHTEEN	)	
ROSEBUD LANE REALTY TRUST,	)	
Plaintiffs	)	
	)	
v.	)	CIVIL ACTION
	)	DOCKET NO. ______
NANCY M. WASHINGTON,	)	
INDIVIDUALLY AND AS TRUSTEE OF	)	
THE SAMUEL S. WASHINGTON 1998	)	
REVOCABLE TRUST, RICHARD V.	)	
FRANKLIN, AND RITA C. FRANKLIN,	)	
Defendants	)	
	)	

PLAINTIFFS' FIRST SET OF DOCUMENT REQUESTS TO DEFENDANT NANCY M. WASHINGTON, INDIVIDUALLY AND AS TRUSTEE OF THE SAMUEL S. WASHINGTON 1998 REVOCABLE TRUST

Plaintiffs James M. Cohen and Michele F. Cohen, Trustees of the Eighteen Rosebud Lane Realty Trust (the "Cohens"), by their undersigned counsel, hereby request and require that Defendant Nancy M. Washington, Individually and as Trustee of the Samuel S. Washington 1998 Revocable Trust, respond to the following requests for production pursuant to Rule 34 of the Mind Rules of Civil Procedure:

INSTRUCTIONS

a. Each request must be answered separately, and a response should not be supplied by reference to another response unless the information provided is intended to be identical in all respects.

b. "You" and "your" shall include Nancy Washington and all of her agents, servants and employees and experts.

c. The term "person" shall include any person, whether natural or artificial, including without limitation any individual, partnership, firm, corporation, association, joint venture, business organization, entity, or any employee or agent thereof.

d. "Documents" is used to the full extent allowed by Rule 34(a), and includes any and all manner of writing, typed, printed, reproduced, filmed or recorded material, and all photographs, pictures, plans, or other representations of any kind of anything pertaining, describing, referring, relating, or concerning, directly or indirectly in whole or in part, to the subject matter of the request for production; the term includes, without limitation:

(i) Papers, books, journals, ledgers, statements, memoranda, reports, invoices, worksheets, work papers, notes, transcription of notes, letters, correspondence, abstracts, checks, diagrams, pictures, drawings, films, photographs, graphic representations, diaries, calendars, desk calendars, pocket calendars, lists, logs, publications, advertisements, instructions, minutes, orders, purchase orders, messages, resumes, summaries, agreements, contracts, telegrams, telexes, cables, recordings, audiotapes, magnetic tapes, transcriptions of tapes or recordings, videotapes, videocassettes, videocassette tapes, e-mail, electronic mail, computer diskettes, material on computers, or any other writings or tangible things on which any handwriting, typing, printing, photostatic, or other forms of communications are recorded or reproduced, as well as all notations on the foregoing;

(ii) Originals and all other copies not absolutely identical; and

(iii) All drafts and notes (whether typed, handwritten, or otherwise) made or prepared in connection with such documents, whether used or not.

e. Each document is to be produced as it is kept in the ordinary course of business, in its original folder, file jacket or cover, or shall be organized and labeled to correspond with the categories of this request.

f. "Communication" shall be construed as including but not limited to conversations (whether face to face, by telephone, or otherwise), meetings, conferences, discussions, negotiations, oral expert opinions, letters, memoranda, notes, reports, and all other oral or written contacts.

g. These Requests shall be deemed continuing so as to require supplemental production as provided for in Rule 26 of the Mind Rules of Civil Procedure. Final supplementary submission must be made no later than a reasonable time prior to the trial of this action.

h. All documents and materials shall be produced at the offices of Sawyer, Shur, Fynn, 100 Middle Street, Portland, Mind 04104, or a mutually agreed-upon location to be determined.

i. If any documents are not available for production because they have been misplaced, discarded, or destroyed, identify which categories cannot be produced for these reasons, identify what documents or kinds of documents cannot be produced, and state fully in writing the reasons that said documents are unavailable.

Requests

1. All correspondence, memoranda, notes, deeds, surveys, plans, title searches, or other documents which relate, in any way, to Nancy Washington's title to the property at issue in Jonesport.

2. All correspondence, memoranda, notes, deeds, surveys, plans, title searches, or other documents which relate, in any way, to the Cohens' title to the property at issue in Jonesport.

3. All surveys, plans, drawings, maps, appraisals, historical information, geological information, erosion information, or other documents which relate, in any way, to the property of either party in Jonesport.

4. All photographs or aerial photographs which relate, in any way, to the property of either party in Jonesport.

5. All photographs, drawings, or other visual images which relate, in any way, to the factory which was located on or near the property of the parties in Jonesport.

6. All correspondence, memoranda, notes, e-mails, or other documents which relate, in any way, to communications between Nancy Washington, her agents or attorneys, and Richard V. Franklin or Rita C. Franklin.

7. All correspondence, memoranda, notes, e-mails, or other documents which relate, in any way, to communications between Nancy Washington, her agents or attorneys, and James M. Cohen or Michele F. Cohen, or the agents or representatives of the Cohens.

8. All correspondence, memoranda, notes, e-mails, or other documents which relate, in any way, to interactions between Richard V. Franklin and Samuel Washington.

9. All correspondence, memoranda, notes, e-mails, or other documents which relate, in any way, to communications between Samuel Washington and the Franklins.

10. All correspondence, memoranda, notes, e-mails, or other documents which relate, in any way, to communications between Sam Washington and Eric Schaeffer.

11. All correspondence, memoranda, notes, e-mails, or other documents which relate, in any way, to the efforts of the Franklins to sell the property at issue to the Cohens or any third party.

12. All communications between Sam Washington or Nancy Washington (or their agents) and a surveyor concerning the properties of the parties in this case.

13. All communications between Sam Washington or Nancy Washington (or their agents) and a real estate broker concerning the properties of the parties in this case.

14. All communications between Sam Washington or Nancy Washington (or their agents) and any municipal officer or employee of the Town of Jonesport concerning the properties of the parties in this case.

15. All communications between Sam Washington or Nancy Washington (or their agents) and any employee or volunteer at an area historical society concerning the properties of the parties in this case.

16. All correspondence, memoranda, notes, e-mails, or other documents which relate, in any way, to communications between Samuel Washington and Carl Newton, the signer of the Surveyor's Certificate referenced in Paragraph 5 of Defendants' Counterclaim.

17. All correspondence, memoranda, notes, e-mails, or other documents which relate, in any way, to communications between you, or your agents, and Carl Mayhew, the author of the Surveyor's Certificate referenced in Paragraph 5 of Defendants' Counterclaim.

18. All correspondence, memoranda, notes, e-mails, or other documents which relate, in any way, to the Surveyor's Certificate referenced in Paragraph 5 of Defendants' Counterclaim.

19. All correspondence, memoranda, notes, e-mails, surveys, plans, deeds, historical documents, or other documents which relate,

in any way, to Samuel Washington's search and research referenced in Paragraph 5 of Defendants' Counterclaim

20. All correspondence, memoranda, notes, e-mails, or other documents which relate, in any way, to communications between Mr. Washington or Mrs. Washington (or their agents or attorneys) on the one hand and surveyor Edgar Myers.

21. All correspondence, memoranda, notes, e-mails, plans, surveys, or other documents which relate, in any way, to the Myers Plan referenced in Paragraph 5 of Defendants' Counterclaim.

22. All correspondence, memoranda, notes, e-mails, plans, deeds, surveys, or other documents which support or contradict the Surveyor's Certificate referenced in Paragraph 5 of Defendants' Counterclaim.

23. All correspondence, memoranda, notes, e-mails, deeds, surveys, or other documents which relate, in any way, to the boundary between the Cohens and the Washingtons in Jonesport, Mind.

24. All documents or other information considered by an expert in forming his or her opinions, any exhibits to be used as a summary of or support for the opinions, and all publications authored by each witness or expert.

STATE OF MIND SUPERIOR COURT

FRANKLIN FRANCHISE MORTGAGE	)	
ACCEPTANCE COMPANY,	)	
Plaintiff	)	
	)	
v.	)	CIVIL ACTION
	)	DOCKET NO.
THE LOWLAND INVESTMENT	)	
GROUP CORP., *et al.*,	)	
Defendants	)	

PLAINTIFF'S FIRST SET OF DOCUMENT REQUESTS ON PARTY-IN-INTEREST, CHARLENE F. SALINGER

Plaintiff Franklin Franchise Mortgage Acceptance Company ("Franklin"), by its undersigned counsel, hereby requests and requires that Party-in-Interest Charlene F. Salinger, Executrix of the Estate of William J. Smith, respond to the following requests for production pursuant to Rule 34 of the Mind Rules of Civil Procedure:

INSTRUCTIONS

a. All documents and materials shall be produced at the offices of Some Fine Attorneys.

b. Production shall be made as the records are kept in the usual course of business, or shall be organized and labeled to correspond with the categories of this request.

c. If any documents are not available for production because they have been misplaced, discarded or destroyed, identify which categories cannot be produced for these reasons, identify what documents or kinds of documents cannot be produced, and state fully in writing the reasons that said documents are unavailable.

d. If any documents are available but are not produced because of an objection, including any objection based on privilege, identify such documents with particularity as to date, subject matter and the nature of the objection or privilege claimed, and state in writing the objection and reasons therefore.

e. If documents called for herein are not available to you because they are in custody or control of a third person, identify the documents or categories of documents and identify the third person in whose possession or control said documents can be found.

f. Produce all documents available by virtue of being in the possession of your officers, attorneys, and your accountants.

g. "You" or "your" shall include any party to whom these requests are propounded, and all of that party's agents, personal representatives, executors, servants, and employees and, unless privileged, counsel for that party.

h. "Documents" means any and all manner of writing, typed, printed, reproduced, filmed or recorded material, and all photographs, pictures, plans, or other representations of any kind of anything pertaining, describing, referring, or relating, directly or indirectly in whole or in part, to the subject matter of the request for production, and the term includes, without limitation:

(i) Papers, books, journals, ledgers, statements, memoranda, reports, invoices, worksheets, work papers, notes, transcription of notes, letters, correspondence, abstracts, checks, diagrams, pictures, drawings, films, photographs, graphic representations, diaries, calendars, desk calendars, pocket calendars, lists, logs, publications, advertisements, instructions, minutes, orders, purchase orders, messages, resumes, summaries, agreements, contracts, telegrams, telexes, cables, recordings, audiotapes, magnetic tapes, videotapes, transcriptions of tapes or recordings, electronic mail, or any other writings or tangible things on which any handwriting, typing, printing, photostatic, or other forms of communications that are recorded or reproduced, as well as all notations on the foregoing;

(ii) Originals and all other copies not absolutely identical; and

(iii) All drafts and notes (whether typed, handwritten, or otherwise) made or prepared in connection with such documents, whether used or not.

Requests

1. All correspondence, memoranda, notes, wills, probate filings, estate documents, probate documents, inventories, or other documents which relate, in any way, to money owed to you in connection with the above-captioned case.

2. All correspondence, memoranda, notes, or other documents which relate, in any way, to communications between William J. Smith, his executrix or agents, and any trustee or beneficiary of the Lowland Golf Mortgagees Realty Trust.

3. All correspondence, memoranda, notes, or other documents which relate, in any way, to communications between William J. Smith, his executrix or agents, and Kenneth Gilson.

4. All correspondence, memoranda, notes, or other documents which relate, in any way, to communications between William J. Smith, his executrix or agents, and Lillian S. Gilson.

5. All correspondence, memoranda, notes, or other documents which relate, in any way, to communications between William J. Smith, his executrix or agents, and Lowland Investment Group Corp.

6. All correspondence, memoranda, notes, or other documents which relate, in any way, to communications between William J. Smith, his executrix or agents, and HFC Corporation.

7. All correspondence, memoranda, notes, or other documents which relate, in any way, to communications between William J. Smith, his executrix or agents, and Attorney Jeffery Clark.

8. All correspondence, memoranda, notes, or other documents which relate, in any way, to communications between William J. Smith, his executrix or agents, and any entity controlled by Kenneth Gilson.

9. The document or documents creating the Lowland Golf Mortgagees Realty Trust, and all amendments and modifications thereto.

10. All correspondence, memoranda, notes, agreements, or other documents which relate, in any way, to the Trustees of the Lowland Golf Mortgagees Realty Trust or to the Trust itself.

11. All correspondence, memoranda, notes, agreements, or other documents which identify the past or present trustees and beneficiaries of the Lowland Golf Mortgagees Realty Trust and the amount of funds which they have invested, loaned, or advanced to the Trust, on behalf of the Trust.

12. All correspondence, memoranda, notes, agreements, or other documents by and between the Trustees and the beneficiaries of the Lowland Golf Mortgagees Realty Trust.

13. All correspondence, memoranda, notes, checks, check registers, agreements, financial statements, audit statements, promissory notes, mortgages, loan documents, or other documents which relate, in any way, to funds loaned or advanced by the Lowland Golf Mortgagees Realty Trust for the benefit of the property at issue in this case.

14. All correspondence, memoranda, notes, checks, check registers, agreements, financial statements, audit statements, promissory notes, mortgages, loan documents, or other documents which relate, in any way, to funds loaned or advanced by the Lowland Golf Mortgagees Realty Trust for any purpose whatsoever.

15. All correspondence, memoranda, notes, checks, check registers, agreements, financial statements, promissory notes, mortgages, loan documents, audit statements, or other documents which relate, in any way, to funds loaned or advanced by trustees or beneficiaries to the Lowland Golf Mortgagees Realty Trust.

16. All checkbooks, check registers, ledgers, balance sheets, profit and loss statements, financial statements, or tax returns which relate, in any way, to the Lowland Golf Mortgagees Realty Trust.

17. All promissory notes, mortgages, loan documents, loan agreements, or other documents which relate, in any way, to any funds loaned to or borrowed by the Lowland Golf Mortgagees Realty Trust.

18. All correspondence, memoranda, notes, agreements, or other documents which relate, in any way, to communications between the Lowland Golf Mortgagees Realty Trust (or its trustees or agents) and the Lowland Investment Group Corp.

19. All correspondence, memoranda, notes, agreements, or other documents which relate, in any way, to communications between the Lowland Golf Mortgagees Realty Trust (or its trustees or agents) and HFC Corporation.

20. All correspondence, memoranda, notes, agreements, or other documents which relate, in any way, to communications between the Lowland Golf Mortgagees Realty Trust (or its trustees or agents) and Lillian S. Gilson.

21. All correspondence, memoranda, notes, agreements, or other documents which relate, in any way, to communications between the Lowland Golf Mortgagees Realty Trust (its trustees or agents) and Kenneth Gilson.

22. All documents which support, in any way, your claim that you have a superior claim over Plaintiff's mortgage to the subject real estate.

23. All correspondence, memoranda, notes, or other documents which relate, in any way, to the Subordination Agreement dated as of January 27, 1998.

24. All correspondence, memoranda, notes, or other documents which relate, in any way, to any contention that the Subordination Agreement dated January 27, 1998, is not valid, legitimate, or enforceable.

25. All correspondence, memoranda, notes, reports, opinions, or other documents which relate to any experts which you intend to call at the trial of this case.

STATE OF MIND SUPERIOR COURT

VALERIE A. SCHMIDT,	)	
Plaintiff	)	
	)	
v.	)	CIVIL ACTION
	)	DOCKET NO. ______
JERRY D. EASON, *et al.*,	)	
Defendants	)	
	)	

DEFENDANT'S FIRST SET OF DOCUMENT REQUESTS TO PLAINTIFF

Defendant Pamela Morin Powers, by her undersigned counsel, hereby requests and requires that Plaintiff respond to the following requests for production pursuant to Rule 34 of the Mind Rules of Civil Procedure:

INSTRUCTIONS

a. Each request must be answered separately, and a response should not be supplied by reference to another response unless the information provided is intended to be identical in all respects.

b. "You" and "your" shall include the Plaintiff and all of her agents, servants and employees, and experts.

c. The term "person" shall include any person, whether natural or artificial, including without limitation any individual, partnership, firm, corporation, association, joint venture, business organization, entity, or any employee or agent thereof.

d. "Documents" is used to the full extent allowed by Rule 34(a), and includes any and all manner of writing, typed, printed, reproduced, filmed or recorded material, and all photographs, pictures, plans, or other representations of any kind of anything pertaining, describing, referring to, relating to, or concerning, directly or indirectly in whole or in part, the subject matter of the request for production; the term includes, without limitation:

(i) Papers, books, journals, ledgers, statements, memoranda, reports, invoices, worksheets, work papers, notes, transcription of notes, letters, correspondence, abstracts, checks, diagrams, pictures, drawings, films, photographs, graphic representations, diaries, calendars, desk calendars, pocket calendars, lists, logs, publications, advertisements, instructions, minutes, orders, purchase orders, messages, resumes, summaries, agreements, contracts, telegrams, telexes, cables, recordings, audiotapes, magnetic tapes, transcriptions of tapes or recordings, videotapes, videocassettes, videocassette tapes, e-mail, electronic mail, computer diskettes, material on computers, or any other writings or tangible things on which any handwriting, typing, printing, photostatic, or other forms of communications are recorded or reproduced, as well as all notations on the foregoing;

(ii) Originals and all other copies not absolutely identical; and

(iii) All drafts and notes (whether typed, handwritten, or otherwise) made or prepared in connection with such documents, whether used or not.

e. Each document is to be produced as it is kept in the ordinary course of business, in its original folder, file jacket, or cover, or shall be organized and labeled to correspond with the categories of this request.

f. "Communication" shall be construed as including but not limited to conversations (whether face to face, by telephone, or otherwise), meetings, conferences, discussions, negotiations, oral expert opinions, letters, memoranda, notes, reports, and all other oral or written contacts.

g. These Requests shall be deemed continuing so as to require supplemental production as provided for in Rule 26 of the Mind Rules of Civil Procedure. Final supplementary submission must be made no later than a reasonable time prior to the trial of this action.

h. All documents and materials shall be produced at the offices of Shur and Nelson, or a mutually agreed upon location to be determined.

i. If any documents are not available for production because they have been misplaced, discarded, or destroyed, identify which categories cannot be produced for these reasons, identify what documents or kinds of documents cannot be produced, and state fully in writing the reasons that said documents are unavailable.

Requests

1. All correspondence, memoranda, notes, deeds, surveys, or other documents which relate, in any way, to the properties owned by either of the Defendants in York.

2. All correspondence, memoranda, notes, or other documents which relate, in any way, to communications between you and any of the Defendants or his or her agents or attorneys.

3. All correspondence, memoranda, notes, or other documents which relate, in any way, to communications between you and any prior owner of the Defendants' properties in York.

4. All correspondence, memoranda, notes, or other documents which relate, in any way, to communications between you and the Town of York concerning any of the properties involved in this case.

5. All correspondence, memoranda, notes, or other documents which relate, in any way, to communications between you and the York Sewer District concerning any of the properties involved in this case.

6. All correspondence, memoranda, notes, deeds, easements, plans, surveys, contracts, invoices, inspections, or other documents which relate, in any way, to the sewer line servicing the property referenced in Paragraph 5 of Plaintiff's Amended Complaint.

7. All correspondence, memoranda, notes, or other documents which relate, in any way, to the knowledge of Defendant Pamela Morin Powers or her predecessors-in-interest that Plaintiff's sewer connection crossed her land.

8. All correspondence, memoranda, notes, deeds, easements, plans, surveys, contracts, invoices, inspections, or other documents which relate, in any way, to the sewer line serving the property of James F. Schmidt, Jr. and Valerie A. Schmidt, referenced in a deed dated August 14, 1965, and recorded in the York County Registry of Deeds at Book 1672, Page 176.

9. All correspondence, memoranda, notes, or other documents which relate, in any way, to communications between you and Mary Abbie Donahue concerning any of the properties at issue in this case.

10. All correspondence, memoranda, notes, or other documents which relate, in any way, to communications between you and Lawrence F. Donahue concerning any of the properties at issue in this case.

11. All documents evidencing the date of death of Mary Abbie Donahue.

12. All documents evidencing the date of death of Lawrence F. Donahue.

13. All correspondence, memoranda, notes, deeds, easements, plans, surveys, or other documents which relate, in any way, to the easement referenced in a deed, dated April 17, 1968, from Mary Abbie Donahue and Lawrence Franklin Donahue to James E. Carter and Edna E. Carter.

14. All correspondence, memoranda, notes, deeds, easements, plans, surveys, or other documents which relate, in any way, to the easement to High Street referenced in the deed dated December 12, 1972 from Alan H. Stenberg and Lee A. Stenberg to you and Lawrence F. Donahue.

15. All correspondence, memoranda, notes, deeds, surveys, or other documents which relate, in any way, to the easement to High Street benefiting your property at issue in this case.

16. All correspondence, memoranda, notes, or other documents which relate, in any way, to communications between you and the present or former owner of the land burdened by the aforementioned easement to High Street in York.

17. All correspondence, memoranda, notes, or other documents which relate, in any way, to communications between Lawrence F. Donahue and the present or former owner of the land burdened by the aforementioned easement to High Street in York, Mind.

18. All correspondence, memoranda, notes, or other documents which relate, in any way, to communications between you or Lawrence F. Donahue with any of the following persons. John W. Bledsoe, Ronaine C. Bledsoe, Lorraine Timlinson, Deborah O'Connor, or Darlene Murphy.

19. All documents which relate, in any way, to your claim to a prescriptive easement in this case.

20. All documents which relate, in any way, to your claim to easement by necessity in this case.

21. All documents which relate, in any way, to your claim to easement by estoppel in this case.

22. All other documents which relate, in any way, to your claim to an easement over the property of any of the Defendants in the above-captioned matter.

23. All documents which relate, in any way, to your claim against the Defendants for trespass.

24. All documents which relate, in any way, to your claim against the Defendants for intentional and/or negligent infliction of emotional distress.

25. All documents which relate, in any way, to any damages you have suffered as a result of your claims in the above-captioned matter.

26. All pleadings which relate to other court cases in which you have been a party.

27. All transcripts of testimony you have given in any deposition, court proceeding, or administrative proceeding.

28. All documents or other information considered by each witness or expert in forming his or her opinions, any exhibits to be used as a summary of or support for the opinions, and all publications authored by each expert in forming his or her opinions, any exhibits to be used as a summary of or support for the opinions, and all publications authored by each expert.

Responding to Document Requests

Real estate litigators should generally hold off on further discovery requests until complete documents have been produced by the opponent and by any third parties whom you have subpoenaed. Make sure that the document production is complete. If you have good reason to believe that the document production is not complete, or if documents are produced to you subject to unreasonable objections, go to the judge immediately to force full and complete production. Many jurisdictions require that the parties "meet and confer" before taking discovery battles up with the Court.

Regardless of whether a "meet and confer" is required by rule, it is always a good idea. Trying to work out a discovery issue with opposing counsel will (1) if successful, save your client the expense of the discovery battle; and (2) if unsuccessful, be used by you to show the judge that you have taken reasonable steps to work this matter out—but that your unreasonable opponent has forced the issue despite your good-faith efforts.

Note: Playing games with document production is not recommended. When receiving a reasonable document request, respond fully. Most lawyers will promptly take issue with an incomplete document production and raise the issue. Most judges do not look favorably upon the practices or credibility of lawyers who play document games. Most clients, furthermore, are not likely to be impressed with legal fees they will have to pay that do not provide any material gain in advancing your case.

There are, of course, legitimate reasons to object to document requests. The foremost reason is to protect information that is privileged or protected by the work product doctrine. It is, in fact, *critical* to ensure that attorney-client privileged communications are not produced. In some jurisdictions, the production of privileged materials can be deemed a *waiver* of the privilege—and require the production of additional privileged materials. Even in jurisdictions that protect inadvertent disclosures, an attorney must often prove that he undertook reasonable efforts to prevent such disclosure. Requesting the return of inadvertently produced privileged documents is also embarrassing and—despite the recovery of materials—divulges sensitive information to the other side.

Note: Attorney-generated documents in a real estate closing, including drafts, are not protected by the work product doctrine. The doctrine is limited to materials prepared in *anticipation* of litigation. A transactional lawyer would be hard-pressed to claim that litigation was anticipated at the time a real estate deal was being negotiated or closed.

The Rules of Civil Procedure allow parties to object to document requests that are neither relevant nor reasonably calculated to lead to the discovery of admissible evidence. Courts, however, do not favor discovery objections based on relevance. It should be reserved for poorly drafted document requests that veer widely off the mark or request completely irrelevant personal materials such as tax returns or confidential business strategy memoranda.

Confidentiality is, in and of itself, not a ground for ultimately withholding documents or discovery—but it *is* a valid objection pending a confidentiality order or agreement. Many jurisdictions now have standard orders that can be sought.

Courts *do* tend to sustain objections where document requests are overly broad and not made with reasonable particularity. Depending on the judge, objections to overly broad requests lead to either the outright granting of the objection or the narrowing of the discovery request. As with all litigation filings, consider what you would do or say if you were on the other side—and tailor your pleading or request accordingly. Limit your requests to appropriate properties, transactions, and time frames.

Another pertinent objection is where document requests are vague or ambiguous. Vague requests use language that is hard to comprehend. Ambiguous requests are susceptible to two or more interpretations. It is always a good idea to reach a written agreement on exactly what is being sought—before bringing such an objection to the attention of the court.

Objections to "unduly burdensome" document requests are appropriate where vast amounts of relevant documents are sought. Such objections are rarely upheld in real estate litigation. It may be successful, however, where the basic information can be obtained from a fewer number of files.

Note: The foregoing objections to document requests are equally applicable to responding to interrogatories and requests for admissions in real estate litigation.

Upon receiving a complete production of documents from the opposing side and third parties, you should quickly master the documents and determine if the facts in these documents make it necessary to amend your strategy. After absorbing the impact of the documents on your story and on the opponent's case, the next step in real estate litigation is typically the filing of interrogatories and requests for admissions.

In real estate litigation, it generally does not make sense to file the interrogatories or requests for admissions until after you have received complete document responses from the other side. The detailed review and analysis of all of the documents from the opponent and from third parties provides very helpful assistance in fashioning interrogatories and admissions and authenticating key documents.

Interrogatories

Interrogatories are written questions propounded upon the other side, to which the opponent must provide written responses under oath. In real estate disputes, interrogatories are valuable to (1) identify the names and addresses of the persons with knowledge; (2) identify key documents; (3) seek answers to basic questions; and (4) nail down the other side's contentions in the case. Because the interrogatory answers will be carefully screened and drafted by an attorney, interrogatories are generally not useful for asking complex questions or pressing argumentative points. Do not force the other side to organize its case by asking complex questions in interrogatories. Hard questions should always be sprung at depositions, where a spontaneous answer is in your best interest.

In other words, use interrogatories for the basics. As most jurisdictions limit the number of interrogatories, do not waste them on topics in which you are sure to get an admission or stipulation. Ask what persons have knowledge about the facts and disputes. Ask for the address and the employer of witnesses you cannot locate. Ask for the identity of documents supporting various positions or assertions. Ask for a privilege log of documents not produced in response to the request for production of documents. Ask about experts the other side will be relying upon at the trial of the case. There may also be other basic questions to which you need simple answers:

- Was there a chain put across the driveway?
- Who put the chain across the driveway?
- When was the chain put across the driveway?

- Who helped install the chain?
- Where was the chain obtained?
- Describe the chain that was placed across the driveway.
- How long have you lived on your property?
- How long has the driveway been at that location?
- How long has the Plaintiff used the driveway?
- State any occasions on which the parties discussed the Plaintiff's use of the driveway.
- Describe in detail what was said.

Stay away from the complex questions:

- Why did you put the chain across the driveway?

You *can* use interrogatories for basic relevant background information, such as the identification of prior depositions, court testimony, trials, and criminal history. Some attorneys prefer to do this face-to-face at depositions, but they often receive a "do not recall" response.

Contention interrogatories are of key importance. This is where the involvement of the opposing attorney can be more help then hindrance. You can ask the other side:

- Describe in detail all legal and factual bases for your contention that Plaintiffs' driveway is on property owned by the Defendant.
- Describe in detail all legal and factual bases for your contention that the Plaintiffs have no right to use the driveway to their home.
- Describe in detail all damages you have suffered as a result of Defendant's alleged negligence.

These are questions that nail down the other side's contentions. Asking these questions at a deposition will likely evoke a vague or ambiguous response. Asking these questions as an interrogatory should elicit a full and complete response that fully elaborates on the other side's position—and nails it down. If you do not get a complete response, seek immediate intervention from the court. Some parties seek to defer responses to contention interrogatories until after the close of discovery. However, the better argument for the court is that the other side has made the contention and should be required to provide its full good-faith basis for doing so.

Accordingly, contention interrogatories are an excellent means for discovering—and pinning the other side to—the basis for its claims and affirmative defenses, its theory of damages, and its calculation of the damages.

As with the document responses, make sure you have full and complete answers to every relevant question. Allowing good discovery to slip away is an error. Good interrogatory answers serve as powerful admissions and stipulations at trial. Examples of interrogatories are as follows:

STATE OF MIND SUPERIOR COURT

VICTOR HEPBURN, *et al.*, Plaintiffs	)))	
v.	))	CIVIL ACTION DOCKET NO. ______
SALLY L. DAVIS, *et al.*, Defendants	)))	

DEFENDANTS' FIRST SET OF INTERROGATORIES
TO PLAINTIFF VICTOR HEPBURN

Defendants Sally L. Davis and Michael A. Antone, by their undersigned counsel, hereby request and require that Plaintiff Victor Hepburn respond to the following requests for production pursuant to Rule 33 of the Mind Rules of Civil Procedure:

INSTRUCTIONS AND DEFINITIONS

a. These interrogatories are continuing in character, so as to require you to file supplementary answers if you obtain further or different information before trial.

b. "You" or "your" shall include the party to whom these interrogatories are propounded, and all of his agents, servants, and employees and, unless privileged, counsel for the party.

c. The term "person" shall mean any individual, partnership, firm, corporation, association, joint venture, business organization, entity, or any employee or agent thereof.

d. "Documents" means any and all manner of writing, typed, printed, reproduced, filmed or recorded material, and all photographs, pictures, plans, or other representations of any kind of anything pertaining, describing, referring, or relating, directly or indirectly, in whole or in part, to the subject matter of the request for production, and the term includes, without limitation:

(i) Papers, books, journals, ledgers, statements, memoranda, reports, invoices, worksheets, work papers, notes, transcription of notes, letters, correspondence, abstracts, checks, diagrams, pictures, drawings, films, photographs, graphic representations, diaries, calendars, desk calendars, pocket calendars, lists, logs, publications, advertisements, instructions, minutes, orders, purchase orders, messages, resumes, summaries, agreements, contracts, telegrams, telexes, cables, recordings, audio tapes, magnetic tapes, videotapes, transcriptions of recordings, electronic mail, e-mail, or any other writings or tangible things on which any handwriting, typing, printing, photostatic, or other forms of communications are recorded or reproduced, as well as all notations on the foregoing;

(ii) Originals and all other copies not absolutely identical; and

(iii) All drafts and notes (whether typed, handwritten, or otherwise) made or prepared in connection with such documents, whether used or not.

e. Whenever you are asked to identify any person, please state with respect to such person: the person's full name, such person's last known business address and telephone number; such person's last known residence and telephone number; such person's present occupation and business affiliation; and such person's occupation and business affiliation as of the time to which your answer relates.

INTERROGATORIES

1. Identify all persons, by full name and address, who have knowledge of any of the claims in your Complaint or in Defendants' Counterclaims. Describe in detail the specific knowledge of each person concerning these claims.

2. State all court cases in which you have been a party, and describe in detail the name of the parties, the name of the court, the case number, and the lawyers involved in each case.

3. Identify all cases in which you have given sworn testimony in a deposition or trial, and describe in detail the name of the court and case number, whether the testimony was at a deposition or a trial, all lawyers who participated in the case, and the location of the transcript of your testimony.

4. Describe in detail all places in which you have lived for six months or more and provide the address and term of residence for each such location.

5. State the date that the Town of Hiram discontinued that portion of Bray Road which currently abuts the land of the Defendants.

6. Describe in detail all properties you own which abut Bray Road in Hiram. Your answer should include the map and lot number of the property, the date that you purchased the property, the name of the prior owners, and the size of the property.

7. For each property that you own along Bray Road in Hiram, state what other public or private roads, ways, or easements can be used to access each such property by foot or motor vehicle.

8. State whether there has ever been a dwelling on any portion of your property or properties abutting Bray Road in Hiram, Mind. If your answer to the foregoing is in the affirmative, describe the dwelling in detail, state whether it was seasonal or year round, state all years in which it was present, and describe in detail the exact location of the dwelling.

9. Describe in detail each and every time that you have traveled across that portion of Bray Road abutting the land of the Defendants. Your answer should include the dates of your use, all witnesses who saw you use the road, and whether you traversed the road by foot, car, truck, or other vehicle.

10. State the date when the portion of Bray Road, abutted by Defendants, first became readily passable by two-wheel-drive automobiles.

11. State the date when the portion of Bray Road, abutted by Defendants, first was plowed.

12. State all times when you have driven across Beaver Cut Dam Road in a motor vehicle.

13. State whether you have ever accessed any of your property on Bray Road in Hiram, Mind, other than by traveling over that portion of Bray Road which abuts land currently owned by the Defendants.

14. Describe in detail all conversations which you have had with officials of the Town of Hiram concerning Bray Road in Hiram, Mind. Your answer should include the date of each such communication, with whom each communication occurred, and the substance of each communication.

15. Describe in detail all legal and factual bases which support your claim to a right to travel across that portion of Bray Road abutted by the property of the Defendants.

16. Describe in detail the substance of any admission by any party or any alleged agent of a party. Your answer should include the name of the person making each such admission, the date and time of the admission, and the names of all witnesses to the admission.

17. Describe in detail all communications and agreements you have or have had with other persons, who abut Bray Road, concerning the use of the road.

18. State whether you have ever proposed a subdivision or real estate development in the Town of Hiram. Your response should include the name of the subdivision or development, the date that you proposed it, a description of the development or subdivision, and the outcome of your proposal.

19. State whether you have ever proposed a subdivision or real estate development anywhere else in the United States. Your response should include the name of the subdivision or development, the date that you proposed it, a description of the development or subdivision, and the outcome of your proposal.

20. Describe in detail all legal and factual bases for your contention, set forth in Paragraph 13 of your Amended Complaint, that you "do not have adequate right of access to [your] property aside from Bray Road."

21. Describe in detail all legal and factual bases for your contention, set forth in Paragraph 14 of your Amended Complaint, that the "Defendants have no right to gate Bray Road . . ."

22. Describe in detail all legal and factual bases for your contention, set forth in your first affirmative defense to Defendants' Counterclaim, that "Defendants' Counterclaim fails to state a claim for relief against Plaintiffs upon which relief may be granted."

23. Describe in detail all legal and factual bases for your contention, set forth in your second affirmative defense to Defendants' Counterclaim, that "Plaintiffs or their predecessors in title have continuously used the Bray Road for more than 20 years."

24. Describe in detail all legal and factual bases for your contention that you have a prescriptive easement over that portion of Bray Road in Hiram, Mind, which is abutted by the property of the Defendants.

25. Itemize and detail the date and amount of all damages you are claiming in the above-captioned matter.

26. State whether you have ever been convicted within the past 15 years of a crime which either (a) was punishable by death or imprisonment for one year or more or (b) involved dishonesty or false statement.

If so, state the nature of the crime, the punishment (if any), the date of the offense, the court which adjudicated the conviction and the relevant circumstances.

27. Identify all experts that you expect to call at the trial in this case and describe in detail the subject matter to which each expert is expected to testify, the substance of the facts and opinions to which each expert is expected to testify, and the grounds for each expert opinion. Identify the data or other information considered by each expert in forming the opinions, any exhibits to be used as a summary of or support for the opinions, the qualifications of each expert, including a list of all publications authored by each expert within the preceding ten years, and the compensation to be paid for the study and testimony.

28. If you state a claim of privilege as to any of your answers to Defendants' First Set of Interrogatories, Defendants' First Set of Admissions, or Defendants' First Set of Document Requests, state the basis for the privilege. If the claim relates to a privileged document, state the date, person or persons who prepared or participated in preparing the document, the name and address of any person to whom the document was shown or sent, the general subject matter of the document, the present or last known location and custodian of the original of the document, and the basis for the claim of privilege with respect to the document. If the claim of privilege relates to a communication, state the date, place, and persons involved in the communication, the subject matter of the communication, and the basis for the claim of privilege with respect to that communication.

STATE OF MIND SUPERIOR COURT

MICHAEL A. LITZ and MARGARET M. SUSHIMI	)	
Plaintiffs	)	
	)	
v.	)	CIVIL ACTION
	)	DOCKET NO. ______
ANTHONY J. NIXON and BONNIE NIXON,	)	
Defendants	)	
	)	

PLAINTIFFS' FIRST SET OF INTERROGATORIES
TO DEFENDANTS

Plaintiffs Michael A. Litz and Margaret M. Sushimi, by their undersigned counsel, hereby request and require Defendants Anthony J. Nixon and Bonnie Nixon to respond to the following interrogatories pursuant to Rule 33 of the Mind Rules of Civil Procedure:

INSTRUCTIONS AND DEFINITIONS

a. These interrogatories are continuing in character, so as to require you to file supplementary answers if you obtain further or different information before trial.

b. "You" or "your" shall include the parties to whom these interrogatories are propounded, and all of their agents, servants, and employees and, unless privileged, counsel for the parties.

c. The term "person" shall mean any individual, partnership, firm, corporation, association, joint venture, business organization, entity, or any employee or agent thereof.

d. "Documents" means any and all manner of writing, typed, printed, reproduced, filmed or recorded material, and all photographs, pictures, plans, or other representations of any kind of anything pertaining, describing, referring, or relating, directly or indirectly, in whole or in part, to the subject matter of the request for production, and the term includes, without limitation:

(i) Papers, books, journals, ledgers, statements, memoranda, reports, invoices, worksheets, work papers, notes, transcription of notes, letters, correspondence, abstracts, checks, diagrams, pictures, drawings, films, photographs, graphic representations, diaries, calendars, desk calendars, pocket calendars, lists, logs, publications, advertisements, instructions, minutes, orders, purchase orders, messages, resumes, summaries, agreements, contracts, telegrams, telexes, cables, recordings, audio tapes, magnetic tapes, videotapes, transcriptions of recordings, electronic mail, e-mail, or any other writings or tangible things on which any handwriting, typing, printing, photostatic, or other forms of communications are recorded or reproduced, as well as all notations on the foregoing;

(ii) Originals and all other copies not absolutely identical; and

(iii) All drafts and notes (whether typed, handwritten, or otherwise) made or prepared in connection with such documents, whether used or not.

e. Whenever you are asked to identify any person, please state with respect to such person: the person's full name, such person's last known business address and telephone number; such person's last known residence and telephone number; such person's present occupation and business affiliation; and such person's occupation and business affiliation as of the time to which your answer relates.

INTERROGATORIES

1. Identify all persons, by full name and address, who have knowledge of any of the claims in Plaintiffs' Complaint or Defendant's Counterclaim. Describe in detail the specific knowledge of each person concerning these claims.

2. State whether Defendant Bonnie Nixon claims an easement over Plaintiffs' property in Naples.

3. Describe in detail all legal and factual bases for your claim that Defendant Anthony L. Nixon and/or Defendant Bonnie Nixon has an easement by necessity over Plaintiffs' property in Naples, Mind.

4. Describe in detail all legal and factual bases for your claim that Defendant Anthony L. Nixon and/or Defendant Bonnie Nixon has an implied easement over Plaintiffs' property in Naples, Mind.

5. Describe in detail all legal and factual bases for your contention that Defendant's easement by necessity and/or implied easement over Plaintiffs' property is approximately twenty feet in width.

6. Identify every parcel of property which Marjorie D. Nixon purchased or sold in Naples, Mind. Your answer should include the date of each transaction and the book and page of each transaction.

7. Identify every parcel of property which Robert F. Nixon purchased or sold in Naples, Mind. Your answer should include the date of each transaction and the book and page of each transaction.

8. Identify every parcel of property which Eleanore L. Nixon purchased or sold in Naples, Mind. Your answer should include the date of each transaction and the book and page of each transaction.

9. Identify every parcel of property which Defendant Anthony J. Nixon purchased or sold in Naples, Mind. Your answer should include the date of each transaction and the book and page of each transaction.

10. Identify every parcel of property which Defendant Bonnie Nixon purchased or sold in Naples, Mind. Your answer should include the date of each transaction and the book and page of each transaction.

11. Describe in detail all parcels of property currently owned by either Defendant Anthony J. Nixon or Defendant Bonnie Nixon in Naples, Mind. Your answer should include the date of acquisition of the property, the manner in which the property was acquired, and the book and page of any property which was purchased.

12. Describe in detail all evidence on the face of the earth which would suggest that Defendant Anthony J. Nixon and/or Defendant Bonnie Nixon has ever used an easement across the land of Mr. Litz and Ms. Sushimi in Naples, Mind.

13. Describe in detail all occasions upon which either of the Defendants has used an easement by necessity and/or implied easement over Plaintiffs' property in Naples, Mind.

14. Describe in detail all communications by you or your agents to C.N. Brown Company, to the Naples Planning Board, or to third parties alleging that you have an easement over the land of Plaintiffs in Naples, Mind. Your answer should include the date of the communication, a description of the type of communication (letter, oral, or otherwise), all

persons present at the time of the communication, and the substance of the communication.

15. State when you first learned of the proposed transaction between Plaintiffs and C.N. Brown Company, and describe in detail all actions you or your agents have taken in connection with this proposed transaction.

16. Describe in detail any physical impediments or characteristics which might prevent access from State Route 11 across the land that Defendants acquired from Robert F. Nixon and Eleanore L. Nixon by deed dated April 21, 1999, to the land which Defendant Anthony J. Nixon acquired from Marjorie D. Nixon in 1994 (by a deed recorded in the Cumberland County Registry of Deeds, Book 11527, Page 202).

17. Describe in detail any necessity for which Defendant Anthony J. Nixon requires an easement across the land of Plaintiffs for access, ingress, egress, or the installation of any utilities.

18. Describe in detail all legal and factual bases for your contention, set forth in Paragraph 11 of your Counterclaim, that the "easement by necessity and implied easement owned by Anthony J. Nixon encompasses the right to install utilities essential for most uses . . ."

19. Describe in detail any use to which Defendant Anthony J. Nixon has ever put the land which he acquired from Marjorie D. Nixon in 1994 (by deed recorded in the Cumberland County Registry of Deeds, Book 11527, Page 202).

20. Describe in detail the exact location, using either metes and bounds description, reference to a survey, or any other precise descriptive means, of the alleged approximately twenty-foot-wide easement that either Defendant Anthony J. Nixon or Marjorie D. Nixon claim to have used to traverse the property currently owned by Plaintiffs in Naples, Mind.

21. Describe in detail the exact location of the path or route, referenced in Paragraph 9 of your Counterclaim, which is "approximately 20 feet in width from Route 302 to the Nixon parcel."

22. Describe in detail all actions taken by the Plaintiffs, as set forth in Paragraph 10 of your Counterclaim, which "have sought to interfere with and extinguished Anthony J. Nixon's easement by necessity and implied easement . . ."

23. Describe in detail all legal and factual bases supporting your contention, set forth in your First Affirmative Defense, that the "allega-

tions set forth by Plaintiffs against Bonnie Nixon for failure to state a cause of action upon which relief can be granted."

24. Describe in detail all legal and factual bases supporting your contention, set forth in your Second Affirmative Defense, that the "allegations set forth in Count I must fail for failure to state a cause of action for which relief can be granted."

25. Describe in detail all legal and factual bases for your contention, set forth in your Third Affirmative Defense that the "allegations set forth in Count II must fail for failure to state a cause of action for which relief can be granted."

26. Describe in detail all legal and factual bases for your contention, set forth in your Fourth Affirmative Defense, that the "allegations set forth in Count III must fail for failure to state a cause of action for which relief can be granted."

27. Identify all experts that you expect to call at the trial in this case and describe in detail the subject matter as to which each expert is expected to testify, the substance of the facts and opinions to which each expert is expected to testify, and the grounds for each expert opinion. Identify the data or other information considered by each expert in forming the opinions, any exhibits to be used as a summary of or support for the opinions, the qualifications of each expert, including a list of all publications authored by each expert within the preceding ten years, and the compensation to be paid for the study and testimony.

28. If you state a claim of privilege as to any of your answers to Plaintiffs' First Set of Interrogatories to Defendants, Plaintiffs' First Requests for Admissions to Defendants, or Plaintiffs' First Set of Document Requests to Defendants, state the basis for the privilege. If the claim relates to a privileged document, state the date, person or persons who prepared or participated in preparing the document, the name and address of any person to whom the document was shown or sent, the general subject matter of the document, the present or last known location and custodian of the original of the document, and the basis for the claim of privilege with respect to the document. If the claim of privilege relates to a communication, state the date, place, and persons involved in the communication, the subject matter of the communication, and the basis for the claim of privilege with respect to that communication.

Responding to Interrogatories

Interrogatories must be responded to fully and under oath, signed by the party or an officer or manager of a corporate entity. The failure to fully provide persons with knowledge may lead to sanctions or the exclusion of witnesses or documents. Similarly, the failure to disclose information may preclude your use of it at trial. Therefore, full and complete answers are the best course of action.

Where an interrogatory requires you to cull through voluminous documents, many jurisdictions allow you to simply identify and produce the documents, in the manner they are kept in the normal course of business.

As with responses to document requests, you can refuse to answer an interrogatory by objecting to it based on relevance, vagueness, or burdensomeness. Such objections should be used sparingly, where appropriate.

Requests for Admissions

The third type of useful written discovery in real estate litigation is requests for admissions. While often neglected by real estate litigators, requests for admissions should virtually always be submitted to the other side. Admissions have two great benefits: (1) to obtain admissions that reduce the scope and costs of the case and (2) to authenticate key documents and potential exhibits. As set forth in the Advisory Committee Notes to the Federal Rules, parties should use admissions to narrow issues for trial and to simplify the proof of the remaining issues. Admissions are used as evidence at trial and as evidence for summary judgment motions.

Many jurisdictions provide that the failure to timely respond to a request for admissions results in it being deemed admitted. Other jurisdictions provide for the opposing party to reimburse the other side for legal fees incurred to prove an admission that had been improperly denied.

Before filing a request for admissions, review the facts of the case and all of the documents produced by the opponent, the client, and third parties. Gather together these simple undisputed facts in the case and get the other side to admit them. For example:

- Admit that Mr. Smith owns the house and surrounding land at 10 Main Street.

- Admit that Mr. Jones owns the house and surrounding land at 12 Main Street.
- Admit that the property of Mr. Smith abuts the property of Mr. Jones.
- Admit that Mr. Jones has lived on his property for 13 years.
- Admit that Mr. Jones mows his lawn up to a hedge of trees.
- Admit that there is a hedge of trees with orange marks on them.
- Admit that the predecessors-in-title to both Mr. Smith and Mr. Jones mutually placed the orange marks on the trees.
- Admit that the predecessors-in-title to Mr. Smith and Mr. Jones treated the hedge of trees, with orange marks, as their mutual boundary line.
- Admit that Mr. Jones has never mowed any of the lawn on the other side of the hedge of trees.

Look at the opposing party's answer to your complaint. Add to your request for admissions any simple allegations that you believe the other side improperly denied in the answer.

The request for admissions should also authenticate all important documents: correspondence, e-mails, surveys, plans, appraisals, deeds, chains of title, or anything else that you will be relying upon at a hearing or trial:

- Admit that the document, attached to Plaintiff's Complaint as Exhibit A, is a true and accurate copy of a letter which you received on or about October 10, 2009.
- Admit that the document, attached hereto as Exhibit B, is a true and accurate copy of a survey of your land performed by the Acme survey company and dated October 9, 2009.
- Admit that the document, attached hereto as Exhibit C, is a true and accurate copy of an e-mail which you sent to the Plaintiff on October 11, 2009.

You can also use a request for admissions to lay a foundation for the admissibility of an exhibit. For example, you can ask for an admission that a document was kept in the ordinary course of business or that the document was prepared under the authority of the author or sending entity.

Make sure that all of your admissions and other stipulations are submitted timely and properly to the court for use in a summary judgment hearing or trial. Examples of requests for admission follow.

STATE OF MIND SUPERIOR COURT

JAMES M. COHEN AND MICHELE F. COHEN, TRUSTEES OF THE EIGHTEEN ROSEBUD LANE REALTY TRUST, Plaintiffs	)	
v.	)	CIVIL ACTION DOCKET NO. ______
NANCY M. WASHINGTON, INDIVIDUALLY AND AS TRUSTEE OF THE SAMUEL S. WASHINGTON 1998 REVOCABLE TRUST, RICHARD V. FRANKLIN, AND RITA C. FRANKLIN, Defendants	)	

PLAINTIFFS' FIRST SET OF REQUESTS FOR ADMISSIONS TO DEFENDANTS NANCY M. WASHINGTON, INDIVIDUALLY AND AS TRUSTEE OF THE SAMUEL S. WASHINGTON 1998 REVOCABLE TRUST

Plaintiffs James M. Cohen and Michele F. Cohen, Trustees of The Eighteen Rosebud Lane Realty Trust, by their undersigned counsel, request and require Defendant Nancy M. Washington, Individually and as Trustee of The Samuel S. Washington 1998 Revocable Trust to respond to these Requests for Admissions pursuant to Rule 36 of the Mind Rules of Civil Procedure.

A. Instructions

a. Each Request for Admission should be answered separately and fully in writing. You must set forth each request in full immediately preceding your answer or objection thereto.

b. Each Request for Admission is deemed admitted unless, within 30 days after service of the Request for Admissions, you serve upon the party requesting the admission a written answer or objection addressed to the matter, signed by you or your attorney.

c. If objection is made to any of the Requests for Admissions, the reasons therefore shall be stated. The answer shall specifically deny the matter set forth in detail or set forth in detail the reasons why you cannot truthfully admit or deny the matter. A denial shall fairly meet the substance of the requested admission, and when good faith requires that you qualify an answer or deny only a part of the matter for which an admission is requested, you shall specify so much of it as is true and qualify or deny the remainder.

d. You may not give lack of information or knowledge as a reason for failure to admit or deny unless you state that you have made reasonable inquiry and that the information known or readily obtainable by you is insufficient to enable you to admit or deny.

e. Pursuant to Rule 37(c), if you fail to admit the genuineness of any document or the truth of any matter as requested hereunder, and if the party requesting the admissions thereafter proves the genuineness of the document or the truth of the matter, the requesting party may apply to the Court for an order requiring you to pay the reasonable expenses incurred in making that proof, including reasonable attorney's fees.

B. Requests for Admissions

1. Admit that a true and accurate copy of a survey by E.E. Myers, dated November 22, 1989, and entitled "Plan of Helen Dunbar Land; Jonesport, Mind, To Be Conveyed" (the "Myers Plan"), is attached to Plaintiff's Complaint as Exhibit A.

2. Admit that the document, attached to the Plaintiff's Complaint as Exhibit G, is a true and accurate copy of a letter sent by Plaintiff's counsel to your counsel on or about December 28, 2006.

3. Admit that neither you nor your counsel ever responded to the letter dated December 28, 2006, attached to Plaintiff's Complaint as Exhibit G.

4. Admit that the document, attached hereto as Exhibit A, is a true and accurate copy of a Boundary Agreement between Richard V. Franklin and Rita C. Franklin, on the one hand, and Lillian Huntley, on the other hand, which is dated July 31, 2001, and recorded in the Washington County Registry of Deeds at Book 2548, Page 187.

5. Admit that Richard C. Franklin owned Plaintiffs' property at the time they entered into the aforementioned Boundary Agreement on July 31, 2001.

6. Admit that the document, attached hereto as Exhibit B, is a true and accurate copy of a Warranty Deed between Richard V. Franklin and Rita C. Franklin and James M. Cohen and Michele F. Cohen, which is dated September 5, 2002, and recorded in the Washington County Registry of Deeds at Book 2664, Page 97.

7. Admit that the document, attached hereto as Exhibit B, is the deed to the Plaintiffs' property at issue in this case.

8. Admit that the document, attached hereto as Exhibit C, is a true and accurate copy of a Warranty Deed between Helen L. Dunbar and Richard V. Franklin and Rita C. Franklin, dated November 30, 1989, which is recorded in the Washington County Registry of Deeds at Book 1612, Page 261.

9. Admit that the document, attached hereto as Exhibit C, is for the property currently owned by the Plaintiffs.

10. Admit that Helen Dunbar had the Myers Plan done in 1989 and recorded in the Washington County Registry of Deeds in February 1990.

11. Admit that Helen Dunbar used the Myers Plan as a basis for describing the property she sold to Richard V. Franklin and Rita C. Franklin.

12. Admit that the document, attached hereto as Exhibit D, is a true and accurate copy of a Notice filed with the Washington County Probate Court reflecting, among other things, that Theresa R. Dunbar died on January 7, 1974, and that Helen L. Dunbar is the Personal Representative of her Estate.

13. Admit that the document, attached hereto as Exhibit E, is a true and accurate copy of a Warrant and Inventory for the Estate of Theresa R. Dunbar, dated January 7, 1974.

14. Admit that Theresa R. Dunbar acquired most of the land, now owned by the Plaintiffs, in the 1930s.

15. Admit that the document, attached hereto as Exhibit F, is a true and accurate copy of a deed between Arthur H. Rogers and Theresa R. Dunbar, dated September 29, 1945, which is recorded in the Washington County Registry of Deeds at Book 464, Page 151.

16. Admit that the document, attached hereto as Exhibit F, is for property currently owned by the Plaintiffs.

17. Admit that the document, attached hereto as Exhibit G, is a true and accurate copy of a deed between William B. Nichols and Arthur R. Rogers, dated August 1939, which is recorded in the Washington County Registry of Deeds at Book 428, Page 237.

18. Admit that the document, attached hereto as Exhibit G, is for property currently owned by the Plaintiffs.

19. Admit that the document, attached hereto as Exhibit H, is a true and accurate copy of a deed by and between Arthur R. Rogers and Theresa R. Dunbar, dated March 20, 1934, which is recorded in the Washington County Registry of Deeds at Book 400, Page 331.

20. Admit that the document, attached hereto as Exhibit H, is for property currently owned by the Plaintiffs.

21. Admit that the document, attached hereto as Exhibit I, is a true and accurate copy of a deed by and between Marcus R. Peterson and Theresa R. Dunbar, dated March 20, 1934, which is recorded in the Washington County Registry of Deeds at Book 400, Page 330.

22. Admit that the document, attached hereto as Exhibit I, is for property currently owned by the Plaintiffs.

23. Admit that the document, attached hereto as Exhibit J, is a true and accurate copy of a deed by and between Theresa L. Kelley and Marcus R. Peterson dated November 8, 1920, which is recorded in the Washington County Registry of Deeds at Book 346, Page 40.

24. Admit that the document, attached hereto as Exhibit J, is for property currently owned by the Plaintiffs.

25. Admit that the document, attached hereto as Exhibit K, is a true and accurate copy of a deed by and between A.B. Kelley and Theresa L. Kelley (wife of A.B. Kelley), dated January 3, 1888, which is recorded in the Washington County Registry of Deeds at Book 304, Page 31.

26. Admit that the document, attached hereto as Exhibit K, is for property currently owned by the Plaintiffs.

27. Admit that the document, attached hereto as Exhibit L, is a true and accurate copy of a deed by and between Edward M. Sawyer and Arthur R. Rogers, dated August 18, 1915, which is recorded in the Washington County Registry of Deeds at Book 321, Page 193.

28. Admit that the document, attached hereto as Exhibit L, is for property currently owned by the Plaintiffs.

29. Admit that the document, attached hereto as Exhibit M, is a true and accurate copy of the first page of a deed by and between Mansfield Packing Company and William S. Nichols, dated November 20,

1924, which is recorded in the Washington County Registry of Deeds at Book 377, Page 534.

30. Admit that the document, attached hereto as Exhibit M, is for property currently owned by the Plaintiffs.

31. Admit that the document, attached hereto as Exhibit N, is a true and accurate copy of a Sallyff's Sale Deed, dated March 30, 1910, which is recorded in the Washington County Registry of Deeds at Book 212, Page 458.

32. Admit that the document, attached hereto as Exhibit N, is for property currently owned by the Plaintiffs.

33. Admit that the document, attached hereto as Exhibit O, is a true and accurate copy of a Warranty Deed by and between The Bent Family Trust and Samuel S. Washington, Trustee of the Samuel S. Washington 1998 Revocable Trust, dated January 5, 1989, which is recorded in the Washington County Registry of Deeds at Book 2308, Page 217.

34. Admit that the document, attached hereto as Exhibit O, is Defendant's deed to her property.

35. Admit that the document, attached hereto as P, is a true and accurate copy of a Corrective Deed from Barbara K. Young to The Bent Family Trust, dated January 5, 1999, which was recorded in the Washington County Registry of Deeds at Book 2308, Page 214.

36. Admit that the document, attached hereto as Exhibit P, is for property currently owned by Defendant Washington.

37. Admit that the document, attached hereto as Exhibit Q, is a true and accurate copy of a Quitclaim Deed from John S. Bent and Mary Linda Bent to The Bent Family Trust, dated January 12, 1993, which is recorded in the Washington County Registry of Deeds at Book 1852, Page 224.

38. Admit that the document, attached hereto as Exhibit Q, is for property currently owned by Defendant Washington.

39. Admit that the document, attached hereto as Exhibit R, is a true and accurate copy of the first page of a Warranty Deed from Roger C. Taylor and Geraldine M. Taylor to John S. Bent and Mary Linda Bent, dated August 25, 1989, which is recorded in the Washington County Registry of Deeds at Book 1594, Page 239.

40. Admit that the document, attached hereto as Exhibit R, is for property currently owned by Defendant Washington.

41. Admit that the document, attached hereto as Exhibit S, is a true and accurate copy of a Warranty Deed from Herbert C. Allen and Mary E. Allen to Roger C. Taylor and Geraldine M. Taylor, dated July 1,

1988, which is recorded in the Washington County Registry of Deeds at Book 1520, Page 271.

42. Admit that the document, attached hereto as Exhibit S, is for property currently owned by Defendant Washington.

43. Admit that the document, attached hereto as Exhibit T, is a true and accurate copy of a deed from Thomas A. King and Katherine M. King to Herbert C. Allen and Mary E. Allen, dated June 30, 1983, which is recorded in the Washington County Registry of Deeds at Book 1232, Page 204.

44. Admit that the document, attached hereto as Exhibit T, is for property currently owned by Defendant Washington.

45. Admit that the document, attached hereto as Exhibit U, is a true and accurate copy of a deed from Frederick S. Ryan, Jr. and Barbara J. Ryan to Thomas A. King and Katherine M. King, dated August 1, 1977, which is recorded in the Washington County Registry of Deeds at Book 1003, Page 268.

46. Admit that the document, attached hereto as Exhibit U, is for property currently owned by Defendant Washington.

47. Admit that the document, attached hereto as Exhibit V, is a true and accurate copy of a deed from George A. Alley and Roxie S. Alley to Thomas A. King and Katherine M. King, dated September 12, 1972, which is recorded in the Washington County Registry of Deeds at Book 772, Page 72.

48. Admit that the document, attached hereto as Exhibit V, is for property currently owned by Defendant Washington.

49. Admit that the document, attached hereto as Exhibit W, is a true and accurate copy of a deed from George A. Alley to George A. Alley and Roxie S. Alley, dated September 27, 1971, which is recorded in the Washington County Registry of Deeds at Book 729, Page 24.

50. Admit that the document, attached hereto as Exhibit W, is for property currently owned by Defendant Washington.

51. Admit that the document, attached hereto as Exhibit X, is a true and accurate copy of a Deed from John M. Alley to George A. Alley and Alberta Alley, dated August 13, 1965, which is recorded in the Washington County Registry of Deeds at Book 625, Page 72.

52. Admit that the document, attached hereto as Exhibit X, is for property currently owned by Defendant Washington.

53. Admit that the document, attached hereto as Exhibit Y, is a true and accurate copy of a deed from H. John Young to John M. Alley

and Arlena B. Alley, dated October 12, 1953, which is recorded in the Washington County Registry of Deeds.

54. Admit that the document, attached hereto as Exhibit Y, is for property currently owned by Defendant Washington.

55. Admit that the document, attached hereto as Exhibit Z, is a true and accurate copy of a Quitclaim Deed from Alton V. Rogers to John Young, dated May 25, 1953, which is recorded in the Washington County Registry of Deeds at Book 514, Page 40.

56. Admit that the document, attached hereto as Exhibit Z, is for property currently owned by Defendant Washington.

57. Admit that the document, attached hereto as Exhibit AA, is a true and accurate copy of a Deed from Alton V. Rogers to H. John Young, dated November 7, 1950, which is recorded in the Washington County Registry of Deeds at Book 501, Page 238.

58. Admit that the document, attached hereto as Exhibit AA, is for property currently owned by Defendant Washington.

59. Admit that the document, attached hereto as Exhibit BB, is a true and accurate copy of an Abstract of the Will of Sarah A. Rogers, dated November 14, 1944, which is recorded in the Washington County Registry of Deeds at Book 5, Page 255.

60. Admit that the document, attached hereto as Exhibit BB, relates to property currently owned by Defendant Washington.

61. Admit that the document, attached hereto as Exhibit CC, is a true and accurate copy of a deed from Ida Woodward, Edith Beal, Fred Rogers, Grace Waugh, Minnie Whitney, and Helen Rogers, Heirs of the late Charles E. Woodward, to Sarah A. Rogers, dated November 30, 1934, which is recorded in the Washington County Registry of Deeds at Book 417, Page 80.

62. Admit that the document, attached hereto as Exhibit CC, is for property currently owned by Defendant Washington.

63. Admit that the document, attached hereto as Exhibit DD, is a true and accurate copy of a Deed from A.B. Kelley to Charles E. Woodward, dated November 30, 1895, which is recorded in the Washington County Registry of Deeds at Book 251, Page 32.

64. Admit that the document, attached hereto as Exhibit EE, is a true and accurate copy of a letter from Michael R. Leonard to Samuel S. Washington, dated September 4, 2001, with handwritten notes from Mr. Washington.

65. Admit that Mr. Mayhew relied on deed and/or title research from Samuel S. Washington in drafting the Surveyor's Certificate, attached to Plaintiff's Complaint as Exhibit EE.

STATE OF MIND SUPERIOR COURT

BERNARD L. WHIPPLE, *et al.*,	)	
Plaintiffs	)	
	)	
v.	)	CIVIL ACTION
	)	DOCKET NO. ______
JAMIE B. GOLDBERG, *et al.*,	)	
Defendants	)	
	)	

DEFENDANT JAMIE B. GOLDBERG'S FIRST SET OF REQUESTS FOR ADMISSIONS TO PLAINTIFFS

Defendant Jamie B. Goldberg, individually and as Trustee of the Jamie B. Goldberg 1992 Trust (the "Goldbergs"), by his undersigned counsel, requests and requires Plaintiffs to respond to these Requests for Admissions pursuant to Rule 36 of the Mind Rules of Civil Procedure.

Instructions

a. Each Request for Admission should be answered separately and fully in writing. You must set forth each request in full immediately preceding your answer or objection thereto.

b. Each Request for Admission is deemed admitted unless, within 30 days after service of the Request for Admissions, you serve upon the party requesting the admission a written answer or objection addressed to the matter, signed by you or your attorney.

c. If objection is made to any of the Requests for Admissions, the reasons therefore shall be stated. The answer shall specifically deny the matter set forth in detail or set forth in detail the reasons why you cannot truthfully admit or deny the matter. A denial shall fairly meet the substance of the requested admission, and when good faith requires that you qualify an answer or deny only a part of the matter for which an admission is requested, you shall specify so much of it as is true and qualify or deny the remainder.

d. You may not give lack of information or knowledge as a reason for failure to admit or deny unless you state that you have made reasonable inquiry and that the information known or readily obtainable by you is insufficient to enable you to admit or deny.

e. Pursuant to Rule 37(c), if you fail to admit the genuineness of any document or the truth of any matter as requested hereunder, and if the party requesting the admissions thereafter proves the genuineness of the document or the truth of the matter, the requesting party may apply to the Court for an order requiring you to pay the reasonable expenses incurred in making that proof, including reasonable attorney's fees.

Requests for Admissions

1. Admit that Plaintiff Bernard L. Whipple lives on Cove Road in Boothbay Harbor, Mind.

2. Admit that Plaintiff Mary Whipple does not live in Boothbay Harbor, Mind.

3. Admit that, from 1987 through 2004, Jamie B. Goldberg walked across Plaintiffs' property to access the dock, runway, and float adjacent to their property.

4. Admit that, prior to 1987, Dr. and Mrs. Raymond E. Buchanan walked across Plaintiffs' property to access the dock, runway, and float adjacent to their property.

5. Admit that Dr. Raymond E. Buchanan is the husband of Suzanne R. Buchanan.

6. Admit that William H. Pierce, Sr. died on October 10, 1976.

7. Admit that a true and accurate copy of the Will of William H. Pierce, Sr. is attached hereto as Exhibit A.

8. Admit that William H. Pierce, Sr. was married to Clara C. Pierce.

9. Admit that the children of William H. Pierce Sr. were the same people as the children of Clara C. Pierce.

10. Admit that the reservation, in the deed from the Estate of William H. Pierce, Sr. to T. Scott Kennedy and Judith C. Kennedy, purports to benefit the heirs of Clara C. Pierce, Sr.

11. Admit that the intent of the reservation, in the deed from the Estate of William H. Pierce, Sr. to T. Scott Kennedy and Judith C.

Kennedy, was to give the heirs of William H. Pierce, Sr. an easement over the property to use the adjacent dock, runway, and float.

12. Admit that the intent of the reservation, in the deed from the Estate of William H. Pierce, Sr. to T. Scott Kennedy and Judith C. Kennedy, was to give the heirs of Clara C. Pierce an easement over the property to use the adjacent dock, runway, and float.

13. Admit that William H. Pierce, Sr. and Clara C. Pierce had four children: Philip C. Pierce, Margaret R. Harris, William H. Pierce, Jr., and Carolyn R. Simmons.

14. Admit that Margaret R. Harris was the daughter of William H. Pierce, Sr. and Clara C. Pierce.

15. Admit that Philip C. Pierce was the son of William H. Pierce, Sr. and Clara C. Pierce.

16. Admit that William H. Pierce, Jr. was the son of William H. Pierce, Sr. and Clara C. Pierce.

17. Admit that Carolyn R. Simmons was the daughter of William H. Pierce, Sr. and Clara C. Pierce.

18. Admit that Clara C. Pierce died on April 25, 1961.

19. Admit that, at the time of her death, the heirs of Clara C. Pierce were Philip C. Pierce, Margaret R. Harris, William H. Pierce, Jr., and Carolyn R. Stein.

20. Admit that Carolyn R. Stein subsequently changed her name to Carolyn R. Simmons.

21. Admit that Carolyn R. Simmons died on August 6, 1976.

22. Admit that, at the time of her death, the heirs of Carolyn R. Simmons were David G. Stein, Betty H. Rosenberg, Carolyn H. Hanson, and William R. Stein.

23. Admit that a true and accurate copy of the Will of Clara C. Pierce is attached hereto as Exhibit B.

24. Admit that, at the time of his death, the heirs of William H. Pierce, Sr. were the following: Philip C. Pierce, William H. Pierce, Jr., Margaret R. Harris, David Gordon Stein, Betty Stein Rosenberg, Carolyn Stein Hanson, and William Pierce Stein.

25. Admit that the Executors of the Estate of William H. Pierce, Sr. sold the property currently owned by the Plaintiffs with the following language included in the deed:

> The above-described premises are conveyed subject to a certain right-of-way which is described as follows:

A right-of-way running from the terminus of Cove Road, southwesterly to the wharf extending into Hodgdon's Cove; the southerly boundary of said way being a 12 foot parcel of land owned by Pomerantz and Ramsey and which extends S. 72° 38' W. two hundred eighty six and one-tenth (286.1) feet from a pipe in cement at said terminus, to a bolt in an off-shore ledge. The north boundary of said way begins at a pipe in rocks located N. 26° 28' E. and eleven and two-tenths (11.2) feet from aforementioned pipe in cement and runs thence S. 72° 38' W. one hundred forty-four and two-tenths (144.2) feet to a pipe in large rocks; thence S. 78° 01' W. eighty and eight-tenths (80.8) feet to a pipe in rocks at high water mark, which pipe is also four and five-tenths (4.5) feet northerly from the wharf.

The right to maintain or replace the dock, runway and float, within the westerly extension of the S. 78° 04' W. line, on the north, and the westerly extension of the S. 72° 38' W. property line of the land herein conveyed, shall be a part of the right-of-way herein granted.

The use of the above described right-of-way and the dock, runway, and float shall be restricted to the owner or owners of the premises described in the Deed of Chester A. Swett to Clara C. Pierce dated October 24, 1939, and recorded in Lincoln County Registry of Deeds, Book 427, Page 458 (the "Swett Deed"), which owners currently are Philip C. Pierce, William H. Pierce, Jr., Margaret R. Harris, David Gordon Stein, Betty Stein Rosenberg, Carolyn Stein Hanson, and William Pierce Stein and their guests. The right-of-way and the use of the float, runway, and dock shall be subject to the following restrictions:

(1) There shall be no cutting of trees or bushes on said right-of-way without the permission, in writing, of the owners of the land over which the right-of-way passes.

(2) The right to the use of said right-of-way shall be by foot only.

(3) The routine maintenance of the dock, runway, and float shall be borne equally by the owners of Lot 12 and the owners of the land over which the right-of-way passes and any other users of said dock, runway, and float. See Boothbay Harbor Tax Map #13, Parcel #12.

(4) The owners of Lot 12 shall always hold harmless the owners of the land over which the right-of-way passes from any claim

arising out of the use of said right-of-way, dock, runway, and float by the owners of Lot 12 and their guests.

(5) These restrictions shall be binding on any and all owners of Lot 12, provided, however, that neither said owners nor their guests may use the right-of-way nor the dock, runway, and float during such time as they are in violation of said restrictions.

26. Admit that the purpose of the language, set forth in Paragraph 22 of the Goldberg Counterclaim, was to benefit the Pierce heirs.

27. Admit that the Contract for Sale of Real Estate, by and between the Estate of William H. Pierce, Sr. and the Kennedys, expressly provided that a "Right-of-Way shall be granted to the owners of Lots 12 and 19 on the Boothbay Harbor Tax Map #13 and to the owners of Lots 12, 13, and 15 on Map #25 over a parcel of land 20' x 260' on lot #17 bounded on the southeast by Parcel 18 and on the northwest by Lot 17 extend 100' from the waters of Sexton Cove to the Town Road, including the use of the dock, float, and runway."

28. Admit that the right-of-way set forth in the contract, dated October 11, 1977, and attached to the Goldberg Counterclaim as Exhibit E, purports to benefit the property owned today by the Goldbergs.

29. Admit that the reference in the contract, dated October 11, 1977, and attached to the Goldberg Counterclaim on Exhibit E, to Map 13, Lot 12 refers to what is now the Goldberg property.

30. Admit that Clara C. Pierce died on April 25, 1961, leaving the property to the four children of William H. Pierce, Sr. and Clara C. Pierce: Philip C. Pierce, Margaret R. Harris, William H. Pierce, Jr. and Carolyn R. Stein (later to be known as Carolyn R. Simmons upon her marriage).

31. Admit that the heirs of Clara C. Pierce crossed over the property now owned by the Whipples and used the dock, runway, and float at issue.

32. Admit that on September 8, 1978, William H. Pierce, Jr., as one of the four heirs of Clara C. Pierce, conveyed his one-fourth interest in the "Swett Property" (see Exhibit D to the Goldberg Counterclaim), along with the purported easement, to Charlotte R. Blaney and Margaret Pierce.

33. Admit that the deed from William H. Pierce, Jr. to Charlotte R. Blaney and Margaret Pierce was recorded in the Lincoln County Registry of Deeds at Book 970, Page 276.

34. Admit that a true and accurate copy of the deed from William H. Pierce, Jr. to Charlotte R. Blaney and Margaret Pierce is attached to the Goldberg Counterclaim as Exhibit H.

35. Admit that the deed from William H. Pierce, Jr. to Charlotte R. Blaney and Margaret Pierce contains the following language:

> Meaning and intending to describe the same premises as Chester A. Swett conveyed to Clara C. Pierce by warranty deed dated October 24, 1939, and recorded in Lincoln County Registry of Deeds in Book 427, Page 458.
>
> Together with a certain right-of-way which is described as follows:
>
> A right-of-way running from the terminus of Cove Road, southwesterly to the wharf extending into Hodgdon's Cove, the southerly boundary of said way being a 12 foot parcel of land owned by Pomerantz and Ramsey and which extends S. 72° 38' W. two hundred eighty-six and one tenth (286.1) feet from a pipe in cement at said terminus, to a bolt in an off-shore ledge. The north boundary of said way begins at a pipe in rocks located N. 26° 28' E. and eleven and two tenths (11.2) feet from aforementioned pipe in cement and runs thence S. 72° 38' W. one hundred forty-four and two tenths (144.2) feet to a pipe in large rocks; thence S. 78° 04' W. eighty and eight tenths (80.8) feet to a pipe in rocks at high water mark, which pipe is also four and five tenths (4.5) feet northerly from the wharf.
>
> The right to maintain or replace the dock, runway, and float, within the westerly extension of the S. 78° 04' W. line, on the north, and the westerly extension of the S. 72° W. property line of the land herein conveyed, shall be a part of the right-of-way herein granted.
>
> The use of the above described right-of-way and the dock, runway, and float shall be restricted to the owner or owners of the premises described in the Deed of Chester A. Swett to Clara C. Pierce dated October 24, 1939, and recorded in Lincoln County Registry of Deeds, Book 427, Page 458, which owners currently are Philip C. Pierce, William H. Pierce, Jr., Margaret R. Harris, David Gordon Stein, Betty Stein Rosenberg, Carolyn Stein Hanson, and William Pierce Stein and their guests. The right-of-way and the use of the float, runway, and dock shall be subject to the following restrictions:

(1) There shall be no cutting of trees or bushes on said right-of-way without the permission, in writing, of the owners of the land over which the right-of-way passes.

(2) The right to the use of said right-of-way shall be by foot only.

(3) The routine maintenance of the dock, runway, and float shall be borne equally by the owners of Lot 12 and the owners of the land over which the right-of-way passes and any other users of said dock, runway, and float. See Boothbay Harbor Tax Map #13, Parcel #12.

(4) The owners of Lot 12 shall always hold harmless the owners of the land over which the right-of-way passes from any claim arising out of the use of said right-of-way, dock, runway, and float by the owners of Lot 12 and their guests.

(5) These restrictions shall be binding on any and all owners of Lot 12, provided, however, that neither said owners nor their guests may use the right-of-way nor the dock, runway, and float during such time as they are in violation of said restrictions.

36. Admit that on or about September 8, 1978, Charlotte R. Blaney; Margaret Pierce; Margaret R. Harris; Phillip C. Pierce (Margaret and Phillip being sister and brother of William M. Pierce); David G. Stein; Carolyn H. Hanson; William R. Stein (the last three being three of the four children of Carolyn R. Stein (Simmons), sister of William R. Pierce, Jr.) conveyed their interest to the "Swett Property" and the purported easement to Charles S. Yentsch and Clarice M. Yentsch.

37. Admit that the deed from Charlotte R. Blaney; Margaret Pierce; Margaret R. Harris; Phillip C. Pierce; David G. Stein; Carolyn H. Hanson; William R. Stein to Charles S. Yentsch and Clarice M. Yentsch was recorded in the Lincoln County Registry of Deeds at Book 970, Page 282.

38. Admit that a true and accurate copy of the deed from Charlotte R. Blaney; Margaret Pierce; Margaret R. Harris; Phillip C. Pierce; David G. Stein; Carolyn H. Hanson; William R. Stein to Charles S. Yentsch and Clarice M. Yentsch is attached to the Goldberg Counterclaim as Exhibit I.

39. Admit that on or about September 8, 1978, Betty H. Rosenberg, as the last of the four children of Carolyn R. Stein (Simmons), conveyed

all of her interest in the "Swett Property" and the purported easement to Charles S. Yentsch and Clarice M. Yentsch.

40. Admit that the deed from Betty H. Rosenberg to Charles S. Yentsch and Clarice M. Yentsch was recorded in the Lincoln County Registry of Deeds at Book 970, Page 279.

41. Admit that a true and accurate copy of the deed from Betty H. Rosenberg to Charles S. Yentsch and Clarice M. Yentsch is attached to the Goldberg Counterclaim as Exhibit J.

42. Admit that Charles S. Yentsch and Clarice M. Yentsch regularly crossed over the Whipple lot and used the dock, runway, and float at issue.

43. Admit that Suzanne R. Buchanan regularly crossed over the Whipples' property and used the dock, runway, and float.

44. Admit that Dr. Raymond Buchanan regularly crossed over the Whipples' property and used the dock, runway, and float.

45. Admit that, historically, improvements and maintenance of the dock, runway, and float at issue have been paid in equal amounts by the Whipples, the Goldbergs, other abutters, and their predecessors-in-interest.

46. Admit that the Goldbergs and their predecessors, the Buchanans, have used the dock, runway, and float at issue in this case and have paid their pro rata share of the cost of all improvements and maintenance to the dock, runway, and float.

47. Admit that on September 17, 1986, Ben's Boatyard sent Mr. Whipple a $21,300 proposal to replace the old dock, to build a new runway, to build a new float, and for other work.

48. Admit that the document, attached to the Goldberg Counterclaim as Exhibit N, is a true and accurate copy of a September 17, 1986, proposal from Ben's Boatyard to Bernard L. Whipple.

49. Admit that Bernard Whipple, Raymond E. Buchanan, and Peter Warren accepted the September 17, 1986, Ben's Boatyard proposal and each signed the contract with Ben's Boatyard.

50. Admit that a true and accurate copy of the contract executed by and between Ben's Boatyard, Bernard Whipple, Raymond E. Buchanan, and Peter Warren is attached to the Goldberg Counterclaim as Exhibit P.

51. Admit that Ben's Boatyard subsequently sent other bills to Raymond E. Buchanan and Peter Warren for dock improvements and maintenance.

52. Admit that the Goldbergs, or their predecessors-in-interest, always paid their pro rata share of all invoices for the cost of the dock improvements and maintenance.

53. Admit that on June 24, 2004, the Whipples forwarded bills for dock maintenance to their neighbors and asked that their neighbors pay their pro rata share of such maintenance.

54. Admit that a true and accurate copy of a letter which Bernard Whipple wrote to Peter Warren, dated June 24, 2004, is attached to the Goldberg Complaint as Exhibit Q.

55. Admit that Ben's Boatyard, for many years, improved, repaired, and maintained the dock, runway, and float at issue in this case.

56. Admit that the deed from the Executors of the Estate of William H. Pierce, Sr. to T. Scott Kennedy and Judith C. Kennedy, attached to the Goldberg Counterclaim as Exhibit C, purports to convey an easement over what is now the Whipple lot to the Goldberg lot.

57. Admit that Plaintiffs do not believe that the deed, attached to the Goldberg Counterclaim as Exhibit C, creates an easement because the beneficiaries of the purported easement were strangers to the deed.

58. Admit that, prior to 2004, Plaintiffs believed that Defendant Goldberg had an easement over their property to access the dock, runway, and float at issue in this case.

59. Admit that, prior to 2004, Defendant Goldberg paid his pro rata share of the cost of improving, preparing and maintaining the dock, runway, and float at issue in this case.

60. Admit that the statements in your lawyer's letter dated May 3, 2005, and attached to the Goldberg Counterclaim as Exhibit S, are accurate with respect to the Goldbergs and the Goldberg lot.

61. Admit that the documents, attached hereto as Exhibit C and bates-stamped KBL 1 through KBL 18, are true and accurate copies of invoices from Ben's Boatyard (other than the handwritten notes) related to the dock, runway, and float at issue in this case.

62. Admit that the survey, attached hereto as Exhibit D, is a true and accurate copy of a survey of Plaintiffs' property dated September 1985.

63. Admit that the survey, attached hereto as Exhibit D, was commissioned by the Plaintiffs.

STATE OF MIND DISTRICT COURT

MIND FOREST TRUST, Plaintiffs	))	
	)	
v.	)	CIVIL ACTION
	)	DOCKET NO. ______
JOAN BRONSON, *et al.*, Defendants	)))	

PLAINTIFF'S FIRST SET OF REQUESTS FOR ADMISSIONS TO PARTIES-IN-INTEREST DELMER J. BARK AND KELLY-JEAN BARK

Plaintiff Mind Forest Trust, by its undersigned counsel, requests and requires Parties-in-Interest Delmer J. Bark and Kelly-Jean Bark to respond to these Requests for Admissions pursuant to Rule 36 of the Mind Rules of Civil Procedure.

Instructions

a. Each Request for Admission should be answered separately and fully in writing. You must set forth each request in full immediately preceding your answer or objection thereto.

b. Each Request for Admission is deemed admitted unless, within 30 days after service of the Request for Admission, you serve upon the party requesting the admission a written answer or objection addressed to the matter, signed by you or your attorney.

c. If objection is made to any of the Requests for Admissions, the reasons therefore shall be stated. The answer shall specifically deny the matter set forth in detail or set forth in detail the reasons why you cannot truthfully admit or deny the matter. A denial shall fairly meet the substance of the requested admission, and when good faith requires that you qualify an answer or deny only a part of the matter for which an admission is requested, you shall specify so much of it as is true and qualify or deny the remainder.

d. You may not give lack of information or knowledge as a reason for failure to admit or deny unless you state that you have made reasonable inquiry and that the information known or readily obtainable by you is insufficient to enable you to admit or deny.

e. Pursuant to Rule 37(c), if you fail to admit the genuineness of any document or the truth of any matter as requested hereunder, and if the party requesting the admissions thereafter proves the genuineness of the document or the truth of the matter, the requesting party may apply to the Court for an order requiring you to pay the reasonable expenses incurred in making that proof, including reasonable attorney's fees.

Definitions

a. "Writ of Execution" means the Writ of Execution, dated November 23, 2004, and recorded by you in the Hancock Registry of Deeds at Book 4074, Page 75.

b. "Property" means the land on Beaver Dam Road in Bar Harbor, Mind, at issue in this case, which was purchased by Defendant Joan Bronson on November 22, 2005.

c. "Mortgage" means the Mortgage, secured by the Property, which Defendant Joan Bronson gave to Plaintiff on December 12, 2006, and which is the subject of the above-referenced foreclosure action.

Request for Admissions

1. Admit that you recovered a judgment against Defendant Joan Bronson and W. David Andrews, II, on September 14, 2004, in the Mind Superior Court for Waldo County, Docket No. RE 2004-001 (the "Judgment").

2. Admit that the Judgment arose as a result of the failure of Defendant Joan Bronson and W. David Andrews II to pay a mortgage on property located at 175 Sand Point Road in Bar Harbor, Mind.

3. Admit that you filed a Writ of Execution against Defendant Joan Bronson and W. David Andrews II after obtaining the Judgment.

4. Admit that you obtained a Writ of Execution against Defendant Joan Bronson and W. David Andrews II arising from the Judgment on November 23, 2004 (the "Writ of Execution").

5. Admit that a true and accurate copy of your Writ of Execution, dated November 23, 2004, is attached hereto as Exhibit A.

6. Admit that your Writ of Execution on Defendant Joan Bronson and W. David Andrews II was recorded at the Hancock Registry of Deeds on November 23, 2004, at Book 4074, Page 75.

7. Admit that you obtained an Order Approving Attachment and Trustee Process against Defendant Joan Bronson and W. David Andrews II on September 13, 2005.

8. Admit that a true and accurate copy of the Order Approving Attachment and Trustee Process is attached hereto as Exhibit B.

9. Admit that the Order Approving Attachment and Trustee Process was recorded in the Hancock County Registry of Deeds on September 15, 2005, at Book 4294, Page 212.

10. Admit that the Order Approving Attachment and Trustee Process is related to the case in which the Writ of Execution was obtained.

11. Admit that Defendant Joan M. Bronson bought property on Beaver Dam Road in Bar Harbor, Mind, on November 22, 2005 (the "Property").

12. Admit that a true and accurate copy of the Quitclaim Deed with Covenant, wherein Defendant Joan M. Bronson purchased the Property, is attached hereto as Exhibit C.

13. Admit that Defendant Joan Bronson's deed for the Property is recorded at the Hancock Registry of Deeds at Book 4353, Page 133.

14. Admit that Defendant Joan M. Bronson mortgaged the Property to Plaintiff Mind Forest Trust on December 12, 2006 (the "Mortgage").

15. Admit that a true and accurate copy of Defendant Joan M. Bronson's mortgage of the Property to Plaintiff Mind Forest Trust is attached hereto as Exhibit D.

16. Admit that Defendant Joan M. Bronson's Mortgage to Plaintiff Mind Forest Trust is recorded at the Hancock Registry of Deeds at Book 4659, Page 215.

17. Admit that the foreclosure of the Property is the subject of Plaintiff's claim in the above-captioned matter.

18. Admit that you are claiming in this foreclosure case that your Writ of Execution, attached hereto as Exhibit A, has a higher priority than Defendant Bronson's Mortgage to the Plaintiff, a copy of which is attached hereto as Exhibit D.

19. Admit that both the Writ of Execution (dated November 23, 2004) and the Order Approving Attachment and Trustee Process (dated

September 12, 2005) were recorded in the Hancock County Registry of Deeds before Defendant Joan Bronson purchased the Property on Beaver Dam Road in Bar Harbor, Mind.

20. Admit that you did not record any liens, attachments, judgments, writs, or other encumbrances on the Property between the time it was purchased on November 22, 2005, and the date it was mortgaged to Plaintiff Mind Forest Trust on December 12, 2006.

21. Admit that you re-recorded your Writ of Execution, dated November 23, 2004, on June 7, 2007.

22. Admit that a true and accurate copy of the re-recorded Writ of Execution is attached hereto as Exhibit E.

23. Admit that the re-recorded Writ of Execution was recorded at the Hancock County Registry of Deeds at Book 4778, Page 316.

24. Admit that you re-recorded the Writ of Attachment so that it would encumber properties purchased by Defendant Joan Bronson and W. David Andrews II, after the date of the original recording of the Writ of Execution.

25. Admit that the re-recorded Writ of Execution was filed in the Hancock County Registry of Deeds after Plaintiff recorded its Mortgage on the Property on Beaver Dam Road in Bar Harbor, Mind.

26. Admit that the Plaintiff's Mortgage has a higher priority, in connection with Plaintiff's foreclosure proceeding on the Property at issue in this case, than your Writ of Execution or Order Approving Attachment and Trustee Process.

Responding to a Request for Admissions

In responding to a request for admissions, you must admit or deny each admission or explain in detail why you cannot admit or deny it. If the reason for failure to admit or deny is a lack of information, you must make a diligent effort to gather the information before you make such a response:

> After a reasonable inquiry was conducted of all information within her custody or control, Defendant Joan Bronson cannot admit or deny Request for Admission No. 1 due to a lack of information.

Objections to requests for admissions are appropriate based on relevance, privilege, or the aforementioned objections. However, given the binding effect of admissions and the risk that an improperly answered admission may be deemed admitted, this may not be a wise course.

CHAPTER 11

Depositions

Faith is a fine invention
When Gentlemen can see
But Microscopes are prudent
In an Emergency
—Emily Dickinson

Once you have mentioned the documents and received fully responsive interrogatory answers and admissions, the next step is taking depositions. A deposition is where a person or corporate representative is placed under oath and required to orally respond to questions asked by the attorney. A transcript of all questions and answers is made by a court reporter.

TAKING THE DEPOSITION

The purpose of depositions is to obtain detailed information, to anticipate what the witness will say at trial, to obtain admissions, and to nail down the deponent's testimony for summary judgment and trial. The deposition will also give you advance notice of a witness's mannerisms and credibility at trial.

Before launching into depositions, draft a detailed deposition plan. Take careful stock of your case. Review the story, documents, and all of the other side's responses to your interrogatories and requests for admissions. Make a careful list of everything that remains to be proven or discredited. Beside each point, identify the witness or witnesses who are going to accomplish this task.

Depositions are very expensive. Determine a reasonable deposition budget before beginning. Younger litigators often make the mistake of spending more on depositions than is warranted by the value of the case, or by the property at issue. Cost parameters, therefore, need to be worked out prior to undertaking these examinations.

Many lawyers who take and defend depositions like to videotape the proceedings. In real estate trials—where the deponent is likely to be available for trial—this is not generally worth the additional expense. Use videotaping where the witness will not be available or where credibility is a big issue.

Try to avoid deposing witnesses who are *not* hostile to your case. Deposing an independent witness has the adverse effect of prematurely identifying the witness, preparing the other side on what the witness will say, and exposing that person's relative strengths and weaknesses. It also gives the other side an advanced opportunity to cross-examine the witness.

Accordingly, if the witness is in-state or available for trial, interview the witness outside of the presence of your opponent. If the witness is willing, ask him to sign a statement or affidavit setting forth the beneficial facts in your case. The existence of such an affidavit gives you extra comfort that the witness will stick to the story. In the unfortunate event that the witness changes the story at trial, use the statement or affidavit for impeachment.

In making the decision to launch into depositions, it is important to consider the order in which they will be taken. Start with people who are less important and less biased. This will enable you to get a clearer picture of the facts, given that there is a lesser risk of the witness hiding the truth or being evasive. The beginning deponents should also be people who would likely be more forthcoming and generous in filling in factual blanks, i.e., people with less at stake to lose.

End with the more important deponents—the opposing parties and their expert witnesses. Before taking these depositions, you may want to obtain questions and themes from your experts, or have your experts present at these depositions. Assume, for example, that you are in a dispute as to whether an old, ambiguous shore easement gives the holder the right to construct a dock. You should begin by interviewing and/or deposing predecessors-in-title and neighbors about the historical use of the easement and what the original parties intended. You should end by deposing the opposing party and his surveyor or title expert. At these later depositions, try to pin down the opponent into an admission that there has historically been a dock at the end of the easement.

Make an outline of your questions prior to the deposition. Plan to explore as many points as possible with the witness, given that witness's factual knowledge and experience.

Start the deposition with general concepts. Ask nonspecific open-ended questions:

- What is your full name?
- What is your address?
- Are you represented by a lawyer here today?
- Do you have problems hearing or understanding questions?
- Have you ever been deposed before?
- When?
- Ever given other testimony under oath?
- Describe your educational background.
- Briefly describe your work history.

At the beginning of the deposition, you are seeking to build rapport with the deponent. You want to build a relationship with him. You ask a question and get an answer. You ask another question and get an answer. Question. Answer. Question. Answer. Build a rhythm and a limited relationship of trust. Get the deponent in the habit of responding to your questions so that you can move in for the "kill" by putting words in his mouth:

- You bought your property five years ago, did you not?
- The property you bought five years ago has ten acres of land, right?
- Would it be correct to say that the property you bought ten years ago has 1,000 feet of road frontage on Route 1?
- Last year, you sold three of your ten acres to Mr. Finiker, correct?
- It would be fair to say, would it not, that the property that you sold to Mr. Finiker does not have any road frontage on Route 1?
- In fact, the property you sold to Mr. Finiker does not have frontage on any public road, right?
- So, it would be fair to say that you sold Mr. Finiker a landlocked piece of property, correct?

The best way to put words in a deponent's mouth is to use deeds, surveys, and other documents in your deposition outline. To save time, include three copies of each of the deposition exhibits with your deposition outline. The first copy of the deposition exhibit should have your questions written right on it, and the key words underlined. The second copy of the exhibit is to mark and show the witness. The third copy of the exhibit is a courtesy copy for your opposing counsel. With the actual documents in front of everyone, it is much easier to guide the deponent into giving exact answers which you want:

- I am handing you a document that has been marked Deposition Exhibit 1. Is Deposition Exhibit 1 a true and accurate copy of the Purchase and Sale Agreement that you signed on October 1, 2009?
- That's your signature on page 4, is it not?
- Would it be fair to say that you read and reviewed the entire contract before you signed it?
- Turning your attention to Paragraph 3, you expressly agreed to buy the office building at 111 Commercial Street, did you not?
- Paragraph 7 says, does it not, that you will close the purchase within ten days?
- You specifically agreed, in Paragraph 4, to pay $3,700,000 for the office building, correct?
- You never paid this money, did you?
- It says, in Paragraph 3, that my client has the right to specifically perform the contract, does it not?
- Now, Paragraph 5 of the Agreement you signed says that—if you default on this agreement—my client can sue you for legal fees, correct?

Make sure that the questions and answers are clear, concise, and unambiguous. Confusing questions—and vague answers—are not useful at trial.

Note that the "admission" or "pinning down" questions call for a "Yes" or "No" response. This is because you are pushing words into the deponent's mouth—for later use at summary judgment and trial.

In order to discover facts and fill in gaps, it is best to proceed chronologically through events. Questions and deposition exhibits should flow in the order that the events occurred. This puts the witness at ease and generally produces the greatest amount of factual information.

When the witness says something important to your case, it is a good idea to summarize the statement and get the witnesses to agree that your summary is correct. Other exercises in gathering admissions from the witness, however, need not be chronological. You should spring these on the witness before he is ready for them. **Note**: For an admission to be effective, it is a must that it be specific and clear. Avoid compound questions and multiple phrases.

DEFENDING THE DEPOSITION

Obviously, you need to be very cognizant of these techniques when *defending* a deposition. Spend a lot of time preparing your client. The following is a checklist of items to discuss with the deponent-to-be:

Questions

Answers Under Oath

- Court reporter
- Prior deposition experience
- Prior courtroom experience
- Medical problems
- Hearing problems
- Drugs affecting memory, speech
- Listen carefully to questions
    - Can take breaks (after answer)
    - No hurry
    - Hear/Understand/Don't know
- Don't volunteer
- Don't allow rapport
- Don't get angry
- Types of objections
    - Protect record
    - Don't answer
- Don't let them put words in your mouth
    - Careful saying "yes" or "no"
    - Use your own words
    - Don't say "Absolutely"
    - No jokes
    - No snide comments
    - Straightforward answers

- Do not bring papers or files with you
- Go through themes of the case
- Anything you do not want asked?
  - Skeletons in the closet?
  - Criminal issues?

Explain how the deposition works. Opposing counsel will be asking questions. You will be sitting next to your client. The client will be answering the questions under oath. A court reporter and/or videographer will be recording everything. Take time to make sure that the deponent understands the entire process.

Spend time going through all of the deponent's prior depositions and courtroom experiences. Determine whether there is any prior sworn testimony that can be used to contradict or impeach the witness's position in the case. Learn whether there is any witness statement or any affidavits that could be characterized as a problem.

Discuss whether there are any medical problems or any other issues that may pose a problem at the deposition. Does the witness have any problems with hearing? Is one ear better than the other? Does the witness take any medications that could affect memory or speech?

Advise the deponent to listen very carefully to each question of the opposing counsel. Assuming that the deposition is not videotaped, the deponent should be counseled to take his time to answer a question. The deponent should never substantively answer a question that is not heard. If the witness cannot hear the question, the only appropriate answer is "I did not hear the question." Many witnesses with hearing problems are embarrassed about their medical condition. They attempt to fill in words or guess at the question asked. This is very dangerous in a deposition. If the deponent does not fully and completely hear a question, emphasize that there is nothing wrong with saying so.

Similarly, a witness should never provide a substantive answer to a question that is not fully understood. The only proper answer to a question not fully understood is "I do not understand the question. Would you kindly rephrase it?" As with hearing problems, many witnesses do not want to admit that they do not understand every question. This leads to providing an answer that is not meant to go with the question. There have been many instances where a witness gave a positive answer to a question that he would have answered negatively had he fully understood the question.

You should also counsel your client not to answer questions to which he does not know the answer. If your client does not, in fact, know the answer, the only truthful and appropriate answer is "I do not know." While there are isolated situations in which not knowing an answer can make the deponent look silly or can be damaging, a truthful answer of "I do not know," under most circumstances, will not hurt the case.

The deponent must thoroughly understand that before answering a question, he must (1) hear the question; (2) understand the question; and (3) know the answer. Advise your client to pause before answering each question and consider these issues. You should further explain that *you* need this hesitation in order to have the opportunity to object to questions that are vague, ambiguous, lacking foundation, or eliciting privileged information. Explain that in order for you to do your job, the client needs to do his part.

In addition, it is important to emphasize to the deponent that he must answer questions in his own words and must not volunteer information. A simple answer of "yes" or "no" allows the opposing party to lead the witness and put words in his mouth. The witness should be trained to truthfully answer the question briefly, in his own words, and then stop. While there is a natural tendency of a nice person to volunteer information, the deponent should be carefully cautioned against doing so at the deposition. Volunteered information can only hurt one's case. A deposition is not the time to go into detail espousing a party's position or to recite your persuasive case. While a trial is to provide a person with his day in court, a deposition is for one thing and one thing only: to damage your case. Volunteering information can hurt; at best, it leads to many more questions.

As set forth above, a well-prepared opposing attorney will work hard at the beginning of every deposition to build a wonderful rapport with your client. With the rapport in place, a typical deponent can be led by the nose within twenty minutes. Do not let this happen. If you need to call a break in the deposition, do so at an appropriate moment. Make sure your client sticks to the true and accurate story, and does not allow anyone to "lead" the testimony.

After failing to build a rapport, the skillful deposition taking attorney may then attempt to make the deponent angry. An angry deponent does the one thing you cannot allow a deponent to do: fail to think. Make sure that your client never becomes angry or disoriented. Again, if your client is not thinking, take a break at an appropriate moment.

You should also ensure that the deponent is intimately versed in every detail of the story. Do *not* assume that just because your client knows the story—and because it is true—that every detail has sunk into his skin. Once the "bright lights" of the deposition or trial have begun, the average person becomes flustered in the new setting. Even the best-known aspects of the story become murky. You have probably seen children who spent hours memorizing lines to a play only to forget everything when it came time for a public performance. This is all too common with an unprepared client, but preventable with careful presentation and pre-deposition practice.

One last objective in preparing a witness for a deposition: Check for surprises. Give the witness a confidential opportunity to disclose embarrassing details such as prior criminal activities. This will give you a chance to head the problem off at the deposition, or to have the information disclosed in a better light.

At the deposition itself, you are not a potted plan (as attorney Brendon Sullivan became famous for stating during his defense of Colonel Oliver North's examination before a congressional committee). You should interpose objections to questions that are vague, ambiguous, confusing, misleading, or lacking in foundation. Objections to these types of questions are simply to "protect the record" so that the deponent's answers cannot be automatically used at trial. For example, consider the question: "Isn't it true that the boundary is clear?" This could mean clear in the deed or clear on the face of the earth. If it is clear in the deed—but not on the face of the earth—a "Yes" answer to this ambiguous question could seriously hurt your case. Interpose an objection before the witness responds, so that the ambiguity of the question can be dealt with by the court before the other side uses it as an admission at trial. The failure to do so waives the objection.

These objections should be brief and to the point: "Objection. Ambiguous question." Lawyers sometimes improperly make a "speaking" objection such as "your question is putting words into my client's mouth. We all know that the boundary on the face of the earth is badly monumented." These speaking objections inappropriately warn the client what not to say at the deposition. They should be rarely made, if ever. The attorney taking the deposition should consider an immediate call to the court seeking an order to prevent speaking objections and/or sanctions.

The defending attorney may also instruct his client not to answer a question that violates privilege or is otherwise outrageous. These objections are reserved for situations where the deponent is your client. If your client is asked at a deposition about confidential conversations between the two of you, you should grab your client's arm and instruct him not to answer. The examiner, if he wishes to press the issue, should ask the witness whether he intends to follow this instruction. This will create a record that the examiner can then bring to the court's attention for a ruling.

At the conclusion of the deposition, the court reporter will ask if the deponent wants to read and sign the deposition. The answer is always "Yes." After the deposition transcript is prepared, you will have a set period of time to review it. Both the lawyer and the deponent should carefully review the transcript. As the deposition is under oath, you should also correct any inaccurate answers. It is far better to correct a wrong answer than to leave it standing for summary judgment or trial. The other side can, of course, impeach the witness at trial for changing answers after the transcript has been reviewed.

CHAPTER 12

The Motion for Summary Judgment

Invincibility lies in the defense; the possibility of victory in the attack.
—Sun Tzu

Most real estate cases have enough undisputed facts for a whole or partial Motion for Summary Judgment. If you have a good motion, you should file it. If you win, you avoid or reduce the high cost of trial. If you lose, you have simply paid to prepare for trial a little early. With a good motion, you have also educated the judge to your issues and—with a strong motion—there is little loss of momentum.

The following items are often ripe for a motion for summary judgment:

- Enforcement of an unambiguous purchase and sale agreement
- Enforcement of an unambiguous easement
- Enforcement of an unambiguous right of access
- Determination of an easement by necessity
- Interpretation of a deed
- Dismissal of a late-filed or unperfected lien
- Dismissal of a time-barred cause of action

Even where the entire case is not susceptible to a Motion for Summary Judgment on all issues, it generally makes sense to file a Partial Motion for Summary Judgment on issues that are winnable as a matter of law. A partial victory saves time, saves trial cost, and has the effect on momentum of steamrollering the other side's confidence and chances of winning.

Once you have decided that a motion for summary judgment is likely to be a good idea, sketch out every issue on which you have a good chance of winning—and then immediately gather together the facts and law that support the undisputed facts and law that supports your position. The sources of facts are the following:

- Statements in an answer admitting allegations in the complaint
- The opponent's statements in any pleading
- Documents that have been authenticated as part of an answer to the complaint or a request for admissions, or at a deposition
- Interrogatory answers
- Responses to a request for admissions
- Affidavits

Gathering these facts should not be a problem since proving the story has been your top priority from the moment you started gathering your experts and drafting your complaint. If you have been consistent, these admissions should fall right into your lap.

Carefully sketch out the factual and legal arguments for the motion for summary judgment before gathering all of the proof. You must determine exactly what you need for facts and law before completing the writing. Often, experienced real estate litigation attorneys pull together all of the facts and try to cram them into an uncoordinated motion. Sketch out the motion. Determine the exact factual and legal elements for each claim. After ensuring that you have obtained what you need, draft the motion.

As with your complaint, the motion for summary judgment should have a very powerful first paragraph, or "press release." The first paragraph should simply and clearly express to the court what you want—and why you should get it: "The Defendant has wrongfully blocked the access to the home of Sam and Sherry Milner. The undisputed deeds in this case clearly demonstrate, as a matter of law, that the Milners have a clear and ambiguous easement to their home, over the Defendant's property. The Milners request that the Court grant their Motion for Summary Judgment and declare that the Milners have an unambiguous right, under the easement, to use the driveway to their home."

The motion should then dive into the facts. The facts are based on your story. As with any well-written story, the facts should be easy and enjoyable to read. Keep the sentences short, and use power writing. Stay away from complicated clauses as often as possible. Begin with nouns and move quickly to verbs. If this seems confusing, read a novel or short story by Ernest Hemingway before drafting a motion for summary judgment in a real estate case.

The Facts section or story is, by far, the most important part of the motion for summary judgment. This is where the court will make its initial decision. While it is true that law professors always teach that the decision should be made on the law and legal precedents, it is more true that judges are human. As with all people, they make decisions based on the facts and based on fundamental fairness. Most judges will quietly tell you that it is the facts that win a case—as long as there is enough law upon which to hang one's hat.

In short, the Facts portion of the Motion for Summary Judgment should read like a well-written story. It should be easy and stimulating to read. It should be convincing and persuasive, without embellishment or exaggeration.

Every sentence of the Facts portion of the brief should cite to a source. If your jurisdiction requires the use of a Statement of Material Facts, a cite to the Statement should be at the end of every factual sentence. If your jurisdiction does not require a Statement of Material Facts, there should be a cite at the end of every sentence in the Facts to an admission, deposition statement, or other authoritative fact.

Note: Put the Facts in regular type (except to emphasize) and the authorities in italics. This way, the judge understands and appreciates that your facts are well documented, without disturbing the flow of the brief. The judge's eyes can easily jump over the italicized portions of the brief, and his clerk can later go back and check to ensure that each cite is authoritatively supported.

As set forth above, you want the judge to be well in your camp by the time he reads the facts. However, the judge is presumably well trained and is going to want to see enough law to know that his tentative decision, based on the facts, is well grounded.

The next section of the brief will be on the law. The Law section is where you document that your facts are, based on the law, sufficient to win your case.

Present the key statutes and cases clearly. After each important case, devote at least one paragraph to plainly expressing how the facts of that case are analogous to the issue before the Court.

You do not need to have a lot of law. In real estate cases, it is more important to have cases that are on point. Given the age of many real estate principles, courts are generally not deterred by older precedents, as the black letter law, in some real estate areas, has been consistent for a substantial period of time.

As a general rule in real estate cases, cite to the case in the jurisdiction that is more on point, and cite to a case in any jurisdiction that has virtually identical facts and a holding that is consistent with the results you are seeking.

Again, brevity and straightforwardness are well received by the courts in real estate litigation. Use the Facts portion of the brief to sell your case. Use the Law portion of the brief to let the judge know that his initial impression from the Facts portion is correct. The following exemplars of Motions for Summary Judgment are set forth on the next few pages:

- Easement by Necessity/Implied Quasi-Easement
- Chain of Title
- Public Ways/Prescriptive Easements/Abandonment

EASEMENT BY NECESSITY

STATE OF MIND SUPERIOR COURT

MICHAEL A. LITZ and	)	
MARGARET M. SUSHIMI,	)	
Plaintiffs	)	
	)	
v.	)	
	)	CIVIL ACTION NO.
ANTHONY J. NIXON and	)	
BONNIE NIXON,	)	
Defendants	)	
	)	

PLAINTIFFS' MOTION FOR SUMMARY JUDGMENT ON COUNT I AND ON DEFENDANT'S COUNTERCLAIM

Defendant Anthony J. Nixon claims that he has an easement by necessity and/or implied easement over the property of Plaintiffs Michael A. Litz and Margaret M. Sushimi by virtue of a 1957 deed in which his grandmother, and predecessor-in-title, landlocked herself by selling her road frontage on Route 302 in Naples to Plaintiffs' predecessor-in-title. Defendant's grandmother, however, un-landlocked herself in 1958 by purchasing abutting property along Route 11 in Naples. Mr. Litz and Ms. Sushimi move this Court to declare, as a matter of law, that any easement by necessity and/or implied easement held by Marjorie D. Nixon in 1957 was fully extinguished by her subsequent purchase in 1958 and that the Defendant has no easement over their property.

I. The Facts

Plaintiffs Michael A. Litz and Margaret M. Sushimi own property at the corner of State Routes 302 and 11 in Naples. *Plaintiffs' Statement of Undisputed Material Facts in Support of Plaintiffs' Motion for Summary Judgment on Count I and on Defendant's Counterclaim (the "Statement") ¶¶ 10, 11.* Defendant Anthony J. Nixon owns land behind the property of Mr. Litz and Ms. Sushimi (the "back property"). *Statement ¶¶ 13, 19, 29.* Mr. Nixon claims that he has an easement by necessity or implied easement over the property of Mr. Litz and Ms. Sushimi to Route 302. *Statement ¶¶ 1–7.* This claim to an easement is wholly derived from the fact that Marjorie D. Nixon, Anthony Nixon's grandmother and predecessor-in-title, landlocked herself in 1957. *Statement ¶ 5.* Mr. Litz and Ms. Sushimi move this Court to declare that any easement by necessity or implied easement was extinguished, as a matter of law, when Marjorie D. Nixon, in 1958, purchased an abutting property with plentiful road frontage on State Route 11.

The story begins in 1957. Early in 1957, Marjorie D. Nixon owned property, including some of the property now owned by Mr. Litz and Ms. Sushimi, in Naples. *Statement ¶¶ 12, 13, 18.* On May 16, 1957, Marjorie D. Nixon sold the portion of her property that abutted State Route 302. *Statement ¶ 13.* As a result of this conveyance, her "back property" was landlocked—in other words, she had no access to either State Route 11 or to State Route 302. *Statement ¶ 13.*

On March 28, 1958, Marjorie D. Nixon purchased property adjoining her existing "back property" in Naples. *Statement ¶¶ 14, 17.* This adjoining property contained seventy-five feet of road frontage on State Route 11. *Statement ¶¶ 15, 16.* In other words, Marjorie D. Nixon's so-called "back property" or "landlocked" land (now owned by Defendant Anthony J. Nixon) was *not* landlocked as of March 28, 1958. *Statement ¶¶ 13–19.* Specifically, Marjorie D. Nixon, after March 28, 1958, could readily and sufficiently access her "back property" by driving from State Route 11 over the property that she purchased on that date. *Statement ¶¶ 20–21.* As a result of a series of conveyances in April, July, and November of 1965, Marjorie D. Nixon acquired an additional twenty-one feet of frontage on Route 11, thus increasing her total Route 11 frontage to ninety-six feet. *Statement ¶¶ 22–25.* In fact, Marjorie D. Nixon's July 20, 1965 deed also contains an express right-of-way that goes from State Route 11 to the "back property":

> Together with right-of-way over and along the westerly side of the property conveyed to the said Marjorie D. Nixon by Flagg Lumber, Inc. in its latest deed to wit: April 26, 1965, said right-of-way to permit these Grantees, their heirs, successors, and assigns the right of ingress and egress over and along a road and drive as presently laid out along and across the said westerly portion of the land of this Grantor.

Statement ¶ 23.

Thus, any easement by necessity, created by Margaret D. Nixon's actions in landlocking herself in 1957, was *extinguished* when she purchased abutting property with ample road frontage on State Route 11.

Defendant Anthony J. Nixon is the current owner of his grandmother's "back property." He obtained this property from his grandmother on June 21, 1994. *Statement ¶¶ 13, 19, 30.* Anthony J. Nixon acknowledges that his grandmother purchased abutting property in 1958 and acknowledges that this abutting property has frontage on State Route 11. *Statement ¶¶ 15–18, 26.* However, Anthony J. Nixon contends that passage from the "back property" to the abutting property on State Route 11 is blocked by a brook. *Statement ¶ 32.*

The fact that there is a brook on the subject property does not, in any way, mean that access from State Route 11 to the "back property" is not readily or sufficiently accessible. *Statement ¶ 33.* In fact, the brook can be readily and sufficiently crossed by means of a culvert, and the cost of this culvert would be a relatively minor expense of the overall development of the property. *Statement ¶ 34.*

All of the deeds demonstrate that the property purchased by Marjorie D. Nixon on March 28, 1958, enabled her to obtain direct access to and from State Route 11, a public way, to her "back property" without the need to trespass on the land of any third party. *Statement ¶¶ 14–17, 20–21.*

The boundary between the parties in this case is covered by trees and undergrowth except for a small portion of a gravel parking lot which extends onto the Defendant's property. *Statement ¶ 37.* There is absolutely no evidence on the face of the earth indicating a road or a path from the Defendant's property, over Plaintiffs' property, to State Route 302. *Statement ¶ 38.* There is also no evidence of any pathways, roads, tracks, or indentations in the ground or any clearing of undergrowth that would suggest vehicular or other usage, crossing from Defendant Anthony Nixon's property, to State Route 302. *Statement ¶ 39.* Mr. Nixon has never built anything on the "back property." *Statement ¶ 31.*

Mr. Litz and Ms. Sushimi are currently trying to sell their property in Naples, Mind, to C.N. Brown Company *Statement ¶ 40.* This sale is subject to the approval by the Town of Naples of a site review plan. *Statement ¶ 41.* Defendant Anthony J. Nixon is attempting to hold up this sale by extorting money from the Plaintiffs.

Specifically, Mr. Nixon's counsel has copied C.N. Brown's counsel on a letter claiming that Nixon has an easement running through the middle of the property. *Statement ¶ 42.* Mr. Nixon has also challenged the site plan review based on the alleged easement. *Statement ¶ 43.* The Naples Board of Appeals, however, ruled against Mr. Nixon. *Statement ¶ 44.* There is no grant of any easement recorded at the Cumberland County Registry of Deeds.

II. The Law

The Defendant Has Wrongfully Claimed That He Has an Easement by Necessity and/or Implied Easement Over the Property of Mr. Litz and Ms. Sushimi

There are two kinds of implied easements under the law. *Taylor v. Nutter*, 687 A.2d, 632, 636 (Me. 1996); *Frederick v. Consolidated Waste Services, Inc.*, 573 A.2d 387, 389 (Me. 1990); *Bowers v. Andrews*, 557 A.2d 606, 609 (Me. 1989). The first type of implied easement is an easement by necessity. *Frederick*, 573 A.2d at 389; *Bowers*, 557 A.2d at 609. This implied easement is created by strict necessity and arises when a common grantor conveys a lot that is landlocked by the grantor's surrounding land, and cannot be accessed by a road or highway. *Frederick*, 573 A.2d at 389; *Bowers*, 557 A.2d at 609. Under the law, an easement by necessity lasts only so long as the necessity lasts, and is extinguished when the necessity ends. *LeMay v. Anderson*, 397 A.2d 984, 989 (Me. 1979); *Rumill v. Robbins*, 77 Me. 193, 195 (Me. 1885).

The second type of an implied easement is a quasi-easement. The quasi-easement can be implied "when a common grantor severs real estate, conveying part of it and retaining the balance . . . and the circumstances at the time of the conveyance denote the grantor's intent to subject the retained land (the servient estate) to an easement benefiting the conveyed land (the dominant estate)." *Frederick v. Consolidated Waste Services, Inc.*, 573 A.2d 387, 389 (Me. 1990); quoting *Bowers v. Andrews*, 557 A.2d, 606, 609 (Me. 1989); *see also Robinson v. Mind Central Railroad Co.*, 623 A.2d 626, 627 (Me. 1993). This type of an easement has not been alleged by Defendant Anthony Nixon.

In the present case, Nixon's claim to an easement by necessity and/or implied easement is based upon the same thing: Marjorie D. Nixon's landlocking of her own property in 1957. The resulting implied easement by necessity lasted until 1958, when her purchase of abutting property extinguished the easement as a matter of law.

Nixon's Claim to An Implied Easement by Necessity Fails, as a Matter of Law, Because the Necessity Terminated in 1958

An easement by necessity is, as set forth above, one type of an implied easement. *Morrell v. Rice*, 622 A.2d, 1156, 1158 (Me. 1993). "An easement by necessity is created only when: (1) a grantor conveys a parcel of land out of a larger, divided parcel; (2) the conveyed lot is 'landlocked' by the grantor's surrounding land; and (3) relief in the form of an easement across the grantor's land is available." *Jordan v. Shea*, 2002 ME 36, ¶ 26; citing *Shadan v. Town of Skowhegan*, 1997 Me. 187, ¶¶ 8–9; *Amodeo v. Francis*, 681 A.2d, 462, 465 (Me. 1996).

The key to an easement by necessity is that the grantor or seller must, at the time of the conveyance, have conveyed to the buyer a lot "that is 'landlocked' by the grantor's surrounding land and cannot be accessed from a road or highway." *Shadan v. Town of Skowhegan*, 1997 ME 187, ¶ 8.

The law is also unequivocal that an easement by necessity terminates when the necessity is extinguished. *LeMay v. Anderson*, 397 A.2d, 984, 989 (Me. 1979); *Whitehouse v. Cummings*, 83 Me. 91, 98 (Me. 1890); *Rumill v. Robbins*, 77 Me. 193, 195 (Me. 1885); *see also* 25 Am. Jur. 2d *Easements* § 108, at 679 (1996) ("an easement of necessity lasts only as long as the necessity continues.").

The Supreme Court has made it crystal clear that termination of the necessity extinguishes the easement: "The recognized rule in Mind with respect to ways of necessity is that termination of the necessity extinguishes the easement." *LeMay*, 397 A.2d at 989.

In *LeMay*, the parties claiming an easement by strict necessity subsequently acquired abutting land that would allow them to build a road from their landlocked land, over the new property, to the public highway. The Court found that this "forecloses a finding of strict necessity." *Id.* at 989 (reiterating that an easement of necessity terminates when the necessity is extinguished).

Similarly, the Supreme Court in *Rumill* also set forth that the ending of the necessity terminates the easement by necessity. In that case, a landlocked property owner claimed an easement by necessity over his neighbor's land. The municipality subsequently laid out a public way to the property owner's land. The Court held that the connecting of the formerly landlocked property to a public way, ends any right-of-way by necessity. *Rumill*, 77 Me. at 195.

It is the inescapable conclusion of these precedents that the acquisition of road-accessible adjoining property, by the owner of a landlocked parcel, will extinguish an easement by necessity. Because the law sanctions such easements only where there is a strict necessity for their existence, it logically follows that the easement terminates when the strict necessity is alleviated.

This is exactly the situation with the case at bar. Marjorie Nixon, in 1957, landlocked herself by selling off all of her frontage on State Route 302. At the time, she could have conceivably claimed an easement by necessity over the property she had sold.[1] Subsequently, Mrs. Nixon purchased an abutting property in 1958 which provided her with access to State Route 11. Her seventy-five feet of frontage on State Route 11 was increased to ninety-six feet in 1965. Thus, Marjorie Nixon's purchase of abutting property—with ample frontage on a public way—*extinguished* any easement of necessity which may have been created in 1957. Accordingly, Defendant Anthony J. Nixon, Marjorie D. Nixon's grandson and successor-in-title, cannot have an easement by necessity over Mr. Litz and Ms. Sushimi, who are successors-in-title to the Route 302 frontage sold by Marjorie Nixon in 1957. There was then, and is now, direct non-trespassory access to and from State Route 11, for the remainder of Marjorie D. Nixon's property, across the parcel acquired in 1958.

Defendant seeks to derail the clear extinction of the easement by necessity by alleging that there is a brook between the "back property" which Marjorie D. Nixon retained in 1957 and the abutting property, with Route 11 frontage, she purchased in 1958. The presence of such a brook, however, does not circumvent the extinction of the necessity. Courts have constantly reiterated that a necessity must be based on *strict* necessity, and not a mere convenience.

An easement by necessity will not be granted unless there is a *strict* necessity of access to the landlocked parcel over the grantor's remaining land. *Shadan v. Town of Skowhegan*, 1997 ME 187, ¶ 9, citing *Morrell v. Rice*, 622 A.2d, 1156, 1158 (Me. 1993); *see also Frederick v. Consolidated Waste Services, Inc.*, 573 A.2d 387, 389 (Me. 1990) (an easement

1. At common law, only the grantee could claim an implied easement, not the grantor who carelessly landlocked herself.

by necessity is created by strict necessity); *Ouellette v. Bolduc*, 440 A.2d 1042, 1046 (Me. 1982) ("Easements will not be implied in the construction of deeds, or contracts for the purchase and sale of lands, unless the easement be one of strict necessity."); *York v. Golder*, 147 A.41 (Me. 1929) (in determining the necessity, it must be shown" to be one of "strict necessity"); *Hildreth v. Googins*, 39 A.550 (Me. 1898) ("Implied grants of this character are looked upon with jealousy, construed with strictness, and are not favored, except in cases of strict necessity, and not from mere convenience"); *Whitehouse v. Cummings*, 83 (Me. 1890) 91, 98 (easements of necessity must be one of strict necessity and not one of mere convenience).

"In the absence of strict necessity for an easement . . . at the time of the severance of the unity of title, the law will not imply one." *Frederick v. Consolidated Waste Services, Inc.*, 573 A.2d 387, 389 (Me. 1990), citing *O'Connell v. Larkin*, 532 A.2d 1039, 1042 n.5 (Me. 1987). "Mere convenience, however great, will not suffice." *Ouellette v. Bolduc*, 440 A.2d 1042, 1046 (Me. 1982); *see also Littlefield v. Longley*, 128 A.285 (287) (Me. 1925) (convenience alone cannot give a right-of-way).

In *Littlefield*, the Court reaffirmed the longstanding rule that "where land borders on the ocean, a public highway, there exists no way of necessity even over a grantor's land, although such passage by water may not be as convenient as a passage by land, since necessity and not convenience is the test." *Id.* at 286–87, citing *Hildreth v. Googins*, 91 Me. 227, 228 (Me. 1898); *Kingsley v. Gouldsborough Land Improvement Co.*, 86 Me. 279, 280 (Me. 1894). The Court went on to clearly set forth that an easement of necessity cannot be found to exist without a strict necessity—in other words, "the expense to be incurred in utilizing" a route to a public way must be "grossly in excess of the total value of the estate itself . . . . " *Littlefield*, 128 A. at 287.

The more recent case of *Ouellette v. Bolduc* reaffirms this principle: "the test of necessity is whether the party claiming the easement can at reasonable cost on his own estate create a substitute." *Ouellette*, 440 A.2d at 1046, citing *York v. Golder*, 147 A. 41 (Me. 1929).

Even more recently, the Law Court in *Shadan* refused to find an easement by necessity where an allegedly landlocked property owner failed to prove that he had no alternate means of access to his land over another road, even though the alternate road was in poor condition. *Shadan v. Town of Skowhegan*, 1997 ME 187, at ¶ 9. The Court reiterated that an easement by necessity must be premised upon *strict* necessity. *Id.*

In the present case, it is undisputed that, as of 1958, Marjorie Nixon's formerly landlocked property adjoined a parcel she owned with road frontage. The fact that there is a brook between the back property and the road does not overcome the hurdle of strict necessity. The minimal cost of crossing a brook does not involve the kind of strict necessity required, as a matter of law, to create an easement of necessity. While it would have been convenient for Marjorie Nixon to have an easement by necessity over the land now owned by Mr. Litz and Ms. Sushimi, she would not have been entitled to such an easement where her abutting property had readily available access to a public way.

The Supreme Court of Alabama dealt with a case with similar facts in *Oyler v. Gilliland*, 382 So. 2d 517 (Ala. 1980). There, Gilliland acquired an easement by necessity over Oyler's property. Gilliland, however, subsequently purchased an abutting property which had access on a public road. There was no physical road from Oyler's "back property," over his abutting property, to the public road. Under the circumstances—which were strikingly similar to the case at bar—the Supreme Court of Alabama found that Oyler's easement by necessity was extinguished when he purchased abutting property with road frontage:

> By its very nature, an easement of necessity is extinguished once the necessity ceases.
>
> . . . .
>
> The law in this case is well settled. If one has a way through his own land, he cannot impose a "way of necessity" through his neighbor's land, unless his own way is not reasonably adequate or its cost is prohibitive. . . . Mere inconvenience or mere cost, as the basis for using another's land to get access to one's own property, falls short of meeting this test.
>
> . . . .
>
> [We] hold that the Gillilands have not met their burden of proof as to why their acquisition of adjoining property which abuts a public road does not extinguish their "way of necessity" across Oyler's land. At most, the evidence shows that their continued use of the way across Oyler's land is more convenient and will spare them the expense of building their own road.

Id. at 519.

The *Oyler* case reveals the fundamental logic problem with Defendant's claim that an easement still exists over the land of Mr. Litz and Ms. Sushimi. In *Oyler*, the court recognized (as do courts) that easements by necessity are, by their very nature, temporary, insofar as they last only as long as the necessity which creates them. *Oyler*, 382 So. 2d at 519. This creates a variety of logical consequences, including, for example, that easements by necessity cannot be the subject of permanent injunctions. *Id.* The facts of *Oyler* reveal that the owner of a servient tenement, Oyler, sought to block his neighbor, Gilliland, from a way across his property despite a lower court injunction in 1977 allowing Gilliland to use the way by necessity. Furthermore, Oyler blocked access in apparent contempt of a court order allowing such access to Gilliland. However, Oyler showed that Gilliland's necessity to use the way had, in fact, ended long before Gilliland purchased abutting property with road access in 1996. *Id.* The *Oyler* court recognized, on the basis of a map depicting the disputed properties and the availability of access over his land, that indeed Gilliland had extinguished his way by necessity when he acquired adjoining property which abutted a public road, subsequent to his acquisition of the parcel adjacent to Oyler's land. *Id.* The court therefore discharged the 1977 injunction and expunged Oyler's contempt order because he was correctly exercising his right to exclude his trespassing neighbor, since no easement by necessity had existed since 1966. *Id.* at 519–20.

The *Oyler* case reveals the consequences of the temporary nature of easements by necessity, i.e., that they exist only so long as necessary, and that as soon as the holder loses the necessity, he loses the easement. Because Mind courts have also recognized, on the basis of *LeMay* and *Rumill*, that the termination of the necessity extinguishes the easement, it is impossible for the Defendant to assert that Marjorie Nixon had any necessity for an easement over the land of Mr. Litz and Ms. Sushimi, subsequent to Ms. Nixon's 1958 acquisition of the parcel providing road access over her own land to her back lot. It is immaterial whether the parcels are now, or were then, held separately or zoned separately, provided there is common ownership.[2] The relevant inquiry is whether the owner of a landlocked parcel has access to her land without trespassing

---

2. It is well settled law in states that have considered the issue that the subsequent acquisition of an adjoining parcel by a common owner, where the later purchase provides road access, will serve to terminate an easement by necessity, without any consideration as to whether or not the parcels are "merged" for any other purpose. See Pender v. Matranga, 752 A.2d 77, 82 (Conn. App. Ct. 2000); Hart v. Jacobacci, 16 Conn. Supp. 71, 73 (Conn. C.P. 1948); Abbott v. Stewartstown, 47 N.H. 228, 230 (1866). Defendant's claim, that his other abutting parcel somehow does not give the back lot access because it may be held as a separate parcel, is therefore inaccurate.

over the land of another. In 1958, Marjorie Nixon acquired just such access for her back lot by purchasing her parcel along State Route 11.

On point, Nixon claims an easement by necessity over the property of Mr. Litz and Ms. Sushimi arising from a landlocking of the "back property" in 1957. His grandmother, who owned the "back property," bought an abutting property in 1958 with seventy-five feet of road frontage on Route 11. In 1965, she purchased more abutting property increasing the road frontage on Route 11 to ninety-six feet.

Under these facts, Nixon's 1957 easement by necessity was extinguished in 1958. Any necessity which existed in 1957 no longer existed in 1958. The fact that Nixon would have to build a new road from the "back property" to Route 11 does not mean that strict necessity still exists—it just means that Nixon and/or his predecessor-in-title has to go through the inconvenience of building a road over a brook. To its credit, Mind law requires a showing of *strict* necessity before a property owner is permitted to seize an easement over a neighbor's property without any notice or express writing. It mocks more than a hundred years of consistent precedents to suggest that a strict necessity was not extinguished in this case, or to suggest that it is a hardship to build a road over a brook.

Indeed, courts throughout this country have repeatedly held that the presence of a brook does *not* justify or create an easement by necessity. In *Collins v. Ketter*, 719 P.2d 731 (Colo. App. 1986), the Colorado court ruled that the appellants did not have an easement by necessity to cross their neighbor's bridge and road where the appellants could build a bridge over a stream on their *own* land in order to connect to a public way. *Id.* at 733. The court—noting that "implied easements are not looked upon with favor by the courts"—gave no credence to the fact that it would be "more convenient for [appellants] to traverse the length of [the neighbor's] road and cross his bridge, than to construct a bridge of their own directly across the stream and onto the road." *Id.*

As with the case at bar, the presence of a stream or brook does not create an easement by necessity. Such an easement can only be found where *strict* necessity exists. It *cannot* be found where a party is simply unwilling to build a bridge across a stream.

The Supreme Court of Nebraska came to a virtually identical conclusion in *Badura v. Lyons*, 23 N.W.2d 678 (Neb. 1946). There, the court refused to find an easement by necessity where the party seeking the easement could access a public way by building a seventy-eight-foot bridge over a drainage ditch near the Platte River. The court found that the "mere fact that the road over which they formerly traveled would be more convenient, or that to create the new way would necessitate an expenditure of some money, are not sufficient reasons to warrant an easement by necessity . . . , especially so when the expense to create the new way is reasonable and not disproportionate to the value of the . . . property." *Id.* at 685.

Similarly, the Court of Appeals of Maryland (Maryland's highest court) reached a similar conclusion in *Condry v. Laurie*, 41 A.2d 66 (Md. 1945). In *Condry*, plaintiffs were denied an easement by necessity where they could access a public road by building a bridge over the creek in the rear of their property. Echoing the words of courts in Mind and across the country, the Maryland Court of Appeals firmly stated that the cost of bridging the creek did not constitute the type of strict necessity needed to create an implied easement of necessity:

> [The] court will not recognize a way of necessity if another road to a public highway can be made without unreasonable expense, even though the other road may be much less convenient. Mere inconvenience will not be sufficient to justify the finding of a way of necessity. It is only [in cases] of strictest necessity, where it would not be reasonable to suppose that the parties intended the contrary, that the principle of implied easement can be invoked.

Id. at 68.

Nixon's case of an easement by necessity boils down to the fact that he does not want to pay for installing a Buchanan and building a road over a brook. Cases in Mind and throughout the country have reiterated that this does not meet the test of strict necessity. While it would clearly be convenient for Mr. Nixon to demand a free easement that runs over the middle of his neighbor's property to Route 302, such access is not necessary: Defendant's grandmother, Marjorie Nixon, always had the ability to cross over her abutting property to State Route 11. Accordingly, no necessity existed at the time of the conveyance.

Nixon's Alleged Implied Easement Is Simply a Reiteration of the Easement by Necessity

As set forth above, an implied easement *includes* an easement by necessity and a quasi-easement. Mr. Nixon's claim to an implied easement is repetitive of his claim to an easement by necessity. Accordingly, Mr. Nixon's claim to an implied easement fails, as a matter of law, for the same reasons that he cannot have an easement by necessity.

In their Interrogatory No. 3, Mr. Litz and Ms. Sushimi asked Mr. Nixon to "detail all legal and factual bases" for his claim that he "has an easement by necessity over Plaintiffs' property in Naples." They also asked Mr. Nixon, in Interrogatory No. 4, to "[d]escribe in detail all legal and factual bases for your claim that Defendant Anthony J. Nixon and/ or Defendant Bonnie Nixon has an implied easement over Plaintiffs' property in Naples, Mind. Defendants answered, in substantive part, as follows:

> The implied easement arose when the Nixon parcel was retained after conveyance of the front parcel. The Nixon family accessed the retained land via Route 302. We could not access it from any other land because of the brook. Even today, the parcel cannot be accessed because there is a bridge across the brook. The Route 11 property has structures which would block the path and route of travel and the Route 11 parcels are subject to life estates. We access that land, usually by car, but sometimes by foot. We brought in fill, we use it for recreation and we granted rights to others to use the property.

Interrogatory No. 3, as set forth above, relates to Defendant's claim to an easement by necessity. Interrogatory Nos. 1 and 2 relate only to witnesses and to Mrs. Nixon's lack of a claim, nothing else. Thus, Mr. Nixon's claim to an implied easement—which he claims "arose when the Nixon parcel was retained after conveyance of the front parcel" in 1957—appears to be a reiteration of his claim to an easement by necessity.

Even if he is making a claim to a separate quasi-easement, such a claim would also be barred as a matter of law.

A quasi-easement, which is a subspecies of an implied easement, is recognized where "(1) the 'property when in single ownership [must have been] openly used in a manner constituting a 'quasi-easement' (defined in *Brown* 106 Me. [97] at 101, 75 A.382 [at 384]), as existing conditions on the retained land that are *apparent* and *observable* and the retention of which would clearly benefit the land conveyed; (2) the common grantor, who severed unity of title, must have 'manifested an intent that the quasi-easement should continue as a true easement,' to burden the retained land and to benefit the conveyed land; and (3) the owners of the conveyed land must have continued to use what had been a quasi-easement as a true easement." *Robinson v. Mind Central Railroad Co.*, 623 A.2d 626, 627 (Me. 1993) (emphasis added), citing *Frederick v. Consolidated Waste Services, Inc.*, 573 A.2d 387, 389 (Me. 1990); *Bowers v. Andrews*, 557 A.2d 606, 608 (Me. 1989). A quasi-easement is also subject to the requirement that the easement be "important for the enjoyment of the conveyed quasi-dominant parcel." *Bowers*, 557 A.2d at 609, citing 3 *Powell on Real Property* § 411(2) (1985 & Supp.1988). The *Bowers* court also stated that quasi-easements "are existing conditions in the land retained, the continuance of which would be so clearly beneficial to the land conveyed that they would be presumed to be intended. These easements must be such as are apparent in the sense as being indicated by objects which are necessarily seen or would be ordinarily observable by persons familiar with the premises." *Bowers*, 557 A.2d at 608 n.2, citing *Brown v. Dickey*, 75 A.382, 384 (Me. 1909); *Tiffany on Real Property* § 781 (3d ed. 1939 & Supp. 1989).

Thus, a quasi-easement occurs where (1) a portion of property is sold and the remainder of the property is retained; (2) the intention of the parties at the time of the partial sale is to have an easement; (3) the easement is an apparent and observable condition on the face of the land; and (4) the parties continue to use the easement.

In the event that Mr. Nixon claims a quasi-easement as part of his implied easement claim, his claim fails due to the admitted facts in this case. First, Mr. Nixon makes no claim that the parties to the 1957 conveyance ever intended to create an easement. His answer to Interrogatory No. 4 contains no such allegation.

Second, Mr. Nixon's Interrogatory Answer No. 4 fails to claim that in 1957—or now—there is or was, or ever has been, any observable condition on the face of the earth showing the location of any such easement. In fact, Mr. Nixon concedes that the property is "tarred" and that there is no physical evidence of an easement on the face of the earth. He further concedes that he has "never built anything" to preserve any such easement.

The fact that Mr. Nixon might desire such an easement or that Mr. Nixon may or may not have accessed such land over the years since 1957 has nothing to do with the fact that there was no manifest intention of the parties to create an easement in 1957 and that there is no observable condition on the face of the earth showing such an easement ever existed.

Even if Mr. Nixon can provide evidence of such easement—and he cannot—such an easement would still fail because such an easement is not important to the enjoyment of the "back property." As in the situation of the easement by necessity, Marjorie Nixon, Mr. Nixon's grandmother, could easily access her "back property" by means of State Route 11. Her enjoyment of the property, therefore, was not limited to access across the land now owned by Mr. Litz and Ms. Sushimi.

Accordingly, Mr. Nixon's claim to an implied easement fails because this term (as he uses it) is simply another way of stating an easement by necessity. In the event that he is referring to a quasi-easement, his claim fails due to the admitted facts that the parties to the 1957 conveyance never manifested an intention to create an easement, that there is no physical evidence on the face of the earth of such an easement, and that easement at issue is not important to the enjoyment of the "back property" since access could be accomplished (as of 1958) from State Route 11.

III. Conclusion

For all the reasons set forth above, the Court should grant Count I of Plaintiffs' Complaint as a matter of Summary Judgment, dismiss Defendant's Counterclaim, and declare that Mr. Nixon does not have an easement by necessity or implied easement over the land of Mr. Litz and Ms. Sushimi in Naples.

PRIORITY OF LIENS AND MORTGAGES

STATE OF MIND BUSINESS AND CONSUMER DOCKET

WATER'S EDGE TRUST, Plaintiff	)	
v.	)	PLAINTIFF'S MOTION FOR SUMMARY JUDGMENT AGAINST THE REEDS
JOAN TINER, Defendant	)	
and	)	
WALTER J. REED and KELLY-JEAN REED, Parties-In-Interest	)	
and	)	
GREAT LENDING BANK, INC., Party-In-Interest	)	

Plaintiff Water's Edge Trust ("Water's Edge") asks this Court to confirm that its mortgage on the property of Defendant Joan Tiner has priority over the execution lien of Parties-In-Interest Walter J. and Kelly-Jean Reed (the "Reeds"): (1) because the Reeds' writ of execution was first recorded *before* Ms. Tiner owned the mortgaged property and, thus, did not create an execution lien upon that property; and (2) because the writ was recorded again only *after* Water's Edge's mortgage had been recorded, which created an execution lien that is subordinate to Water's Edge's mortgage.

The Facts

On November 29, 2004, the Reeds recorded a writ of execution against Defendant Joan Tiner in the Hancock County Registry of Deeds.

Statement of Material Facts, filed simultaneously herewith ("*SMF*") *¶ 1*. At that time, Ms. Tiner did not own the property at issue in this case. *SMF ¶ 2*. Almost a year later, on November 22, 2005, Ms. Tiner purchased Eochaidh Stables Farm in Bar Harbor, Hancock County, Mind (the "Property"). *SMF ¶ 3*. At the time Ms. Tiner purchased the Property, she granted three mortgages on the Property to secure debts owed to: (1) the sellers; (2) her attorneys; and (3) Water's Edge. *SMF ¶ 4*. Water's Edge recorded its mortgage on the Property on November 22, 2005. *SMF ¶ 5*.

Ms. Tiner allegedly failed to make payments due to the sellers of the Property and was faced with a foreclosure action. *SMF ¶ 6*. Water's Edge stepped in and refinanced the Property. *SMF ¶ 7*. The three outstanding mortgages were discharged and, on December 12, 2006, Ms. Tiner granted a new mortgage on the Property to Water's Edge to secure a note for $409,255.19. *SMF ¶ 8*.

Six months later, on June 7, 2007, the Reeds re-recorded their November 23, 2004, writ of execution. *SMF ¶ 9*. This second recording occurred after the recording of the Water's Edge mortgage. *SMF ¶ 10*. This was the first action taken by the Reeds to enforce their judgment against Ms. Tiner in the more than two years since they first recorded the writ. *SMF ¶ 11*.

Subsequently, Ms. Tiner failed to pay the $409,255.19 note to Water's Edge. *SMF ¶ 12*. As a result of Ms. Tiner's material breach of the note, Water's Edge brought the present action seeking a declaration of the order of priority of security interests on the Property and foreclosure and sale of the Property. *SMF ¶ 13*. The Reeds were joined as Parties-In-Interest based on their June 7, 2007, recordation of the Writ of Execution dated November 23, 2004. *SMF ¶ 14*.

In response to Water's Edge's complaint in this matter, the Reeds have alleged that they obtained a lien against the Property when they first recorded their writ on November 29, 2004, despite the fact that Ms. Tiner did not own the Property at that time. *SMF ¶ 15*. This allegation is based upon the fact that Ms. Tiner filed a Clerk's Certificate in the Hancock County Registry of Deeds in 2001 providing notice of a lawsuit in which she was seeking to enforce an alleged promise by the prior owners of the Property to sell the Property to her. *SMF ¶ 16*.

For the Court's convenience, a graphical timeline is set forth below:

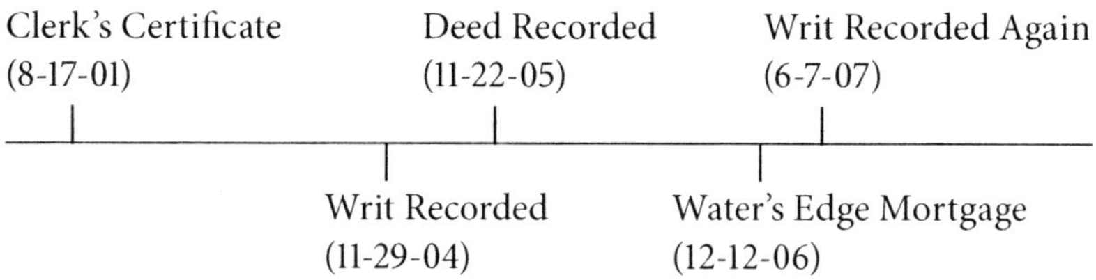

Summary Judgment Standard

A party is entitled to summary judgment where—as here—there is no genuine issue of material fact and the moving party, on the undisputed facts, is entitled to judgment as a matter of law. *See* M.R.Civ.P. 56(c); *see also Levine v. R.B.K. Caly Corp.*, 2001 ME 77, ¶ 4, 770 A.2d 653, 655 (Me. 2001). Summary judgment is appropriate unless there is sufficient evidence in favor of the non-moving party for a jury to return a verdict for that party. *See Biette v. Scott Dugas Trucking and Excavating, Inc.*, 676 A.2d 490, 494 (Me. 1996). If the evidence offered by the non-moving party is merely colorable, or is not significantly probative, summary judgment may be granted. *Id.* Water's Edge is entitled to summary judgment, as a matter of law, in this case because the undisputed material facts establish the priority of its mortgage over the Reeds.

The Law

In this foreclosure action, Water's Edge's mortgage is the first recorded lien against the Property and is therefore entitled to priority over all other claims. It is undisputed that the second recording of the Reeds' writ of execution in June 2007 occurred after the recording of Water's Edge's mortgage in December 2006 and, thus, the execution lien created by that second recording is subordinate to the mortgage. *See* 14 M.R.S.A. § 4454; *U.S. v. Belanger*, 598 F. Supp. 598, 606 (D. Me. 1984) ("The Bank's attachment . . . having been recorded subsequent to Plaintiff's mortgage deed, is of lower priority than Plaintiff's interest"). Therefore, the only issue in dispute is the effect, if any, of the first recording of the writ of execution in November 2004.

The facts are not disputed. At the time the writ was first recorded, Ms. Tiner did not own the Property. A writ of execution cannot attach to property that the judgment debtor does not own. *See Dumont v. J & M Realty Co., Inc.*, 2001 WL 1671513, *1 (Me. Super. 2001) (denying attachment of writ of execution when the judgment debtor had no "legal interest in the property at the time of the attachment" of the writ). Nor does a writ attach after-acquired property. *Id.* Thus, the first recording of the writ did not create a lien against the Property. This is why creditors—such as the Reeds—re-record execution writs, from time to time, in the hope that the debtor may own property at the time of recording.

The Reeds attempt to avoid the result of their lack of diligence in timely re-recording their writ by claiming that the recording of the writ created a lien based upon a Clerk's Certificate that had been recorded in the Hancock County Registry of Deeds by Ms. Tiner evidencing a disputed contract claim between Ms. Tiner and the prior owner of the Property. As a matter of law, a Clerk's Certificate is insufficient to create a property interest to which an execution lien can attach. A Clerk's Certificate merely "gives notice of the claim and does not establish a priority for purposes of enforcing a judgment." *Meng v. Vann*, 2006 WL 2959699, *1 (Me. Super. 2006); *Bank of America v. Finnemore*, No. NEW-RE-04-14, 4 (Me. Dist. Ct. 3, Newport, Aug. 16, 2005) (MacMichael, J.), *aff'd* 2006 ME 97, 902 A.2d 843 (Me. 2006).

Additionally, when Water's Edge recorded its mortgage in December 2006, it did not have actual notice of the writ nor was the writ recorded in the chain of title for the Property. Accordingly, even if a lien was created by the first recording of the writ, that lien would not have priority over Water's Edge's mortgage because Water's Edge did not have actual or constructive notice of the writ when it recorded its mortgage.

A. The First Recording of the Writ Attached No Property Because Ms. Tiner Owned No Property at the Time of the Recording

The fundamental flaw in the Reeds' argument is the simple fact that Ms. Tiner did not own the Property at the time that the writ was first recorded. "A judgment lien creditor stands in the shoes of his judgment debtor so as to reach all assets that could be reached by the debtor. The lien cannot attach, however, to any greater interest than the debtor has." *Biette*, 676 A.2d at 495 (quoting 46 Am. Jur. 2d *Judgments* §§ 370, 380 (1994)). At the time of the first recording, Ms. Tiner had no ability to "reach" the Property. At that time, Ms. Tiner had, at most, a judicially decreed contract to purchase the Property pursuant to the terms of an oral agreement with the previous owners of the Property, the Porters. *See Tiner v. Porter*, 2004 ME 134, ¶¶ 20, 26, 861 A.2d 625 (Me. 2004) (affirming Superior Court's order of "specific performance in the form of a purchase and sale agreement"). Even if Ms. Tiner had recorded a fully executed purchase and sale agreement prior to the first recording (which she did not do), it would not have been sufficient to create a lienable property interest. At common law, a writ of execution does not create a lien "against a mere contractual right or chose in action." 30 Am. Jur. 2d *Executions* § 142.

Mind's execution lien statute, 14 M.R.S.A. § 4651-A, follows this common law principle. Under the statute, a purchase and sale contract is not susceptible to an execution lien because it is not the type of interest "against which a mortgage would be duly perfected if filed in the registry."

> The filing of an execution duly issued by a court of this State or an attested copy thereof with a registry of deeds within 3 years after issuance of the execution creates a lien in favor of each judgment creditor upon the right, title and interest of each judgment debtor in all ***real estate against which a mortgage would be duly perfected if filed in the registry*** and that is not exempt from attachment and execution.

14 M.R.S.A. § 4651-A (emphasis added). Because a mortgage against Ms. Tiner's contractual right to purchase the Property would not have been perfected if filed in the Registry, the Reeds' first recording of the writ did not create a lien on the Property.

A mortgage cannot be perfected when the mortgagor does not have record title to the property offered as security. Mind follows the title theory of mortgages, under which legal title to the property passes to the mortgagee upon delivery of the mortgage deed. *Johnson v. McNeil*, 2002 ME 99, ¶ 10, 800 A.2d 702, 704 (Me. 2002); 33 M.R.S.A. § 767. Under Mind law, a mortgage deed includes covenants that "the grantor was lawfully seized in fee of the premises." 33 M.R.S.A. §§ 767, 768. If the grantor does not have legal title to the property, she cannot convey legal title by mortgage deed and the mortgage cannot be perfected by recording. *Brown v. Guarantee & Trust Safe-Deposit Co.*, 128 U.S. 403, 413 (1888).

Judgment liens are creatures of statute, and "[e]xcept as provided by statute, a judgment is never a lien against property of the judgment debtor." *In re Paolini*, 11 B.R. 317, 319 (Bkrtcy. N.Y. 1981). Because Ms. Tiner did not have legal title to the Property at the time the writ was first recorded, pursuant to Section 4651-A(1) the first recording of the writ did not create a lien on the Property. *See Dumont*, 2001 WL 1671513 at

*1 (denying attachment of writ of execution when the judgment debtor had no "legal interest in the property at the time of the attachment" of the writ); *In re Goff*, 812 F.2d 931, 933 (5th Cir. 1987) ("The judgment lien attaches only to real property in which the judgment debtor has legal title"). Accordingly, Water's Edge is entitled to summary judgment in its favor.

B. Under State Law, the First Recording of the Writ of Execution Does Not Attach After-Acquired Property

The Reeds' first recording of the writ also failed to attach the Property at the time it was subsequently acquired by Ms. Tiner. Because liens are creatures of statute, they attach to after-acquired property only when there is specific statutory authority for such an attachment. *See, e.g.*, 26 M.R.S.A. § 1230; 36 M.R.S.A. § 175-A; 38 M.R.S.A. § 1371. There is no such authority in the execution lien statute, 14 M.R.S.A. § 4651-A. Accordingly, the recording of a writ of execution does not create a lien upon after-acquired property and Water's Edge is entitled to summary judgment in its favor. *See* 14 M.R.S.A. § 4651-A; *Dumont*, 2001 WL 1671513 at *1 (writ of execution did not attach to the property because the owner "acquired the property after the attachment of the original writ"); State Title Standards § 2.02 (reflecting established practice of searching in the buyer's chain of title for prior tax liens, which attach to after-acquired property, but not prior judgment liens, which do not attach to after-acquired property).

C. Water's Edge's Mortgage Is Not Affected by the Reeds' First Recording of the Writ Because That Recording Is Outside the Chain of Title for the Property

Even if the Court finds that the Reeds' first recording of the writ created a lien against the Property by virtue of Ms. Tiner's judicially decreed oral contract to purchase the Property, Water's Edge is protected from the Reeds' writ by Mind's recording statute, 33 M.R.S.A. § 201. Section 201 states in pertinent part that "[n]o conveyance of an estate in fee . . . is effectual against any person except the grantor, his heirs and devisees, and persons having actual notice thereof unless the deed or lease is acknowledged and recorded in the registry of deeds within the county where the land lies . . . ." 33 M.R.S.A. § 201.

Because there is no evidence in the record to demonstrate that Water's Edge had "actual knowledge" of the Reeds' judgment lien on the Property, and because the writ was recorded outside of the chain of title for the Property, Water's Edge's mortgage takes precedence over the Reeds' first recording of the writ. *In re Bruder*, 207 B.R. 151, 156–57 (N.D. Ill. 1997) ("Constructive notice . . . arises only when the encumbrances or conveyances are in the direct chain of title. . . . Chain of title is defined as 'the successive conveyances commencing with the patent from the government or some other source and including the conveyance to the one claiming title.' ") (citations omitted); 59 C.J.S. *Mortgages* § 223 ("A mortgagee . . . is not chargeable with notice of claims or liens placed on the land prior to the date the mortgagor came into title."); *Glen Ellyn Savings and Loan Ass'n v. State Bank of Geneva*, 382 N.E.2d 1267, 1273 (Ill. App. 1978) ("Records need not be searched for deeds, mortgages or other conveyances made by a vendor before he became vested in title and his vendee is not chargeable with constructive notice of matters shown by records not in the chain of title."); 66 Am. Jur. 2d *Records and Recording Laws* § 98 ("To impute to a purchaser notice of an instrument out of the chain of title, because it was put on record, is wholly inconsistent with equitable principles.").

When the writ was first recorded, record title of the Property was held by the Porters, not Ms. Tiner. Thus, if one were to research the chain of title of the Property, one would start in the Grantee's (Ms. Tiner's) index and look back to the deed from the Porters to Ms. Tiner in November 2005. Then one would search through the Grantor's (the Porters') index until the prior conveyance, and so forth. One would never see the writ against Ms. Tiner, which was recorded in November of 2004, almost a year before Ms. Tiner entered the Property's chain of title in November of 2005. Accordingly, Water's Edge is entitled to summary judgment in its favor because any lien that may have been created against Ms. Tiner by virtue of the first recording of the writ was outside the chain of title for the Property, and did not place Water's Edge on constructive notice of an encumbrance on the Property.

Conclusion

There are no disputed material facts, and Water's Edge is entitled to judgment as a matter of law on the undisputed facts. For the above reasons, the Court should grant the Motion for Summary Judgment and enter a declaratory judgment in favor of Plaintiff Water's Edge Trust.

PRESCRIPTIVE EASEMENTS AND ABANDONED ROADS

STATE OF MIND SUPERIOR COURT

MALCOLM MOUNTAIN	)	
PROPERTIES, INC.,	)	
Plaintiff	)	
	)	
v.	)	
	)	CIVIL ACTION NO.______
THE INHABITANTS OF THE	)	
CITY OF ONE SMALL CITY, *et al.*,	)	
Defendants	)	
	)	

PLAINTIFF'S MOTION FOR SUMMARY JUDGMENT

Plaintiff Malcolm Mountain Properties, Inc. ("Malcolm"), pursuant to M.R.Civ.P. 56, moves this Court for summary judgment in its favor because the undisputed facts in this case demonstrate (1) that any public way that may have traversed Malcolm's property in colonial times has long since been abandoned; (2) that Defendants Ellis S. Rose, Gail K. Rose, Gina G. Moon, Peter Moon, and Polly Martin have no claim whatsoever to a private prescriptive easement across the Malcolm property because they have always crossed over the Malcolm property either with permission of the owner or in the mistaken belief there was a public easement across the property; and in the alternative (3) that any private prescriptive easements that may be held by Polly Martin or Ellis Rose are personal to them—and not easements which run with the land.

Facts

There is no historical documentation of the creation of a public way on the Malcolm property. To the extent that a public way ever crossed the Malcolm property, there is no evidence of maintenance of that public way by the City of One Small City at any time. There also is scant evidence of the use of that way after 1919 by anyone other than residents of the Fortunes Rocks neighborhood and their guests, most of whom either mistakenly assumed that there was a public way across the

Malcolm property or were given permission to cross over the Malcolm property by its former owner.

In 1652, the general court of Massachusetts ordered the towns between One Big City and One Medium City, Mind (which at that time was known as Falmouth), to mark a passage along the coast for travel between these localities. *Plaintiff's Statement of Material Facts ("SMF") ¶¶ 1–3.* Generally, the King's Highway ran between One Big City and One Medium City along the high water mark. *SMF ¶¶ 1–3.* In 1664, the Town of Saco—which included present-day One Small City—documented its intent to establish the "King's Highway" between two residential properties along the coastline. *SMF ¶ 4.* The precise location of the King's Highway in present day One Small City is not documented. *SMF ¶ 5.*

The coastal route taken by the King's Highway was not the most direct route between One Big City and One Medium City. *SMF ¶ 6.* The King's Highway was established along the coast as inland travel was dangerous because of the presence of French and Indian forces and because it was less expensive for the towns to mark a path along the coast than to construct an inland route. *SMF ¶ 7.* In 1763, the Treaty of Paris was signed and as a result peace was established between the colonists and the French and Indians. *SMF ¶ 8.* The signing of that treaty made it safe for the colonists to travel from One Big City to One Medium City along a more direct route in the interior of Mind rather than along the coast. *SMF ¶ 9.* Once passage in the interior of Mind was safe, the original King's Highway gradually was abandoned as the route between One Big City and One Medium City and replaced by the Post Road, which generally followed the path of what is now known as Route One. *SMF ¶ 10.*

To the extent that a path continued to cross the Malcolm property after 1763, there is no evidence of any maintenance whatsoever on the Malcolm property by the City of One Small City. *SMF ¶ 11.*

In or about 1902, the Granite Point Road was accepted by One Small City as a public way between Fortunes Rocks and Granite Point. *SMF ¶ 13.* The Granite Point Road replaced any path that may have existed across the Malcolm property as the primary route between Fortunes Rocks and Granite Point. *SMF ¶ 14.*

To the extent that a path continued to cross the Malcolm property after 1763, that path from the southwest boarder of the Malcolm property to Granite Point was washed out at some point in time between the late 1800s and 1919. *SMF ¶ 12.* There is no evidence of any public use or maintenance of a path across the Malcolm property at any time after 1919. *SMF ¶ 22.* There is no evidence of the existence of a public right-of-way across the Malcolm property at any time after 1919. *SMF ¶ 23.*

After the path immediately to the south of the Malcolm Property washed out sometime between the late 1800s and 1919, the path across the Malcolm Property dead-ended at Seal Cove, so-called. *SMF ¶ 24.* Since 1919, the path across the Malcolm Property has been used almost exclusively by residents of the Fortunes Rocks neighborhood and their guests for the limited purpose of accessing Seal Cove. *SMF ¶ 25.* In 1928, a resident of One Small City complained to the City Council about the closing of the Old King's Highway and, shortly after that complaint was made, the City of One Small City agreed to accept the section of the Old King's Highway from Granite Point which is south of the Malcolm property to Beachwood which is south of Granite Point. *SMF ¶ 15.*

In 1979, the City of One Small City conducted an inventory of "public ways because of usage and maintenance by the City of One Small City for many years." That inventory lists the Old King's Highway and states that it extends southwesterly 800 +/− feet from Fortunes Rocks Road to a dead end. *SMF ¶ 16.* The Malcolm property is located more than 800 feet from Fortunes Rocks Road. SMF *¶ 17.* According to the description contained in the 1979 inventory of roads, the Old King's Highway ends as a public way at or near the Malcolm property line. *SMF ¶ 18.* The City of One Small City admitted in its deposition that the town road known as the Old King's Highway dead-ends at or near the northeast border of the Malcolm property and that the Old King's Highway ceases to exist on the face of the earth at or near the northeast border of the Malcolm property. *SMF ¶ 19–20.* There is currently no evidence on the face of the earth of a path across the Malcolm property. *SMF ¶ 26.* Additionally, there are no records that evidence the acceptance of any portion of the King's Highway or the Old King's Highway by the Town of One Small City anywhere on the Malcolm property. *SMF ¶ 21.*

Ms. Polly Martin has been spending her summer vacations in the Fortunes Rocks area of One Small City since 1921, the year she was born. *SMF ¶ 27.* From 1921 until 1930, Ms. Martin's family rented a cottage in the Fortunes Rocks area every summer. *SMF ¶ 28.* In 1930, Ms. Martin's parents purchased property in the Fortunes Rocks area and built their own summer cottage. *SMF ¶ 29.* From the 1920s through the 1940s, Ms. Martin recalls that the Old King's Highway was a path from Fortunes Rocks Road to Seal Beach which consisted of "two ruts with grass growing in the middle." *SMF ¶ 30.* During this time, Seal Beach was used mostly by people who lived in the Fortunes Rocks neighborhood. *SMF ¶ 31.* Sometime in the 1940s, Horace Williams, who at that time owned what is now the Malcolm property, hired a contractor to straighten out a curve in the path from Fortunes Rocks Road to Seal Beach at a point near the property that is now known as 15 Old King's Highway. *SMF ¶ 32.*

In 1975, Ms. Martin inherited her parents' property in Fortunes Rocks. *SMF ¶ 33.* In 1979, Ms. Martin sold that property. *SMF ¶ 34.* In August of 1984, Ms. Martin inherited her aunt's property located at 15 Old King's Highway. *SMF ¶ 35.* Ms. Martin has been living at 15 Old King's Highway for six months each year since the mid 1980s when she inherited her aunt's property. *SMF ¶ 36.*

There is no document granting Ms. Martin an easement to cross the Malcolm property. *SMF ¶ 37.* Ms. Martin claims that she has used the path across the Malcolm Property to access Seal Cove at various times since she began vacationing at Fortunes Rocks in 1921. *SMF ¶ 38.* In the 1970s, Horace Nichols, who was a predecessor in title to Malcolm, put a sawhorse at the location where the path to Seal Beach crossed the northeast boarder of the Malcolm property with a sign attached to it that said "Private—No Parking." *SMF ¶ 39.* That sign remained there until the 1990s when it was replaced with a sign that said "No Trespassing." *SMF ¶ 40.* Horace Williams and his son Edmond Williams, who were the predecessors in title to Malcolm, granted permission to Ms. Martin and other neighbors to cross what is now the Malcolm property and to use Seal Beach. *SMF ¶ 41.* Edmund Williams sent Ms. Martin a letter dated January 24, 1990, confirming the fact that his father had given her permission to cross his property and that he would continue to do so. *SMF ¶ 42.* Ms. Martin does not believe that she needed permission from the Nicholses at that time, or that she currently needs permission from Malcolm, to cross the Malcolm property on what she believes to be a public road. *SMF ¶ 43.*

Mr. and Mrs. Ellis S. Rose have owned the property located at 3 Seal Lane since 1996. *SMF ¶ 44.* There is no document granting the Roses an easement to cross the Malcolm property. *SMF ¶ 45.* Mr. Rose began vacationing at Fortunes Rocks in the late 1960s. *SMF ¶ 46.* From the late 1960s until 1996, Mr. Rose claims he used the path across the Malcolm Property to access Seal Cove one to three times per year. *SMF ¶ 47.*

Mrs. Rose visited Seal Cove for the first time in 1996 when she and her husband were looking at the house at 3 Seal Lane with a Realtor.

SMF ¶ 48. While the Roses were at Seal Cove, the owner of the Malcolm Property at that time, Mr. Williams, greeted them, informed them that Seal Cove and the path across the Malcolm property to Seal Cove were private and that, as long as they were going to be neighbors, they had his permission to use the beach. *SMF ¶ 49.* Since buying their house in 1996, the Roses have understood that, as neighbors of Mr. Williams, they had permission to continue crossing the Malcolm property to visit Seal Cove. *SMF ¶ 50.*

Mr. and Mrs. Peter Moon have owned the property located at 3 Old King's Highway since 1992. *SMF ¶ 51.* There is no document granting the Moons an easement to cross the Malcolm property. *SMF ¶ 52.* From 1989 to 1992, when Mr. and Mrs. Moon visited the Fortunes Rocks area of One Small City prior to purchasing the property at 3 Old King's Highway, they would occasionally ride their bicycles as far as they could on Old King's Highway, stopping at the Malcolm property line. *SMF ¶ 53.*

Shortly after the Moons bought the property at 3 Old King's Highway, they were told by their neighbors that there was a "public road" that ran across the Malcolm property to Seal Beach. *SMF ¶ 54.* Shortly after this information was communicated to the Moons, Mrs. Moon was walking across the Malcolm property when she was stopped by Mr. Nichols who told her that he is allowing his neighbors to walk across his property and, now that Mrs. Moon is a neighbor, she had permission to do so. *SMF ¶ 55.*

Since 1992, the Moons have traversed the Malcolm property on the average of two times per week. *SMF ¶ 56.* Since 1992, the Moons have observed "neighbors, friends and the like" walking across the Malcolm property but have not seen any strangers do so. *SMF ¶ 57.* The Moons believe that there is a public road across the Malcolm property. *SMF ¶ 58.* The Moons do not believe that they need permission of the owner to cross the Malcolm property on what they believe to be a public road. *SMF ¶ 59.* The Moons do not believe that they have a private right to cross the Malcolm property. *SMF ¶ 60.*

In 2001, Donna Labbe, the Mayor of One Small City, wrote a letter to the One Small City Coastal Area Committee Chair and Members stating that the Old King's Highway had not been used for a public highway for approximately 200 years. *SMF ¶ 61.* Mayor Labbe was correct when she stated that the Old King's Highway had not been used for a public way for approximately 200 years. *SMF ¶ 62.*

ARGUMENT

I. There Is Insufficient Evidence to Demonstrate the Creation of a Public Way across the Malcolm Property

In this State, there are three methods by which a public way may be created: (1) by the statutory method of laying out a public way pursuant to 23 M.R.S.A. § 3022 et seq.; (2) by dedication and acceptance; or (3) by prescriptive easement. *See Vachon v. Inhabitants of the Town of Lisbon*, 295 A.2d 255, 259 (Me. 1972); *Town of Manchester v. Augusta Country Club*, 477 A.2d 1124, 1128–29 (Me. 1984).

A. No Public Way Was Created by the Statutory Method

The only evidence that the City of One Small City ever laid out a public way in the vicinity of the Malcolm property is the 1654 document establishing "a highway for the Towne" between two residential addresses that was described as running generally "by high water mark." If such a public way ever crossed the Malcolm property, it did so in the vicinity of the high water mark that existed in 1654. That high water mark has long since been eroded away and is now located hundreds of feet offshore in the Atlantic Ocean.

Moreover, the document purporting to establish a highway in One Small City in 1654 was created 300 years before the Mind legislature enacted the statutory method of laying out a public way. As one would expect, the 1654 document does not satisfy all of the statutory requirements. Additionally, there is absolutely no evidence that the highway established by the 1654 document was ever actually laid out on the face of the earth or used as a public way or, even if it was laid out and used, that it ever crossed the Malcolm property.

B. No Public Way Was Created by Dedication and Acceptance

Dedication of privately owned land for public purposes must be proven by evidence of the grantor's "clear intent to so dedicate—[m]ere acquiescence by the owner in occasional and varying use by the public is not sufficient to establish dedication." *Manchester*, 477 A.2d at 1129. Similarly, acceptance must be proven by evidence of "some affirmative act" by the public. *Id.*

In the instant case, there is no evidence of the dedication of any portion of the Malcolm property as a public way by Malcolm or any of its predecessors in interest. Additionally, the only evidence of the acceptance of any portion of the "Old Kings Highway" by the City of One Small City relates to: (1) the section to the south of the Malcolm property from Granite Point to Beachwood; and (2) the 800+/− foot section which extends from Fortunes Rocks Road to the Malcolm property line. There is absolutely no evidence of dedication or acceptance of a public way anywhere on the Malcolm property.

C. No Public Way Was Created by Prescriptive Easement

A prescriptive easement may be established by continuous use for at least 20 years under a claim of right adverse to the owner, with his knowledge and acquiescence, or a use so open and notorious that knowledge and acquiescence may be presumed. *See Manchester*, 477 A.2d at 1130. Acquiescence in this context means passive assent or submission to the use as opposed to license or permission given with the intention that the use may continue only so long as the owner permits it. *Id.*

The burden is upon the party asserting the existence of the easement to prove that its use was with the owner's passive assent as opposed to with permission or in defiance of the owner's protests. *Id.*; *see also Glidden v. Belden*, 684 A.2d 1306, 1317 (Me. 1996). The party asserting the existence of the easement also must prove that his or her use was adverse—i.e., that he or she disregarded the owner's claim to the property and used it as if it were his or her own. *Glidden*, 684 A.2d at 1318. A trespasser's mistaken belief that he or she is traveling upon a public way "utterly negates the party's intent to claim title" and precludes any assertion that the trespasser's use was adverse to the owner's property rights. *Id.*

Additionally, in order to obtain a prescriptive easement in favor of the *public*, the evidence must demonstrate continuous, adverse, open and notorious use by "people who are not separable from the public generally." *See S.D. Warren Company v. Vernon*, 697 A.2d 1280, 1284 (Me. 1997). Use by neighbors and abutting landowners does not satisfy this requirement. *See Inhabitants of the Town of Kennebunk v. Forrester*, 391 A.2d 831, 833 n.2 (Me. 1978) (to establish a public easement by prescription "the adverse use must be general and not limited to a few specific individuals"); *compare Stickney v. Town of Saco*, 2001 ME 69 (40-year history of paving, plowing, and maintenance of road by city together with use of road consisting of members of the general public driving over it was sufficient to create public easement by prescription).

In the instant case, there is no evidence of the use of a path across the Malcolm property by the general public. The evidence indicates that the limited number of "neighbors, friends and the like" who did cross the Malcolm property to access Seal Beach did so either under the mistaken impression that there was a public road across the Malcolm property or with the permission of the owner. These facts are insufficient to create a public way by prescriptive easement.

II. The Evidence Conclusively Demonstrates That Any Public Way That May Have Existed across the Malcolm Property Was Abandoned Long Ago

The common law states that "a presumption of a public intent to abandon a road may be raised by evidence of nonuse for twenty years or more . . . or acquiescence, even for a few years, in the voluntary discontinuance of an old road combined with the use of a new road." *Shadan v. Town of Skowhegan*, 700 A.2d 245, 247 (1997). In *Shadan*, the Law Court held that evidence of lack of public maintenance together with evidence that the road in question had become impassable was sufficient to support a determination that the road had been abandoned as a public way. *Id.*

In the instant case, the evidence demonstrates that: (1) the City of One Small City has not maintained a road across the Malcolm property at any time; (2) in 1902, the Granite Point Road became the primary route between the Fortunes Rocks area and Granite Point, replacing any path that may have existed across the Malcolm property; and (3) at some point between the late 1800s and 1919, any path that may have existed across the Malcolm property was washed out by a storm from the southwest border of the Malcolm property to Granite Point. All of these facts indicate conclusively that any ancient public way that might have existed across the Malcolm property ceased to be used or maintained as of 1919 at the latest. Thus, pursuant to the common law, any such public way is presumed to have been abandoned in 1939. This presumption is supported by the testimony of Ms. Martin that sometime in the 1940s Horace Nichols, who at that time owned the Malcolm property, hired a private contractor to straighten a curve in the road. If the road had been a public way at that time, this type of private activity would not have been undertaken nor permitted.

The abandonment date of 1939 is arrived at by using the common law presumption of abandonment after 20 years of nonuse. *See Shadan*,

700 A.2d at 247. Under this State's road abandonment statute, which has been on the books since 1975, a public way is presumed abandoned 30 years after a municipality or county ceases to maintain the road. *See* 23 M.R.S.A. § 3028. Under this standard, any public way across the Malcolm property may be presumed to have been abandoned in 1949. In either case, the abandonment of any public way that may have existed across the Malcolm property prior to the effective date of the abandonment statute in 1975 results in the extinguishment of any public easement whatsoever that may have existed across the Malcolm property. *See Martin v. Burnham*, 631 A.2d 1239, 1240–41 (Me. 1993) (all rights in roads abandoned prior to effective date of abandonment statute pass to owners of land that abuts center line of right-of-way).

III. The Evidence Conclusively Demonstrates That Neither Ms. Martin, the Roses, Nor the Moons Have Any Private Right to Cross the Malcolm Property

It is undisputed that no formal easement has been granted to either Ms. Martin, the Roses, or the Moons to cross the Malcolm property. Moreover, neither the Roses nor the Moons have continuously used any portion of the Malcolm property for a period of 20 years under a claim of right adverse to the owner with the knowledge or acquiescence of the owner. The Moons first traversed the Malcolm property in 1992 when they bought their house at 3 Old King's Highway and Mrs. Rose did not walk across the Malcolm property at any time prior to 1996 when she and her husband acquired their property at 3 Seal Lane. Thus, it is clear that neither the Moons nor Ms. Rose can satisfy the 20-year use requirement.

Additionally, the Moons believe that the Old King's Highway is a public way that extends across the Malcolm property and that they do not have any private right to cross the Malcolm property. *See SMF ¶¶ 58–60*. Thus, their use of the Malcolm property to access Seal Beach is not adverse to the owner because, as discussed above, a trespasser's mistaken belief that he is traveling upon a public way "utterly negates the party's intent to claim title" and precludes any assertion that the trespasser's use was adverse to the owner's property rights. *Glidden*, 684 A.2d at 1318. Similarly, Ms. Rose's use of the Malcolm property is not adverse to the owner because she believes that she was granted permission by Mr. Nichols to walk across the property. *See SMF ¶ 50.*

Mr. Rose stated at his deposition that he has vacationed in the Fortunes Rocks area since the late 1960s and from that time until 1996, when he and his wife bought their house at 3 Seal Lane, he walked across the Malcolm property one to three times per year to access Seal Beach. This limited use is insufficient to satisfy the requirement of continuous, open and notorious use necessary to establish a prescriptive easement. *Cf. Great Northern Paper Co. v. Eldredge*, 686 A.2d 1075, 1077–78 (1996) (cutting substantial amounts of wood on adjoining lot and creating two roads in order to haul the cut wood across property of defendant over a period of more than 40 years demonstrated continuous, open and notorious use). Thus, Mr. Rose also does not have any prescriptive right to cross the Malcolm property.

Ms. Martin has always thought that there is a public way across the Malcolm property and has always felt that it is her right as a member of the public to cross the Malcolm property and use Seal Beach. As discussed above, a trespasser's mistaken belief that he is traveling upon a public way "utterly negates the party's intent to claim title" and precludes any assertion that the trespasser's use was adverse to the owner's property rights. *Glidden*, 684 A.2d at 1318. Thus, despite the fact that Ms. Martin claims to have been crossing the Malcolm property on a more or less regular basis for more than 20 years, she has not done so in a manner that is adverse to the owner's claim to the property—i.e., she has not used it as if it were her own. Accordingly, Ms. Martin's historical use of the Malcolm property is insufficient to create a private easement by prescription.

IV. The Evidence Conclusively Demonstrates That Any Right That Ms. Martin Or Mr. Rose May Have to Cross the Malcolm Property Is Personal to Them

It is Plaintiff's position that neither Ms. Martin nor Mr. Rose have any prescriptive right to cross the Malcolm property. If this Court determines that this issue cannot be decided on summary judgment, Plaintiff requests that this Court determine, in the alternative, that any easement that Mr. Rose or Ms. Martin may be found to have after a trial of the facts is personal to them.

An easement may either be a personal right—referred to as an easement "in gross"—or it may be created to benefit a particular piece of property, in which case it is referred to as an easement "appurtenant to" that property. *See ALC Development Corp. v. Walker*, 787 A.2d 770 (Me. 2002). In the instant case, any easement that Ms. Martin or Mr. Rose may arguably possess would have been created by their continuous crossing of the Malcolm property for a period of 20 years.

Ms. Martin has been vacationing at Fortunes Rocks since 1921. She acquired her property in 1984, however, and has been on notice since at least 1990 of Mr. Williams' position that she had no right to cross his property but had his permission to do so; any prescriptive easement that she may have acquired came into existence prior to her ownership of the property at 15 Old King's Highway or, at the very latest, prior to 1990—at which time she had owned her property for only 6 or 7 years. Thus, such an easement, if one exists, must be personal to Ms. Martin and not appurtenant to her property.

Since Mr. Rose did not acquire his current residence at 3 Seal Lane until 1996 (just 9 years ago) any prescriptive easement that he may have acquired cannot be appurtenant to his property. It is a personal right, not one created to benefit the property.

Opposing a motion for summary judgment, or drafting a countermotion, is a similar exercise. Focus immediately on the theme:

> The language of the shore easement is ambiguous in that it contains absolutely no guidance as to whether the Smiths have the right to place a dock at the end of the easement. Accordingly, there are extrinsic facts that need to be described and summary judgment is not appropriate.

or

> The Smiths' easement to the shore is clear and unambiguous. It grants them a right to walk to the shore. Nothing else. Nothing further. The Court should deny the Smiths' Motion for Summary Judgment and rule, as a matter of law, that they have no right under the easement to build a dock on the shore.

You can, of course, make both arguments, in the alternative. However, this is bad form and such differing positions may affect your credibility with the judge. Pick one approach. Argue your facts clearly, and back them up with enough law to persuade the judge that your facts and points are meritorious.

The reply in support of your motion for summary judgment should pick your three strongest arguments. Use them, in order of strength, to explain why the motion should be granted, even in light of the vigorous opposition. Be brief and to the point.

The oral advocacy for motions is very different from that of trials. Motion practice is far more intellectual, and less emotional, than trial advocacy.

Clearly, you have to do some advance work to understand the judge. How long does he give for oral argument? Is he generally prepared? What is his background and level of comfort with real estate cases? Does the judge ask a lot of questions? Does he jump in immediately or give you time to speak?

In preparing your argument for the judge, focus on justice. As with the motion, judges want to feel that they are doing the right thing. Explain the facts in an honest, but persuasive, way that leaves the judge feeling that your client is a poor guy who has been wronged and that fairness requires that those wrongs be immediately remedied—or that there is another side to the story, whereby your client has done everything right, and the motion goes much too far and should be denied.

You need to educate the judge. You know your case better than anyone else. You have worked hard on it for months. The judge, however, knows almost nothing about your case and may have no background in real estate litigation. Summarize the basic facts and the relief sought. Then explain, in simple logical sentences, how this relief is warranted by the facts and the law. As with the reply brief, it is a good idea to limit your argument to these essential points.

Visual aids are very helpful. A survey, a photograph of the property, or a diagram of the chain of title can help the judge understand the context and key concepts.

It is important, in oral argument, to address the positions taken by your opponent. While this does not need to be done in the initial motion, it must be part of your advocacy at the hearing:

> "Your honor, Plaintiff John James asks you to grant summary judgment in his favor and to rule that, as a matter of law, the Town should give him a permit to build a dock. Both the U.S. Army Corps of Engineers and the State have determined that Mr. James's home is a safe location for a dock. There have never been any problems with the dock on the abutting property. While the Town presented

testimony that the proposed dock location is unsafe, none of the Town's witnesses have any certifications in dock safety."

Make the statutes and cases exciting and on point:

> "The state law provides that a Town cannot deny a dock permit unless the proposed location is unsafe. In the recent case of *Burton v. Cross*, the State Supreme Court looked at virtually identical facts and found that a municipality must grant a dock permit where both the federal and state governments have approved permits after performing comprehensive safety evaluations."

Listen very carefully to the judge's questions. These give you critical insights into what the judge is thinking—and the facts and law he needs to render a decision in your favor. If you are asked to make a truthful concession, make it—and then distinguish the situation. Always begin by answering "Yes" or "No"—before explaining why the question is relevant or not relevant.

> Court: I am concerned that granting the dock permit may create a dangerous situation. Didn't the Town find that a dock cannot be safely built in the litigation you propose?
>
> Answer: Yes it did. However, both the federal and state governments found the location to be safe; there has never been a safety problem with the abutting neighbor's dock—and the Town safety engineer *admitted* at his deposition that he was not certified in dock safety and has never liked John James.

In other words, listen carefully to the question, understand the judge's concerns, and explain how these concerns do not apply. Reiterate how justice and fairness supports your position—and that this is supported by the law.

CHAPTER 13

The Trial

He can who thinks he can, and he can't who thinks he can't. This is an inexorable, indisputable law.
—Pablo Picasso

It is not the critic who counts. . . . The credit belongs to the man in the arena, whose face is marred by dust and sweat and blood; who strives valiantly . . . who knows the great enthusiasms, the great devotions; who spends himself in a worthy cause; who at best knows in the end triumph of high achievement, and who at worst, if he fails, at least fails while daring greatly.
Theodore Roosevelt

In his inaugural address, President Barack Obama warned that "greatness is never a given. It must be earned. Our journey has never been one of shortcuts or settling for less. It has not been the path for the faint-hearted, for those who prefer leisure over work. . . . Rather, it has been the risk-takers, the doers. . . ." This is exactly the situation with real estate trials. It is about energy, hard work, momentum, and risk. There are no shortcuts to victory.

Jury trials do not usually add anything material to real estate trials, other than cost. While jury trials are more interesting, there is little that they bring to the real estate case that cannot be found in a judge. Bench trials, of course, are also much shorter and do not involve voir dire, jury instructions, the formality of evidentiary rules—and the long waits typical in trial by jury. As many issues in real estate law are equitable rather than legal, juries may not be the finder of fact on many real estate issues. Jury trials in real estate actions are only preferred in those rare cases where damages are important and the lawyer believes that the jury will render a more favorable award—or where the judge is not trusted with the decision.

Trials are, by far, the most stimulating part of real estate litigation.

> "Is counsel for the plaintiff ready for trial?"
>
> "Is counsel for the defendant ready for trial?

The trial begins with excitement and anticipation. Its two over-arching components are content and delivery. Content—or merit—is not enough to win in and of itself. Delivery is where the trial lawyer shines. In an age of Internet and television, a powerful delivery may overshadow content.

The trial lawyer must present herself as well groomed, professional, and confident. "Confident" is comfortable, but not arrogant or "above others"—assertive, but not aggressive.

The client must also be well-groomed and articulate. The type of grooming depends on the locality. Many parts of the country view facial hair and long-haired men in a negative light. If you are in such a jurisdiction, cut the hair and shave off the beard.

Good eye contact is absolutely essential. The lawyer, client, and witness must always look the questioner and finder of fact in the eye. It is important to avoid "uhs" and stuttering.

If you have a client who looks somewhat sinister—especially in a case involving credibility—it is a good idea to retain a consultant to work with him. This also avoids damaging the client relationship with a frank conversation about how bad he appears.

Specifically, consultants can work with clients to vastly improve presentation by purchasing a new wardrobe, recommending physical grooming, and practicing eye contact and speaking skills. The consultant will generally videotape you and your colleagues putting the client through a series of mock examinations. After each mock examination, the consultant will work with the client to point out improvements and problems with presentation. These mock examinations will also help the lawyer to prepare for trial.

At trial, the advocate must speak with conviction. The finder of fact probably knows little about real estate law or the facts. Credible and experienced lawyers, speaking with conviction, carry the day. As Justice Louis Brandeis, a famous trial lawyer, is often quoted as stating: "We are not won by arguments that we can analyze, but by tone and temper; by the manner, which is the man himself."

Another cardinal rule of trial practice is "Keep it simple." The attorney must boil down complex facts and law into its simplest essence.

Most newspapers in the United States are written on a fifth-grade reading level. This is the everyday language in which people speak. Make sure that your words, especially with a jury, reflect this reality. Do not be condescending, but do speak in everyday language.

At trial, do *not* say: "I represent the plaintiff in a breach of easement case." Instead, say: "I represent Tom Elias, who is unable to get to his home because his neighbor has wrongfully blocked the driveway with a heavy chain."

This kind of statement uses plain and simple language. It conveys a strong message—with strong visual context, passion, and compassion. As Winnie the Pooh is famous for saying: "It is more fun to talk with somebody who doesn't use long, difficult words but rather short, easy words like 'what about lunch?'"

Unlike trials in other types of cases, real estate trials require a lot of visualization. You need to make complex deeds and chains of title readily transparent. The Opening Statement is what you have been waiting for: the chance to tell your story. Bring the finder of fact to the site via plans and images. Introduce the key players and witnesses. Allow the judge and jurors to walk in the shoes of your client and to embrace the problems he confronts.

Immediately after the Opening Statement, put forth your most exciting witness—who can explain and visualize exactly what you need. A strong surveyor is generally a good idea. Have the surveyor go through pictures, aerial photographs, surveys, and whatever else will ensure that the court has a very solid understanding of the problem—and is sympathetic to your proposed solution.

Sometimes it is a good idea to get the client to testify at an early stage in the case. Judges—and, more often, jurors—want to "meet" the client. Putting the client off until the last minute might irk some jurors.

Have your witnesses introduce visual exhibits—which you can refer to in the Closing Argument—that empower your case. Examples of powerful exhibits are the following:

This exhibit shows a shed clearly blocking most of an easement:

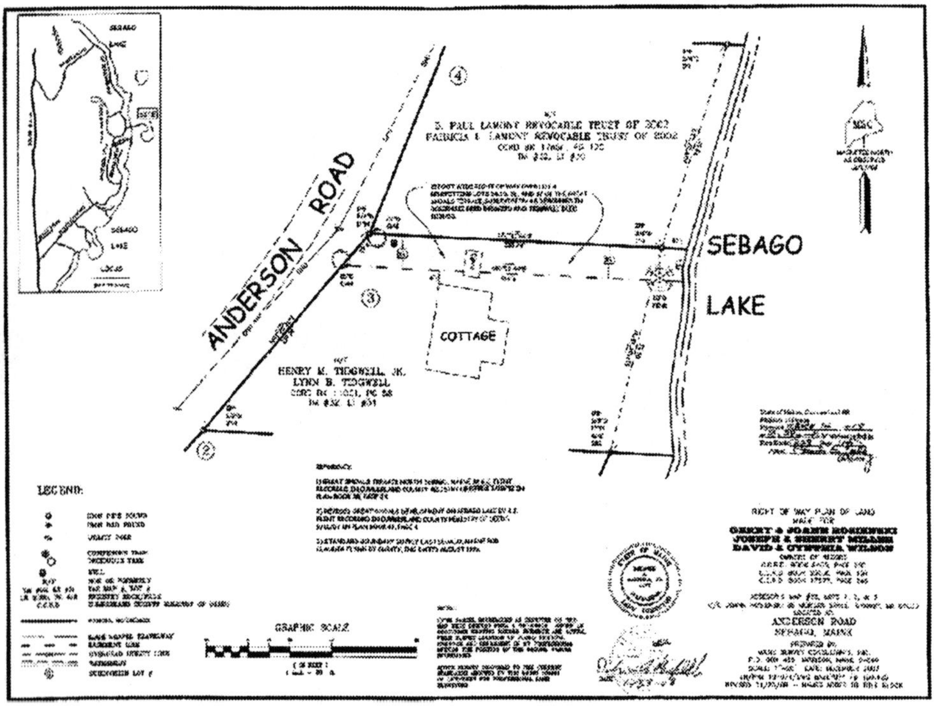

This exhibit plainly shows the incorrect parcel claimed—and the accurate one:

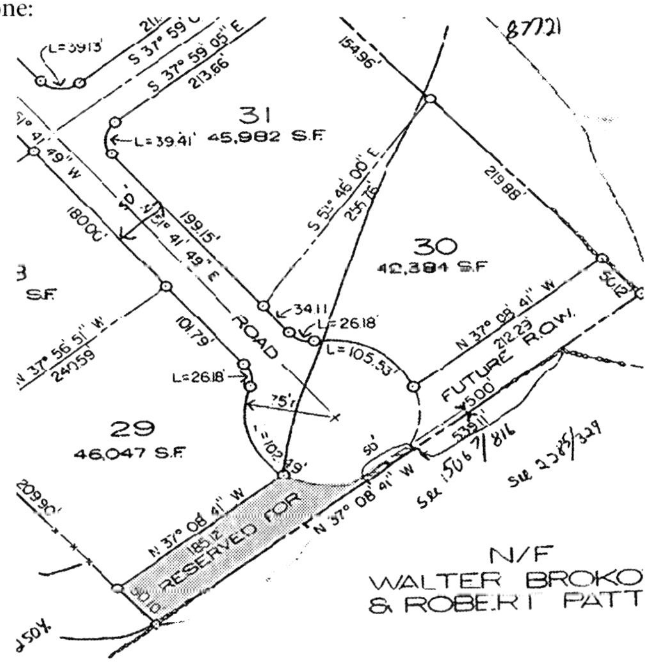

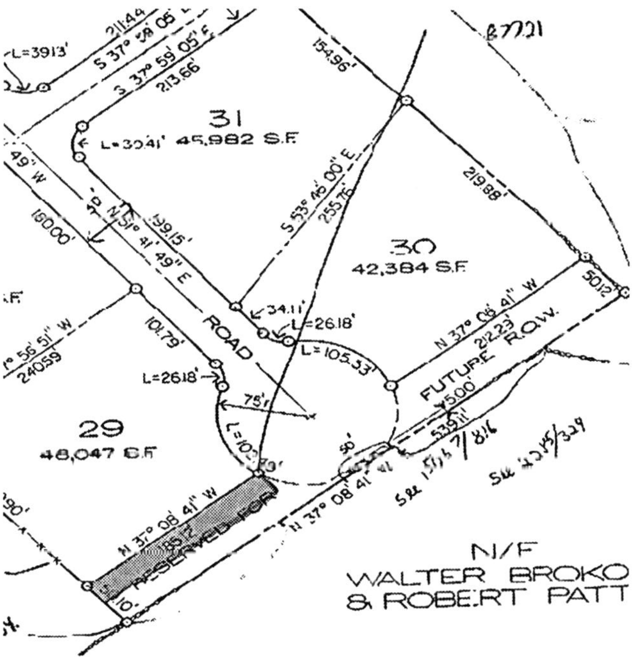

This exhibit shows all of the abutters to the land in question—and their need to have an easement over it:

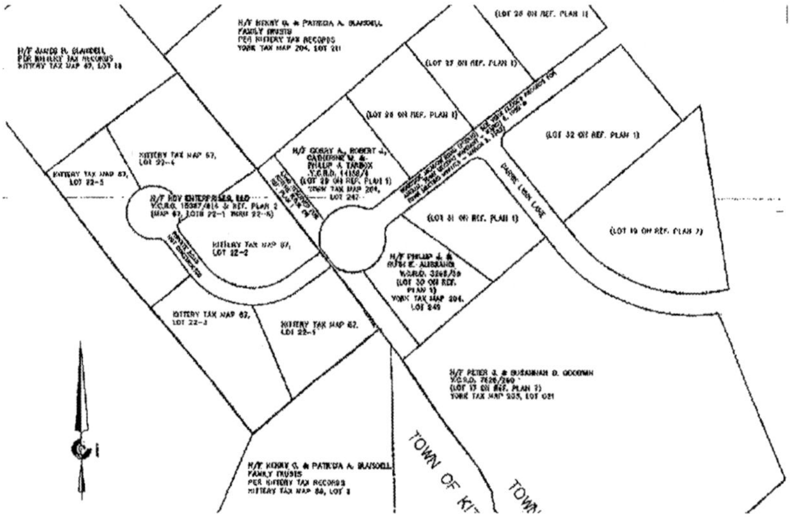

This exhibit nicely lays out the location of all properties in dispute:

This is an exhibit showing the two docks at issue—and the distance between them:

Direct examination in real estate litigation is about empowering your witnesses. Your witnesses should be steeped in the "story" and themes of the case. Spend a lot of time preparing them about their role in this case. A properly prepared and empowered witness is a delight to watch—and a convincing resource.

Be careful about having the other side testify in your portion of the case. If the opposing party can be carefully controlled with a deposition transcript, it may be a good idea to call him into your part of the case—and destroy him prior to the other side's portion of the case. Be careful. If there is a significant chance of the opposing party derailing your momentum, do not use him in your case. Simply cross-examine the opponent in due course.

Cross-examination, as with other types of litigation, needs to be short and carefully controlled. Never ask a question unless you have a deed, survey transcript, or other document setting forth the witness' answer. Lead the hostile witness through all of the helpful evidence—and go for the throat if the hostile witness diverges from his prior documents or testimony.

One of the essential ingredients of a good real estate trial lawyer is flexibility. After your months of rigorous preparation and planning, be ready to change. The exciting thing about real estate litigation is all of its twists and turns. A witness talking about the location of a monument or the history of a marked hedge of trees may break down on the stand. A judge may completely misinterpret what you believe to be a clear and unambiguous purchase and sale agreement. Be ready to handle these unpredictable events and come up with innovative solutions—and a smile. The microwave was invented by a researcher whose chocolate candy bar melted in his pants, after he walked by a radar tube. What looked like a ruined pair of pants and a wasted chocolate bar turned into a revolutionary method of cooking!

Make sure you also have a strong ending to your case. If the case has a major damage component, put a strong damage testimony in at the end. The last witness needs to leave the finder of fact squarely behind your position.

The Closing should be a glorious recapitulation of the promises you make in the Opening, with the evidence confirming all of your promises and the remedy that will right the wrongs. Your confidence and belief in your convictions will sell your case.

CHAPTER 14

Settlements and Consent Final Judgments

We make war that we may live in peace.
—Aristotle

Real estate litigation, unlike any other type of trial law, affords great opportunity in fashioning settlements. The personal injury trial lawyer negotiates dollars and, in the most creative circumstances, works out dollars over time. For the real estate trial lawyer, the sky—or at least the land—is the limit.

The settlement of real estate litigation can change boundaries, move or abandon easements, create dock permits, alter real estate closings, or move buildings. It can accomplish ends that the courts, even with their equitable powers in real estate, would rarely consider. Thus, settlement in real estate litigation should be taken very seriously.

The best time for settlement discussions is at the outset of the case. During the first month of litigation, the parties generally have a basic understanding of the other side's case—and have yet to incur the considerable expense of written discovery, depositions, motions, and trial. Once litigation costs have been calculated, each side's "appetite" for settlement begins to subside. Settlement discussions in the later stages of a real estate case are generally not cost effective. At that point, it is often simpler to just try the case. As a result, many real estate litigators devote the first month of the case to intensive settlement efforts.

Mediation is a much preferred means of settling a real estate case. Perhaps because real estate is so much attached to the concept of the American dream, U.S. landowners tend to be highly attached to their properties, and tensions in real estate disputes can run quite high. Experienced real estate trial lawyers can all tell you stories of combatants who spend hundreds of thousands of dollars fighting over 100 square feet of earth. Mediation allows a neutral party to insert himself between warring litigants and—by use of shuttle diplomacy and one-on-one meetings—resolve intense dilemmas.

Typically the mediator will spend the first thirty to forty-five minutes with all parties and counsel together: going over the rules of the mediation, encouraging the concept of settlement, and listening very briefly to the various positions. At this juncture, you should ask your client to say nothing and to keep a poker face. Even though mediation is always off the record, there is no point giving the other side insights into your client's concerns, fears, or "buttons."

There is no problem at all with your client speaking at length to the mediator in a confidential session where the other side is not present. **Note**: There is a psychological phenomenon whereby a party completely "unloads" on the mediator and—after "saying his peace"—is now ready to settle. It is the attorney's job to ensure that any such terms of settlement are commensurate with a successful settlement strategy—which calculates the relative likelihood of success, the reasonable litigation outcomes, and the cost of the litigation.

An oversimplified settlement strategy, for example, is as follows: If the property at issue is worth $10 million, if the likelihood of success is 60%, and if the estimated cost of the litigation is $100,000, it may make sense to enter into a settlement whereby the real estate is transferred to your client for a payment of around $4.1 million. In any event, all of these parameters must be discussed, in detail, with the client *before* the mediation.

At the mediation itself, it is good strategy to encourage the mediator to spend more time, in the one-on-one shuttle diplomacy, with the other side. It is during the "one-on-one" meetings (with the lawyer present) that most of the arm-twisting occurs. Thus, it is a tactical advantage to have the mediator spend more time with the other side. This can be achieved by acting reasonably and throwing "tidbits" to the mediator that make him feel it is now time to put pressure on someone else.

Make sure you have a complete list of your client's "wants" in advance of the settlement discussions or mediation. Spend substantial time going through the entire list of "wants," no matter how trivial. In a boundary dispute, your client obviously wants the land in contention. Sometimes, however, there is inaccessible property that neither side cares about—but will give one party the minimum lot size or additional setback needed to construct a dwelling under the local zoning ordinance. This is an example of a "win-win" where both sides get what they want: Blackstone gets his proposed solution to the property dispute and Samuels gets enough of Blackstone's worthless land to meet municipal requirements to develop the Samuels parcel. Other possible considerations in resolving boundary disputes are the following:

- Redrawing the boundary between the properties
- Providing both sides with land and/or plant buffers
- Creating or vacating rights-of-way over each other's property
- Creating or vacating scenic easements, view easements, mineral rights, air rights, or other interests
- Imposing or deleting restrictions or covenants on each other's property
- Releasing each person's interest in the opponent's land
- Agreements to consent to development
- Tax considerations

The settlement of partition actions also lends itself to a lot of creativity. If there is a house and land, one person can get the home and the other can take back land and furnishings. Parts of the land can be sold in an orderly manner, and parts of the land can be retained.

The key, regardless of the type of real estate litigation, is to figure out everything you want—and also what you are willing to give up. One recent settlement logjam ended with the transfer of a pick-up truck that one side wanted and the other side planned to discard. Explore everything. If one party is a manufacturer, perhaps the other party is interested in some goods at wholesale prices.

Settlements in real estate cases are best structured as Consent Final Judgments. Unlike settlement in a routine contract case, real estate settlements generally run with the land and are permanent in nature. Accordingly, they are best consummated by a Consent Final Judgment signed by the court and recorded in the Registry of Deeds. Receiving the court's "stamp of approval" on the settlement generally achieves far more than a mere agreement signed by two parties. In many jurisdictions, a court judgment circumvents subdivision laws, transfer taxes, and municipal permitting requirements. While a state, may, for example, require strict oversight for the subdivision of a parcel of property, a court, in a partition action, may physically divide the land among its ten co-tenants without the need for years of hearings before a planning board. Obviously, the partition action must be legitimate and in good faith, and not initiated for the purpose of circumventing the local ordinances.

Similarly, transfers of land generally involve payment of transfer taxes or "stamps." A court decree redrawing property lines or transferring land or property rights generally avoids the need for payments of any fees.

Where a complex settlement or consent judgment is envisioned, it is a good idea to prepare a draft of it prior to the beginning of the mediation. In this manner, you will be able to thrash out your ideas with the client and prevent any angles from being missed. The presence of a draft at the mediation will mean that everyone is working off your script—generally an advantage to the writer. You can also use a side letter agreement for details—such as a minimum sale price in a partition case—that you do not want on the public record.

Regardless of who prepares what, never leave a successful mediation without a writing signed by all parties. In the event the parties do not have time to write up the entire Consent Final Judgment, enter into a written agreement of concepts to be consummated by a judgment entered by the court. Agree that any dispute in composing the judgment will be decided by the mediator in a simple binding arbitration. You may also agree that the losing party, in such a dispute, will pay the legal fees of the prevailing party.

Note: Make sure the client's tax accountant or tax lawyer is consulted on any settlement that involves transfers of money or property.

Examples of Consent Final Judgments follow.

STATE OF MIND SUPERIOR COURT

BERNARD L. WHIPPLE and MARY WHIPPLE, Plaintiffs v. JAMIE B. GOLDBERG, individually and as Trustee of the JAMIE B. GOLDBERG 1992 TRUST; JACQUELINE S. WARREN, individually and as Trustee of the JACQUELINE S. WARREN QUALIFIED PERSONAL RESIDENCE TRUST; FLOYD W. WARREN, individually and as Trustee of the Floyd W. Warren Qualified Personal Residence Trust; DAVID G. STEIN; SUSANNE G. STEIN; JANET K. STEIN; WILLIAM STEIN; and INHABITANTS OF THE TOWN OF BOOTHBAY HARBOR, Defendants	)	CIVIL ACTION DOCKET NO.______

CONSENT FINAL JUDGMENT

This Court, this ____ day of December 2009, hereby ORDERS, ADJUDGES, and DECREES as follows:

1. This Court's Consent Order, dated January 10, 2008, is hereby ratified and affirmed, except where inconsistent with the terms below.

2. By Agreement, Defendants Jamie B. Goldberg, individually and as Trustee of The Jamie B. Goldberg 1992 Trust; Floyd W. Warren, individually and as Trustee of The Floyd W. Warren Qualified Personal Residence Trust; Jacqueline S. Warren, individually and as Trustee of the Jacqueline S. Warren Qualified Personal Residence Trust; David G. Stein; Susanne G. Stein; Janet K. Stein; and William Stein hereby release any and all interest they have in the property of Plaintiffs Bernard L. Whipple and Mary Whipple in Boothbay Harbor, Mind, described in a deed,

dated May 15, 1981, from Phippen Sanborn and Catherine C. Sanborn to Bernard Whipple and Mary Whipple, a copy of which is recorded in the Lincoln County Registry of Deeds at Book 1064, Page 273. This Release includes, without limitation, any and all interest the aforementioned Defendants have in Plaintiffs' adjacent dock, ramp, and float.

3. Defendants David Stein and Susanne Stein are the owners of a twelve-foot-wide lot bordering the ocean, and listed as Lot 18-A on Boothbay Harbor Tax Map 13 and recorded in the Lincoln County Registry of Deeds at Book 1935, Page 194 (the "Stein Lot").

4. The Stein Lot is clearly intended to be access for a dock, ramp, and float, and is not otherwise a buildable lot.

5. Defendants David and Susanne Stein, their heirs and personal representatives, shall promptly convey the Stein Lot, and all rights for an adjacent dock, in equal one-fourth shares, to (a) themselves; (b) Defendants Jamie B. Goldberg, individually and as Trustee of the Jamie B. Goldberg 1992 Trust; (c) Defendants Peter Warren, formerly known as Floyd W. Warren and Jacqueline S. Warren; and (d) Defendants Janet K. Stein and William Stein (collectively the "Four Dock Partners"), or their designees.

6. The Four Dock Partners, their respective heirs and personal representatives, shall construct a dock, ramp, and float extending off the Stein Lot as indicated in the drawing attached hereto as Exhibit A. Plaintiffs shall consent to all permits and approvals required for this dock.

7. Each of these Four Dock Partners shall pay one-fourth of the cost for constructing the dock, ramp, and float off of the Stein Lot.

8. By agreement, Plaintiffs shall promptly pay a total of Eighteen Thousand Four Hundred and Ninety Eight Dollars ($18,498.00) to the Four Dock Partners.

9. Each of the Four Dock Partners, or their designees, shall own an undividable one-fourth interest in the dock, ramp, and float off the Hamblin Lot and shall each be responsible for one-fourth of the cost of all repairs, maintenance, improvements, taxes, and other costs related to the Stein Lot and the adjacent dock, ramp, and float. The Four Dock Partners shall promptly enter into an agreement for the use and enjoyment of the Stein Lot and adjacent dock.

10. All of the terms of this Judgment are permanent and shall run with the land currently owned by the Four Dock Partners and the Plaintiffs.

11. Plaintiffs, their respective heirs and personal representatives, shall modify their existing dock, ramp, and float as shown in the drawing attached hereto as Exhibit A. Defendants shall consent to all permits and approvals required for this modification.

12. Plaintiffs and Defendants Floyd W. Warren and Jacqueline S. Warren (individually and as Trustees of the aforesaid Warren Trusts), their respective successors and assigns, shall have the right, which right shall be appurtenant to and run with their land described herein, to use for ingress, egress, and utilities that portion of Hodgon Cove Road, Plaintiffs' said land, the Warrens' said land, and the Stein Lot which has historically been used for those purposes, and which constitutes the extension between Hodgon Cove Road and Plaintiffs' said land and the Warrens' said land.

13. Paragraph 8 herein shall be fully redacted or otherwise omitted from any attested copy or excerpt hereof which may be recorded in the Lincoln County Registry of Deeds.

14. In all other respects, the above-captioned matter is hereby dismissed with prejudice and without costs.

15. Pursuant to Rule 79(a) the Clerk is hereby directed to enter this Consent Final Judgment on the docket.

____

Justice, Superior Court

STATE OF MIND SUPERIOR COURT

HELEN LONGLEY POTTER AND	)	
JOHN STUART POTTER, TRUSTEES	)	
OF THE HELEN LONGLEY POTTER	)	
2000 TRUST,	)	
Plaintiffs	)	
	)	
v.	)	
	)	CIVIL ACTION NO. _____
GEORGIANA LONGLEY AKZKABAR,	)	
Defendant	)	
	)	

CONSENT FINAL JUDGMENT

Pursuant to the Consent Motion for a Consent Final Judgment, the consent of all counsel, the Mediation pursuant to Mind Rule of Civil Procedure 16(b), and the entire record herein, it is this _____ day of June 2007, hereby

ORDERED, ADJUDGED, and DECREED as follows:

1. The approximately 6.2 acres of real property owned by the parties at 156 Sherman's Point Road in Camden (the "Property") is hereby physically partitioned. The terms of this Consent Final Judgment shall run with the land.

2. Plaintiffs Helen Longley Potter and John Stuart Potter, Trustees of the Helen Longley Potter 2000 Trust ("Potter"), hereby own only the approximately 5.19 acres described in Exhibit A attached hereto and incorporated herein (the "Land Parcel").

3. Defendant Georgiana Longley Akzkabar ("Akzkabar") hereby owns only the approximately 1.01 acres, including the existing home, described in Exhibit B hereto (the "House Parcel").

4. The Plan, attached hereto as Exhibit C and incorporated herein, shows the physical division of the Property, as well as the other easements set forth herein.

5. It is the intention of Potter to market and sell the Land Parcel, and Akzkabar shall not have the right, nor shall she be required, to participate in the marketing and sale of the Land Parcel or the costs thereof.

6. Potter, its heirs and assigns (including subdividees), shall have a permanent thirty (30) foot wide access easement to the shore and for the use and enjoyment of the beach situated to the southeast of the house on the House Parcel (the "Beach and Beach Access Easement"). The Beach Easement and Beach Access Easement is described in Exhibit A attached hereto and incorporated herein. The easement is for the use and enjoyment of the beach and shall be nonexclusive for use of approximately 131 feet of the beach on the House Parcel, commencing where the boundary line between the House Parcel and the land now or formerly of Allen meets the shoreline. The Beach Easement is depicted on the attached Plan. Potter, its heirs and assigns, may clear brush to improve their access and may erect a staircase descending to the beach.

7. Potter, its heirs and assigns (including subdividees), shall have a permanent view easement over the area described in Exhibit B attached hereto and incorporated herein (the "View Easement"). The View Easement is shown on the attached Plan.

8. The View Easement hereby allows Potter, its heirs and assigns (and subdividees), a permanent right to cut and trim trees and vegetation located in the View Easement area, only to the extent permissible by law, including shoreland zoning laws, natural resource protection laws, and other applicable state and municipal laws. Prior to the cutting or trimming of any trees or vegetation located in the View Easement, there must be a site inspection with the Code Enforcement Officer for the Town of Camden, or his delegate, at which time all trees and vegetation approved for cutting must be marked with a particular color tape and at which time all trees and vegetation approved for trimming must be marked with a different color tape. Akzkabar must be notified in writing at least seven days in advance of the date and time of the site inspection and has the right to be present, personally or by a representative, to participate in the site inspection. Akzkabar must also be notified in writing at least seven days in advance of the date and time that any cutting and/or trimming will occur following approval at a site inspection and she shall have the right to be present, personally or by a representative, to oversee the cutting and/or trimming at the time specified in the written notice. No cutting or trimming shall be permitted by Potter unless a proper site inspection and proper notice has occurred.

9. Akzkabar, her heirs and assigns (including subdividees), shall have a permanent access easement over the "existing gravel driveway"

as depicted on the attached Plan (the "Driveway Easement"). Potter, its heirs and assigns, shall have permanent right to relocate the Driveway Easement over the Land Parcel, provided that the relocated driveway shall be the same quality as the existing driveway and provided that it will enter the House Parcel at the location shown, and labeled on the Plan "Relocated Road Entry Location." Potter and Akzkabar, their heirs and assigns, shall share equally in the cost to relocate the Driveway Easement, over the Land Parcel, when it is first relocated. The relocated driveway shall be of the same quality as the current driveway or better. However, if Potter, its heirs and assigns, paves or otherwise improves the driveway over the Land Parcel (as is its right), Akzkabar, her heirs and assigns, shall only be responsible for paying the equivalent costs associated with a gravel driveway similar to the existing driveway.

10. Landmark Corporation shall set monuments on the boundary and easement lines set forth above. Its attached Plan shall be modified to show the monuments, and GPS coordinates of the monuments, and shall be recorded in the Knox County Registry of Deeds. The parties shall share the cost of all of Landmark's work referenced herein.

11. The parties, their heirs and assigns (including subdividees), shall have a permanent easement over each other's parcel for the maintenance of all existing utilities in their present location, including electricity, telephone/cable, and water. The parties, their heirs and assigns, shall have the right to add or relocate existing utilities, at the mover's cost, provided that any work to accomplish such work shall not take place during the months of June, July, August, or September and provided that all areas disturbed by the work are restored to their original condition.

12. To the extent that the location of any utility pole servicing the House Parcel would interfere with the view from a single family dwelling newly constructed on the Land Parcel, Potter shall have the right to relocate said utility pole to a location on the Land Parcel at its cost provided that any work to accomplish such a relocation shall not take place during the months of June, July, August, or September and provided that all areas disturbed by the work are restored to their original condition. Any location of the relocated pole on the Land Parcel cannot interfere with the view of the House Parcel or otherwise unreasonably interfere with the existing structure or mature trees or vegetation on the House Parcel.

13. Akzkabar, her heirs and assigns (including subdividees), shall have a permanent, contingent easement to a four-bedroom subsurface wastewater disposal system on the Land Parcel (for the benefit

of the House Parcel)—at a suitable location determined by Potter—in the event, and only in the event, that the current system serving the House Parcel should fail *and* cannot be adequately replaced, repaired, or restored in its current location and there is no other suitable or permissible location on the House Parcel to relocate a sufficient system. Akzkabar shall pay all costs associated with such Septic System and with restoring the Land Parcel to its original condition.

14. Potter and Akzkabar, their heirs and assigns (including subdividees), shall not oppose any building permits, road permits, or subdivisions on the other party's land, provided that such development is consistent with municipal setbacks.

15. The parties shall identify a qualified independent real estate appraiser (the "Independent Appraiser") to do all work necessary to prepare a valuation of the Property (the "Whole Parcel Value"). The Independent Appraiser shall also determine a value for the House Parcel (the "House Parcel Value") and a value for the Land Parcel (the "Land Parcel Value"), based on everything above and below. The parties shall share equally in the appraisal costs. If the parties cannot agree on an Independent Appraiser within 10 days, then Charles Whittaker, Esquire of Portland shall identify the appraiser who shall serve as Independent Appraiser for all purposes.

16. The materials provided to the Independent Appraiser for appraising the Whole Parcel, the House Parcel, and the Land Parcel shall be as follows:

a. A copy of this Consent Judgment including the exhibit;

b. Letter from Scott Billins at Camden Real Estate Company dated December 15, 2004, including existing updates.

c. Appraisal by Jay Cohen dated March 17, 2005, including existing updates.

d. Appraisal by Pine Tree Appraisal dated May 12, 2005, including existing updates.

e. Detailed information concerning the Town of Camden's claim to public access, including the proposal Ordinance and dispute with the neighbor.

f. The Independent Appraiser shall conduct the appraisal in any way he or she deems fitting, and may use or not use the above information.

17. Unless otherwise agreed by the parties in writing, no other written material shall be provided to the Independent Appraiser. No ex

parte communications may be held with the Independent Appraiser. If additional communication with the Independent Appraiser is desired by either party, the subject of the communication shall be disclosed to the other party, in advance, for pre-approval.

18. Once the Independent Appraiser has determined the Whole Parcel Value, the House Parcel Value, and the Land Parcel Value, Akzkabar shall make the following payments to Potter:

a. If the Whole Parcel Value is greater than the combined value of the House Parcel Value and the Land Parcel Value, then Akzkabar shall pay to Potter one-half ($^1/_2$) of the amount by which the Whole Parcel Value is greater than the combined value of the House Parcel Value and the Land Parcel Value.

b. If the House Parcel Value is greater than the Land Parcel Value, then Akzkabar shall pay to Potter one-half ($^1/_2$) of the amount by which the House Parcel Value is greater than the Land Parcel Value.

c. If the combined total of the two payments set forth in (a) and (b) above is greater than $700,000, then Akzkabar shall only be required to pay a combined total of $700,000 to Potter.

d. If the total payment due from Akzkabar to Potter is $250,000 or less, said amount shall be paid in full within thirty (30) days.

e. If the total payment due from Akzkabar to Potter is $500,000 or less, the first $250,000 shall be paid within thirty (30) days, and the balance shall be paid within one hundred eighty (180) days. However, if Akzkabar receives a distribution of cash from her mother's Estate within the 180 day time period, she shall remit payment of the balance due hereunder up to the amount of the cash distribution from the Estate within 10 days of said distribution.

f. If the total payment due from Akzkabar to Potter is $700,000 or less, the first $250,000 shall be paid within thirty (30) days, the next $250,000 shall be paid within one hundred eighty (180) days, and the balance shall be paid within three hundred sixty (360) days. However, if Akzkabar receives a distribution of cash from her mother's estate within the 360 day time period, she shall remit payment of the balance due up to the amount of the cash distribution from the Estate within 10 days of said distribution.

g. These payments are hereby secured by Akzkabar's interest in the Home Parcel.

19. Potter shall provide a quitclaim bill of sale, without warranties or representations, to Akzkabar for the personal contents contained in the building on the House Parcel. Akzkabar shall make available to Potter any and all photo albums at the Property for her to copy.

20. The existing, undischarged mortgage dated March 12, 2004, recorded at Book 3187, Page 124 shall be released from the Home Parcel within thirty days of Potter receiving the payment of any funds set forth above. Any other mortgages on the Property shall be discharged promptly.

21. Each party shall be responsible, effective immediately, for any real estate taxes, utilities, insurance, or improvements related to her property. As soon as practical, the real property taxes for the Property shall be pro-rated based on the House Parcel Value percentage and the Land Parcel Value percentage to the whole of these combined values.

22. Any and all work commissioned, possessed, or undertaken by either or both of the parties associated with the Property over the past several years, including surveys, topographical studies, wetland studies, architectural studies, soil testing, land planning, dockage feasibility, and other related work shall be made available to both parties regardless of which party commissioned the work.

23. Any amounts in the joint checking account previously established by the parties for the maintenance of the Property will be used to pay any outstanding mutual bills or debts, and the balance shall be split between the parties equally.

24. A certified copy of this Consent Final Judgment shall be recorded at the Knox County Registry of Deeds.

25. In all other respects, any and all other claims in the above-captioned matter are dismissed with prejudice and without costs.

26. The Clerk is instructed to reference this Order on the docket pursuant to Rule 79(a) of the Mind Rules of Civil Procedure.

____

Justice, Superior Court

STATE OF MIND SUPERIOR COURT

JAMES M. WILNER AND MICHELE F. WILNER, TRUSTEES OF THE EIGHTEEN ROSEBUD LANE REALTY TRUST, Plaintiffs v. NANCY M. PIERCE, INDIVIDUALLY AND AS TRUSTEE OF THE SAMUEL S. PIERCE 1998 REVOCABLE TRUST, RICHARD V. ATKINS, AND RITA C. ATKINS, Defendants	))))))))))))))))	CIVIL ACTION NO. _____

CONSENT FINAL JUDGMENT

Pursuant to the Consent Motion for Entry of a Consent Final Judgment, the consent of all counsel, the Mediation pursuant to Mind Rule of Civil Procedure 16(b), and the entire record herein, it is this _____ day of April, 2008, hereby

ORDERED, ADJUDGED, and DECREED as follows:

1. Plaintiffs James M. Wilner and Michele F. Wilner, Trustees of the Eighteen Rosebud Lane Realty Trust ("Wilner"), own the property described in a certain deed recorded in the Washington County Registry of Deeds in Book 2664, Page 97 (the "Wilner Property").

2. Defendant Nancy M. Pierce, Individually and as Trustee of the Samuel S. Pierce 1998 Revocable Trust ("Pierce"), own the property shown as the "Pierce Property" on Exhibit A attached hereto and incorporated herein (the "Pierce Property").

3. The true and correct boundary between the Wilner Property and Pierce Property is as shown on Exhibit A and delineated thereon as "Boundary Line."

4. The parties shall mutually engage a licensed Professional Land Surveyor to set monuments on the boundary set forth above and to pre-

pare a new survey plan depicting the Global Positioning System (GPS) coordinates of the boundary monuments set in accordance with this paragraph. All costs associated with such work shall be shared equally by the parties.

5. Other than what is depicted as the Pierce Property on Exhibit A, Pierce has no right, title, or interest to the property shown on a plan entitled "Plan of Helen Levine Land" by Winston Myers and recorded in the Washington County Registry of Deeds at Hanger 2, Slide 24.

6. The Surveyor's Certificate dated August 19, 2002, and recorded in the Washington County Registry of Deeds in Book 2654, Page 93 is incorrect and is hereby discharged and of no further force and effect.

7. The Certificate of Lis Pendens dated March 16, 2007, and recorded in the Washington County Registry of Deeds in Book 3266, Page 312 is hereby discharged.

8. In all other respects, any and all other claims in the above-captioned matter are dismissed with prejudice and without costs.

9. The Clerk is instructed to reference this Judgment on the docket pursuant to Rule 79(a) of the Rules of Civil Procedure.

____

Justice, Superior Court

AFTERWORD

Final Thoughts

My father, grandfather, and great-grandfather all built buildings and developed property. Most Americans are descended from pioneers and immigrants who risked everything to start a new life in a New World. Our forefathers wanted land. They wanted freedom—and they clearly appreciated the fact that hard work, perseverance, and creativity are the foundations of the American dream.

Our cultural heritage is unique in the world, and our uniqueness distinguishes real estate litigation from all other types of trial practices. To be successful at real estate litigation, you must know and understand property, and appreciate the motives that drive landowners and real estate entrepreneurs.

You must also be an attorney. An attorney who can master the powerful forces at work in this area, who can thoroughly investigate the facts and law at stake, who can bring to bear all of the creativity of the real estate and legal professions, and who can—with conviction and passion—advocate for his or her clients with credibility, simplicity, and directness that would make our forefathers proud.

The rigors and commandments of real estate litigation are tough but doable with hard work, careful thought, and perseverance. As best stated in Deuteronomy:

> [It] is not too hard for you, nor too remote. It is not in heaven, that you should say: "Who will go for us to heaven and bring it down to us, that we may do it?" Nor is it beyond the sea, that you should say: "Who will cross the sea for us and bring it over to us, that we may do it?" No, it is very near to you, in your mouth and in your heart, and you can do it.

INDEX